Fundamentals of the
Options Market

Fundamentals of the Options Market

Michael Williams

McGraw-Hill
New York   San Francisco   Washington, D.C.
Auckland   Bogotá   Caracas   Lisbon   London
Madrid   Mexico City   Milan   Montreal   New Delhi
San Juan   Singapore   Sydney   Tokyo   Toronto

Library of Congress Cataloging-in-Publication Data

McGraw-Hill

A Division of The McGraw·Hill Companies

1 2 3 4 5 6 7 8 9 0   CUS / CUS   0 9 8 7 6 5 4 3 2 1 0

ISBN 007-136318-1

The sponsoring editor for this book was Kelli Christiansen and the production supervisor was Tina Cameron. It was set in New Century Schoolbook by D&G Limited, LLC.

Printed and bound by Custom Printing.

McGraw-Hill books are available at special quantity discounts to use as premiums and sales promotions, or for use in corporate training programs. For more information, please write to the Director of Special Sales, Professional Publishing, McGraw-Hill, Two Penn Plaza, New York, NY 10121-2298. Or contact your local bookstore.

This publication is designed to provide accurate and authoritative information in regard to the subject matter covered. It is sold with the understanding that neither the author nor the publisher is engaged in rendering legal, accounting, or professional service. If legal advice or other expert assistance is required, the service of a competent professional person shoud be sought.

 This book is printed on acid-free paper.

In memory of

John Lawson (F37)

and

John Hauke (T88)

Acknowledgments

Special thanks to Michael Gurwitz, who was instrumental in the completion and editing of this book.

To Karin Swann for her diligent editing of the materials.

To Kelli Christiansen of McGraw-Hill for supporting us throughout this process.

To the following for giving us real-world experience, knowledge, lessons learned, and support throughout our careers: The Pacific Exchange (PCX), Headwaters Capital, Keck Securities, Napoli & Associates, Sheldon Kahn, Barry Goren, Dan Traub, Phil Defeo, Dale Carlson, Catherine Clay, and William Napoli.

To the staff at Market Compass and support staff: Kitric Kerns, Dan Evets, Stephan Choy, Mike Townsend, Keith LaFaver, Lynn Hamburger, and the PCX printing department.

To Michelle M. Swallow for her advice and patience throughout the writing of this book and beyond.

To our family and friends for their undying support.

Amy S. Hoffman
Michael S. Williams

About the Authors

Michael S. Williams is president and CEO of Market Compass, LLC, which specializes in financial education for investors and traders online, via the Internet, and through the PCX Institute. Williams has been an options market maker and floor broker on the Pacific Exchange (PCX) for nearly a decade. He is a frequent speaker at conferences around the country, including the TSAA annual conference, the Options Industry Council seminars, and The Money Show. Michael has also spoken at Weber State and Pepperdine University.

Amy S. Hoffman is a founder and vice president of Market Compass, LLC. She has been an options market maker on the PCX, trading for hedge funds and as an independent market maker. Her financial career began in 1989 as a compliance officer and in-house trader for a large commodities firm. Hoffman is currently an instructor for the PCX Institute and Options Industry Council and can be heard on On24 (online) providing market commentary and analysis.

Contents

Fundamentals of the Options Market

Introduction

The Four Disciplines
of Investing

Introduction

When I began my career on the trading floor of the Pacific Exchange options floor, I asked myself one question repeatedly: "What is the secret?" After a while, I learned that I was wasting too much of my time trying to find an answer to this question when the answer was always right in front of me. There is no secret, only discipline. My boss pounded this concept into my head at the trading firm for which I was working. I watched him trade and was amazed at how easy he made it look. I knew there must be a secret. In the beginning I did not believe him, but I soon learned how true his statement was. Thanks to him and to some other traders at the firm, I soon learned that I had to master the four disciplines in order to be a successful trader. The second thing I learned from them is that you never stop learning, and you never totally master any of the four disciplines. This mastery is a never-ending cycle and a constant journey. Once you have mastered the four disciplines, however, you will make a profit. Trading is a business.

Education

The first discipline is education. The investor or trader must understand how the products work. Education comes in several forms: real-world experience, theoretical or textbook knowledge, and investigation. There are two parts to education: the first is understanding the product, and the second is knowing how to use the product strategically. A course or textbook should describe how something works, then explain how to use it. I have taken several courses where the instructor showed me how something works but never taught the class what it could actually do with that knowledge. I am continually frustrated when someone speaks about trading butterflies (an option strategy that has a low risk with lots of rewards) and fails to tell the student that he or she cannot trade this position as a butterfly but instead must leg into it (putting the position on one step at a time). As a broker and market maker for several years, I have traded a butterfly once. If the instructor had followed through with his teaching, he would have mentioned how one might trade into a butterfly (not just how it works).

Strategy

The second discipline is strategy, or plan of action. Never walk into the market blindly. Always have a strategy or a plan of action. The investor or trader must first decide what his or her market outlook is—whether it is bullish, bearish, neutral, volatile, or uncertain. Once the individual investor has decided what his or her market outlook is, then he or she must decide which strategy will suit this market outlook. Once the trader or invester decides on a strategy, he or she must consider the risk versus reward factors and an exit strategy plan. He or she should always consider "What if?" scenarios.

Execution

The third discipline is execution. The investor or trader needs to execute his or her plan of action or strategy. Many investors suffer analysis paralysis, which is the over-analyzing of a trade. Sometimes they spend too much time looking at technical analyses and feel that they need more confirmations and more data before making a decision. This situation leads to missed opportunities. Your education should be thorough enough to analyze risk versus reward parameters and to make a decision about which strategy suits your investment objectives. The individual investor or trader must also use the right executing software for his or her particular trading strategy. If you were going to be a position trader, then using one of the online brokers would not suffice. If you are going to be a *direct-access trader* (DAT), then you will need access to the right type of execution software. There are brokerage firms that will suit the trading styles of all types of traders.

Risk Management

The last discipline is risk management. This discipline is where we all fail at one point or another. Unfortunately, we are not robots. We are subject to both greed and hope. Greed and hope do not fit into the trader's vocabulary, however. As stock prices decline and the trader or investor is long in the stock, hoping that the stock price goes back up is an oxymoron strategy. Some investors or traders are too greedy and are looking to capitalize on the dot-com phenomenon without being aware of the potential risks that are involved. In many cases, traders commit too much capital to a position—and if the position goes against them, then they are out of the game.

Think of investing as owning a baseball team. You have a certain amount of capital to hire a team, and your goal is to win games and go to the World Series. A owner that spends all of his or her money on the big home-run hitter, assuming that a star alone is enough to win the World Series is effectively, putting all of his or her eggs into one basket, leaving little for pitchers, infield players, outfield players, and a good manager.

When the season is over, the owner's star, home-run hitter might have captured the home-run title, but the team lost 80 percent of its games and came in last in its league. Why? The answer is because the owner's other players could never get on base in order to score runs, and the pitchers lost games because the team had a poor pitching staff. In this case, the owner was greedy and wanted the big home-run hitter—regardless of the cost. A good owner would look for a well-balanced team. He or she wants the team to hit singles and score runs, and he or she needs the pitchers to pitch and win games. Do not lose sight of the object of baseball. You want to go to the World Series, and if you hit home runs on the way, then it is just gravy.

The trading world is the same. The trader wants to hit singles, score runs, and play and win tomorrow. Hitting home runs is just icing on the cake. A good trader is not looking to make a great deal of money in one swoop. If a trader does, that is great. Instead, you should focus on constantly winning small amounts, and then the home runs will come. Hit those singles. Trading is not like playing the lotto or playing the slots. Trading involves being focused, understanding your risk, and managing your position.

What Type of Trader Are You?

Once you have a solid understanding of the four disciplines of successful trading, the next thing that you have to determine is what type of trader you are. Anyone can become an investor, but not everyone can become a successful trader. You must analyze your personality and trading patterns in order to determine what type of trading best suites you. There is no right way or wrong way to trade in the marketplace; rather, there are only successful and unsuccessful traders. There are several types of traders that fit with corresponding personality types:

- **The day trader (in other words, a DAT)**[1]—This person is disciplined, focused, capable of making quick decisions, able to assume considerable capital risk, determined, and optimistic. This type of trader actively trades in and out of the marketplace by using the *National Association of Security Dealers Automated Quotation* (NASDAQ) system, Level II, ECNS, SOES, SelectNet, and DOT execution systems. The DAT must be extremely disciplined and pay close attention to the marketplace at all times. Note that day trading is a high-risk endeavor and a full-time job. Direct-access trading

---

[1]This book is focused on position trading and the use of options. For DATs, we suggest reviewing Chapter 7, and for a more in depth understanding, we suggest reading *How to Get Started in Electronic Day Trading* by David Nassar, who covers the subject thoroughly.

tends to be capital intensive, and positions are intra-day and are closed out prior to the end of the trading day.

- **The swing trader or technical trader**—This person is patient, analytical, and strategic. This trader is a researcher who calls upon historical data and/or experience. This type of trader might hold a position for several days and sometimes months. He or she uses technical analysis software to analyze market activity in order to make buying and selling decisions. This technique is the oldest method of trading. The swing trader, or technical trader, will execute both stock and option strategies in order to take advantage of the best trading positions. Swing traders frequently have full-time jobs aside from their trading activity and might trade from home. Swing traders must be patient and are technically oriented individuals.

- **The position trader**—This person is mathematical (understands probabilities and odds), a problem solver, risk adverse, observant, patient, strategic, and hedges his or her bets. This type of trader uses advanced option strategies to reduce the risk from market exposure in his or her portfolio. Position traders are leverage strategists who are focused on investing minimal capital in order to control a large equity position. These traders tend to hold their positions anywhere from several days up to one year. Generally, market makers, hedge-fund traders, and institutional firms are position traders, but the Internet has enabled individual investors to become position traders. Skilled position trading has the highest rate of *return on investment* (ROI).

How Is Leverage Involved?

Regardless of what type of trader you are, the problem with risk management is that many individual investors do not fully understand how to measure risk. Whenever a person is long or short in the marketplace, he or she is exposed to market directional risk. When the market is closed, the individual investor or trader has no control over the position and has to wait until the following morning to sell or buy back shares—hopefully at the same price at which they closed (which is not guaranteed). To manage this risk, many investors mistakenly believe that stop orders and diversifying will suffice. In reality, stop orders offer little to no protection, and diversifying can actually *increase* risk and make managing a portfolio even more difficult. The first step is to assess risk. Step two, then, is to neutralize or reduce that risk. Option trading is an effective tool for hedging against risk.

To this end, option trading offers an added bonus. Most individual investors purchase stock because they want to gain a profit in the marketplace. This outright purchasing is not only capital intensive, but also (as we have said) it exposes the investor to considerable market risk. By comparison, options require much less capital outlay. For a small, initial investment, the purchaser of options can control a large amount of the underlying asset.

For example, if you were to go into the open marketplace and buy 1,000 shares of XYZ for $35 a share, it would cost you $35,000 (35 × 1000 = 35,000). If you were to buy 10 XYZ Apr 35 calls, however (the right to purchase the underlying asset for a specific price for a given period of time), for $3½ with XYZ trading $35 per share, you are controlling $35,000 of the underlying asset with only $3,000. Each option contract represents 100 shares of the underlying asset (3½ × 100 = $300 × 10 contracts = $3,000 total investment). Essentially, you are controlling the same amount of the underlying asset for a fraction of the cost. As the underlying stock rises in value, the leverage works to your advantage. A 50-cent increase in the underlying asset can equate to a $50 increase in the underlying asset. If the underlying asset decreases in price, the loss is limited to the option purchase price of 3½, or $3,000. Regardless of market conditions, you can never lose more than you paid for the price of the option.

On the other hand, you must remember that when you are selling options, the same leverage can work against you and losses can increase dramatically as the underlying asset increases and/or decreases in value. The advantages of options over stock purchases do not come without tradeoffs. In our example, note that if XYZ does go up in price, the options purchase (when it represents the same number of shares as the stock purchase) will always produce $3,000 less profit (the purchase price of the options). Hence, knowing your options and the leverage that they provide is paramount to option trading. The first step toward determining the risk/reward associated with trading stock options is a foundational knowledge of their characteristics. The following chapters will guide you through the complex and fascinating world of the most popular and most misunderstood financial derivative: the publicly traded stock option.

The Right Education Matters

We are keenly aware of the educational gap between the individual investor and the professional trader. Furthermore, to be a responsible and successful trader, the new generation of individual investors needs the *right* education. Tipster newsletters and unaccredited day-trading courses with the "get rich quick" or "our trading secret" mentality do not apply. Investors need reliable, fundamental information about the markets and risk-limiting strategies that can help them secure their investments. In short, because all investors (market makers and individual traders alike) now have access to the same tools, this book is designed to fill the existing educational void.

For your convenience, we have divided this book into four sections. The first section focuses on the characteristics of options and covers pricing formulas, the Greeks, volatility, building blocks, and the mysterious synthetic phenomena. The second section focuses strictly on strategies. The strategy section is further subdivided into chapters based on market outlook. The typical individual investor has two market outlooks: bullish and bearish. In this section, we will introduce two new outlooks—neutral and volatile—and will describe strategies that correspond to these outlooks. This knowledge will enable the trader to find strategies that more accurately suit his or her market outlook. The third section discusses the role of market makers, how markets are made, the exchanges, their members, accessing and reading quotes, and stock and option execution. The final section of this book discusses setting up a trading station, selecting a broker, finding data service providers, and using available analysis software. In addition, there is also an appendix that includes formulas and tables for easy reference.

There are a great many well-written books about stock options. Unfortunately, the authors of this book believe that they have written principally with the market maker and professional trader in mind. The goal of this book is to create a practical guide for the individual investor. We hope that it serves as a valuable resource tool to help you understand risk management, leverage, strategies, and how to protect profit in an ever-changing market. Most of all, however, in providing you with this resource, we hope that this book not only clarifies for you what stock options are but also helps you effectively *use* them in the marketplace.

Chapter 1

Introduction to Options

Why Stock Options?

Most Americans are aware today of the unprecedented explosion that has taken place in stock investing and ownership over the past 10 years. Whether through their retirement plans at work or in their personal investment accounts at home, a rapidly growing number of American households now own stock in publicly traded companies. Also well documented is the fact that an increasing number of individual investors are actively involved in making their *own* investment decisions, specifically in the area of buying and selling stock. Less widely known, however, is that alongside this escalating interest in personal investing and portfolio management is a growing curiosity about the potential benefits of stock-option trading.

In fact, evidence shows that the excitement of this new opportunity has led many new online traders to rush into trading with a get-rich-quick mentality. The attitude is "buy low, sell high." New traders are so eager to make money in the marketplace that they commit a majority of their capital to a position without taking the time to analyze the risk/reward profile. At this writing, all evidence indicates that the majority of all day traders are losing money. There are several reasons. First, most day traders do not fully understand risk management. Rather, their primary strategy is essentially based on hope. Second, they are committing too much capital to a position, and they are not treating trading as a business. Instead, they treat it as a lotto game. The California Lotto slogan rings so true with the day-trading herd: "You can't win if you don't play!" How many lotto winners do you know?

On the other hand, those who have been less quick to act (the cautious investors among us) have remained on the sidelines, reflecting on what they have heard concerning the inherent risks of option trading. Having read that options are primarily used for speculation and that most will expire as worthless, these investors turn their backs on options and on the potential that they have for enhancing their investment or trading performance. What we can see, then, is that although stock-option trading is steadily gaining legitimacy, many of today's newcomers—the enthusiastic and cautious alike—do not sufficiently understand stock options in order to use them effectively as components of an overall investment strategy.

As professional options traders, we have been buying and selling options for a living for many years. We understand the risks and rewards of options in a way that the individual investor might not, and from that standpoint, we believe that for both the enthusiastic and cautious investor, a sound education in stock-options trading is a necessary investment. From our vantage point, we get to see how investors are using (and, in some cases, abusing) stock options. In addition, options trading can be risky—especially for those who want to use options speculatively in order to create quick wealth. Yet, at the same time, we are more than familiar with the ways in which options can be used to preserve existing wealth and create predictable sources of income. How you use options is what matters. We would like to encourage the enthusiastic and hesitant investor alike to use this book in order to obtain the real facts about stock options. Our strong belief is that individual investors can and should learn how to use stock options intelligently and prudently—and in so doing, they will make themselves available to new horizons in trading and investing. Consider, after all, that although the consequences of an accident or equipment failure can be devastating, most of us drive cars anyway. We have decided that the benefits derived from driving are worth the risk. In both cases, we are all the more likely to benefit if we learn how to be good drivers and when to follow code. Options trading/investing is much the same.

History of Options

The Earliest History

The use of options in an attempt to ensure economic security or financial gain dates back in our history much farther than most people would expect. The first published account of options use was in Aristotle's *Politics*, published in 332 B.C. According to Aristotle, Thales, a fellow philosopher, was said to be the creator of options. Thales was not only a great philosopher but also a great astronomer and mathematician. In response to criticism that his profession had no merit, Thales used his ability to read the stars in order to forecast future weather patterns. His skill enabled him to predict a large olive harvest in the coming year.

Thales, however, had little money and was unable to secure the use of the olive presses for their full value, so he put deposits on all of the presses that existed for miles and miles. In doing so, he used a small amount of money to secure the right to use the presses come harvest season. When olive-picking time came around and the presses were in great demand, Thales was able to sell his options for a great deal more than he paid for them. Unknowingly, perhaps, Thales had created the first option contract. He purchased the right to use the presses, not the presses themselves. In doing so, he was able to use considerably less money than he would have if he purchased the presses themselves. Owning the right gave Thales the ability to use the presses during harvest time himself (or to sell his options when, due to the demand, they would be worth considerably more than when he entered the contract). The seller, on the other hand, was happy to sell the right to use the presses, because it ensured that the seller would receive income whether the harvest was successful or not. In securing a price for the presses, however, the seller gave up the right to charge the customers more for use of the presses during a record harvest. Thales' foresight enabled him to reap this benefit. Clearly, then, Thales was able to redeem philosophy and astronomy from any accusations that its practitioners had their heads in the clouds.

Options sprang up again during the tulip mania of 1636. Tulips were first imported into Europe from Turkey in the 1500s. These brightly colored flowers gained in popularity, and the demand increased for all types of bulbs. By the early 17th century, tulips had become a symbol of affluence; demand began to outweigh supply; and tulip bulb prices rose dramatically. As popularity increased to include all levels of society, Dutch growers and dealers (with Holland being the largest producer of tulip bulbs) began to trade tulip bulb options. With options being less expensive than the direct purchase of the bulbs, greater numbers of people speculated on future price increases. Initially, this strategy proved profitable, because prices did continue to rise. This situation only caused the speculative frenzy to grow. People mortgaged their homes and businesses in order to cash in on the free money. Tulip bulb prices continued to soar even higher.

The bubble burst in 1637. As prices dropped, the buying frenzy became a selling panic. The Dutch economy began to crumble. People lost their homes and their livelihoods, banks failed, and fortunes were lost. Although the real causes of this financial fiasco were greed, reckless speculation, and the use of borrowed funds to invest, people blamed options. This was the first public black eye for options, because tulip options were responsible for enabling people to speculate with small amounts of money and large amounts of leverage. We must remember, then, that leverage can work against a trader just as easily as it can work to his or her favor.

In 1872, an American financier named Russell Sage invented the first call and put stock options. Like today's options, Sage's options gave the holder the right to purchase (call) or sell (put) a set amount of stock at a set price within a given time period. Sage began trading options in an *over-the-counter* (OTC) fashion and made millions of dollars in the process. These options were not standardized, and each contract had specific characteristics that made them difficult to trade out of once they were entered into. For this reason, it was unlikely that anyone aside from the original buyer/seller would trade out of the contract with the option holder. Furthermore, because the public was unfamiliar with stock options, Sage was able to use them to manipulate securities—taking large positions in the underlying stock without the knowledge of the public or the company. At one point, by using stock options to manipulate the security, Sage purchased such a large amount of a company's stock through the use of options that he gained control of the New York City elevated transit lines. After losing a great deal of money by trading options during the stock market crash of 1884, however, Sage stopped trading options altogether. Yet, options continued to trade without him.

The Birth and Rise of Today's Options Industry

By the mid-1900s, in response to the Securities and Exchange Act of 1934 (which itself was a response to the stock market crash of 1929), the Put and Call Brokers and Dealers Association was formed—signaling the beginning of OTC options trading. Public acceptance was extremely limited, and options remained an illiquid investment vehicle as they were not standardized and could not be exercised until their expiration dates.

In 1973, with the creation of the Chicago Board of Options Exchange, call option contracts were finally standardized. With standardization came liquidity, and for the first time in history options became accessible to the general population. The *Options Clearing Corporation* (OCC) was established as the guarantor of traded contracts. As guarantor, the OCC eliminated the concern that the party on the other side of the option contract would default on his or her obligation by guaranteeing each buyer and seller of options performance on their contracts. With the development of standardized option contracts and OCC oversight and guarantees, option trading was ready to flourish. (Refer to Chapter 11, "The Marketplace," for a detailed discussion of market making and market makers.)

One of the most important developments was the institutionalization of the market maker system. Market makers are professional, large-volume options traders whose own trading serves the public customer by creating liquidity and depth in the marketplace. On a daily basis, market makers account for more than half of all options trading volume, and much of this activity is a function of them creating and ensuring a two-sided market with the best bids and offers for public customers.

With an effective infrastructure in place, the remaining hurdle to widespread acceptance of options concerned pricing. You might stand ready to trade a particular option, but only at a fair price. Absent widely accepted methods of evaluating options prices, pricing was arbitrary. Fischer Black and Myron Scholes solved this dilemma around the same time as the establishment of the *Chicago Board of Exchange* (CBOE) when they developed a mathematical formula for calculating the theoretical value of an option. The Black-Scholes model computes the value of an option based on specified inputs related to the various characteristics of an option, such as strike price, price of the underlying asset, time to expiration, risk-free return (interest rate), and the standard deviation (volatility) of the underlying asset. The model's output helps achieve greater accuracy in assessing the fair market value of an option, risks that are associated with a position, and how an option's value changes as market conditions change.

The Black-Scholes model was not the first pricing model developed; however, it was the first model to reduce the number of computations that were necessary for coming up with the values. Combined with the development of the personal computer, the resulting simplicity enabled the model's use in a real-time trading environment. Furthermore, the capacity to determine the risks associated with options trading has given the individual trader the ability to trade by using the same computations that professional traders use. Computational models, therefore, have helped open the business of option trading to a broader public—thereby advancing the growth of the industry.

In 1975 and 1976, with exchange-traded options increasing in demand, the American, Philadelphia, and Pacific stock exchanges began trading call options. By 1977, with call options trading on all U.S. exchanges and their volume increasing, put options were also introduced. As options became more popular, interest in pricing and trading them increased.

In 1979, a new computational formula—the Cox-Rubinstein formula —was developed. Cox-Rubinstein originally developed the model in an attempt to explain the Black-Scholes model to students. Unlike the

Black-Scholes model, however, the Cox-Rubinstein model is a binomial model—which means that at any given point, there are two possible values for an option (based on either an up-tick in the stock or a down-tick in the underlying stock). By totaling the underlying price possibilities and the resulting option price possibilities, the model determines a theoretical price. This formula is better at accounting for American style expiration, which gives the option holder the capability to exercise his or her option early. As more models became available and the ability to fairly assess an options value increased, options became a larger part of the investment portfolio. Valuation models have also given the individual trader the capability to determine the risks that are associated with options trading. Computational models, therefore, have helped open the business of option trading to a broader public—thereby advancing the growth of the industry.

By 1999, a record 507 million option contracts traded across the four U.S. option exchanges—reflecting a veritable explosion in the industry. Today, option trading has evolved into an easy and safe financial instrument and a routine practice for an ever-expanding number of regular participants in financial markets. Furthermore, the advent of the Internet has made it possible for the average investor to trade options at a minimal cost. More than 8.8 million individual investors worldwide have online trading accounts. What many of these traders are learning is that the leverage, which options provide, makes option trading not only a good way to protect an investment but also a powerful way to speculate in the marketplace.

Options: A Conceptual Overview

The intent of this book is to provide the tools that you need to effectively trade stock options. The most basic definition of a stock option is a contract that enables its owner to buy and/or sell stock under certain, specified conditions. As an option investor, you would purchase or sell this right (or option) in order to buy or sell stock; although importantly, this technique is not the same thing as actually purchasing or selling the stock itself. Rather, you are purchasing the right to benefit from movement in the market related to the underlying stock, which will (in turn) influence the public's potential demand for that security. Because an option is defined in terms of its relationship to an underlying security, options are known as derivative products. Now, however, we will focus on familiarizing the reader with options in general.

Options, in their traditional form, evolved as a type transaction between the owner of certain property and a non-owner. The landlord-tenant and lender-borrower relationships, with which the reader is likely much more familiar, are similar types of transactions. In the landlord-tenant situation, the landlord exchanges his or her right to use a portion of his or her property to the tenant for a rental fee. The lender allows the borrower to use the lender's money in exchange for an interest charge and the borrower's pledge to return the borrowed funds pursuant to a schedule of payments.

Owning property brings with it certain consequences that people sometimes refer to as the benefits and burdens of ownership. These consequences include the following:

- The right to benefit from appreciation in the value of the property
- The right to use the property as you see fit
- The risk that the value of the property will decline
- The right to determine when, and at what price, to sell the property

Options are contracts in which specific attributes of ownership are transferred from the owner of the asset to another party in exchange for compensation. Where a benefit of ownership is involved, the owner receives the compensation. Where a risk of ownership is transferred, the owner pays the consideration. Later in this book, we will look in detail at the technical aspects of publicly traded stock. For now, though, let's consider several common examples.

Example: Undeveloped Land

A real estate developer has a problem. He wants to build an apartment complex on a vacant lot that he does not own. In addition to obtaining rights to develop the vacant lot, he will need to obtain certain land-use approvals and a loan commitment from a lender in order to finance construction costs. Additionally, he must raise money from investors. The developer does not want to purchase the vacant lot until he knows that the project will go forward, but he cannot get investors until he has obtained rights to the property. He also cannot get financing until he obtains the land-use approvals. The solution is to purchase the right, but not the obligation (option), to purchase the lot from the owner of the vacant lot by a certain date for an agreed-upon price. With this right, the developer can attempt to put all of the pieces together. If he is successful, he has the resources to exercise his right (option) to buy the property and move forward with the project. If his efforts fail, he just walks away from the project—losing only the amount paid for the option. The motivation of the developer to purchase the option is clear. What can we say about the motivation of the owner of the vacant lot? Why would he sell the option to the developer? There could be two reasons: first, the owner gets to keep the compensation paid for the option; second, the agreed-upon purchase price is likely to be higher than the owner could obtain if he sold the property without first obtaining the land-use approvals. These factors might be sufficient incentive to the owner of the vacant lot to sell the option to the developer. We refer to this type of option as a call option. The purchaser of the option has the right, but not the obligation, to acquire the property for a specific price (prior to a specified date). After that date, the holder of the option no longer has the right to purchase the property. The option is said to expire at that point.

Example: Property/Health Insurance

Auto insurance, health insurance, and homeowner's insurance are all examples of put options. These options transfer the risk of loss from the owner to the seller of the put (the insurance company).

We hope that we have made several important points in this general introduction to options:

- Options have legitimate commercial applications.
- They are similar to other more common transactions such as landlord-tenant and lender-borrower relationships.
- They are not some new casino game designed to suck in the unwary.

With this background in place, we will now focus on how exchange-traded stock options can be intelligently and prudently used to reduce investment risk and increase investment and/or trading profitability.

Chapter 2

Characteristics of Stock Options

Introduction

As we can see from the rather turbulent history of options, the survival of the options industry depended upon the enforced standardization of options contracts. When the doors of the *Chicago Board of Options Exchange* (CBOE) opened in 1973, standardization and government regulation finally made it possible for options to gain legitimacy. Today, specific characteristics of publicly traded stock options contracts, referred to as the terms of the option, enable us to define these option contracts as follows.

A publicly traded stock option, which from this point forward we will simply refer to as a stock option, is a contract. This contract gives the purchaser (in other words, the holder or owner) of that option the right, but not the obligation, to buy or sell shares of the option's underlying security for a specific price per share on or before a specific expiration date. The holder of an option can either exercise the option (buy or sell the underlying security) or sell the option at a profit or loss in the open marketplace. Should the option holder exercise his or her right, the seller of the option is obligated, upon assignment, to sell the underlying asset to the call option holder. Also, in the case of a put option, the seller is obligated to purchase the underlying asset from the holder.

Clearly, upon first encounter, this definition can be rather intimidating. Needless to say, when we start unpacking the definition, we can deduce that stock options have the following characteristics:

1. Stock options are exercisable in relation to a specifically identified underlying security.
2. There are two types of stock options:

    a. Calls—The right to buy the underlying security
    b. Puts—The right to sell the underlying security

3. Stock options have an exercise price (also known as the strike price). This price is known as the established price at which the purchase (in the case of a call) or sale (in the case of a put) of the underlying security will occur upon exercise of the option contract.
4. All stock options have an expiration date. This date is the deadline on which the right to exercise an option ceases to exist (the Saturday following the third Friday of the designated month of the option).

Two additional characteristics are as follows:

5. Stock options can be one of two possible styles: American or European.

NOTE

Note that FLEX options, which we will discuss later in this chapter, have slightly different characteristics.

6. One stock option represents a unit of trade that typically corresponds to 100 shares of the underlying asset.

In this chapter, we will define the various components listed, and in Chapter 4, "Pricing Options," we will see how each characteristic contributes to the price of an option.

Underlying Security

Like stock, you can use options to take a position based on a calculated assessment of movement in the market. Although both stock and options enable taking directional positions, however, options can provide the investor with a comparatively large amount of leverage and far less risk. The purchaser of a stock option is paying for the right to buy or sell stock and is not paying for the stock itself. For this reason, we refer to stock options as derivative products—products for which the value is essentially derived from the characteristics and value of a related stock (known as the underlying security).

The underlying security, then, is the specific stock upon which an option contract is based. When an XYZ call is exercised, XYZ stock is bought. When an XYZ put is exercised, XYZ stock is sold. (You should also remember that a trader can buy or sell calls and puts without actually purchasing stock.)

> ### NOTE
>
> A stock index represents more than one underlying security. Index options are based on an average of the stocks that make up that particular index. For the sake of simplicity, most index options settle for cash, because it would be difficult to deliver the correct percentage of all of the underlying stocks of which the index is made.

The Two Types of Stock Options

Option type refers to whether an option is a call or a put. This distinction is extremely important, because call and put options give their owners different rights and their sellers different obligations.

Call Option

A call option offers its holder the capability to purchase that option's underlying stock at the designated strike price until the option's expiration date. For example, the owner of an XYZ March 50 call has the right to purchase XYZ for $50 on or before its expiration in March.

1. The purchaser of a call option is speculating the following:

   a. That the underlying stock will increase in value
   b. That the option is undervalued and will increase in value due to changes in the pricing variables. If so, the purchaser will be able to exercise the right to buy the underlying security from the call seller for less than the price at which it is trading on the open market. The purchaser will then be in a position to profit from either selling or holding the higher-priced stock. As an alternative to exercising the call, the holder can choose to sell the option for a premium prior to expiration. The option's value itself increases relative (among other things) to an increase in the underlying security.

2. The seller, or writer, of a call is obligated (upon assignment) to sell the underlying stock to the call purchaser. As opposed to the purchaser, the seller of a call option is speculating the following:

   a. That the underlying stock price will stay the same price or decrease in value
   b. That the option is overvalued and will decrease in value due to changes in the pricing variables. Under such conditions, the option itself would decrease in value and/or expire as worthless. The seller then relies on not having to fulfill the contractual obligation to the buyer, thereby profiting from the sale of the option. If the option holder does exercise his or her right to buy the underlying security for the specified strike price, however, then the seller must sell 100 shares of XYZ for $50 a share for each call exercised. The party that is exercising the call does not care whether the seller sells XYZ holdings that he or she already owns, goes out to the market to purchase those shares, or borrows the shares from a broker.

Put Option

The owner of a put option has the right to sell that option's underlying stock for the designated strike price until the option's expiration date. For example, the owner of a XYZ March 40 put has the right to sell XYZ for $40 on or before its March expiration.

1. The purchaser of a put option is speculating the following:

   a. That the underlying asset will decrease in value
   b. That the option is undervalued and will increase in value due to changes in the pricing variables. If so, he or she will then be able to exercise his or her option—and the put seller will have to buy the stock from the put buyer at a higher price than the current trading pricein the open marketplace. As a result of a decline in the price of the underlying security, the right to sell the underlying security at a price higher than its current trading price would become more valuable. The put holder is then able to simply sell

the option at a premium of the original purchase price, thereby profiting from the stock's decline.

2. The seller, or writer, of a put is obligated (upon assignment) to purchase the underlying stock from the put purchaser. As opposed to the purchaser, the seller of a put option is speculating the following:

   a. That the underlying stock price will stay at the same price or increase in value
   b. That the option is overvalued and will decrease in value due to changes in the pricing variables

If the put option were to decline in value due to an increase in the price of the underlying security and/or a decrease in volatility, the put seller could either purchase the put for less than he or she sold it or let it expire as worthless and collect the entire premium received for the sale. The seller (writer) of a put is obligated to buy the underlying stock from the put purchaser, regardless of the price at which the underlying stock is currently trading in the open marketplace.

Strike Price/Exercise Price

The exercise price, or strike price, is the specific price at which the shares of the underlying security can be bought or sold by the purchaser of the option. The exercise price is a fixed price and will not change as the underlying security changes in price. When an option is exercised, the option writer (seller) is obligated to sell (in the case of a call option) or buy (in the case of a put option) a specified number of shares of the underlying security at a per-share price that is equal to the exercise price. The importance of the strike price is illustrated in Figure 2-1, as we can see from this

Figure 2-1   *Exercise prices and exercising options.*

Examples:

Call Option Exercise Price

• If the *holder* of 1 May 50 call option wanted to exercise that option, s/he would pay $5,000 to buy 100 shares of stock for $50/share. (One option contract typically corresponds to 100 shares of the underlying. See Unit of Trade)

• If the *writer* of 1 May 50 Call option were assigned on that option, s/he would be obligated to sell 100 shares of XYZ for $50/share.

Put Option Exercise Price

• If the *holder* of a May 70 put option decided to exercise the option, s/he would receive $7,000 for selling 100 shares of stock for $70/share.

• If the *writer* of a May 70 Put option were assigned on that option, s/he would have to buy 100 shares of stock for $70/share or $7000.00.

example, the strike price is the purchase and sale price of the underlying upon assignment and/or exercise.

Strike-Price Increments.   As with the other constituent parts of stock options, strike prices have a standardized format. Strike-price increments for listed exchange options are established by using uniform increments that all of the U.S. exchanges employ. There are three strike-price increment levels: 2.5, 5, and 10. The assignment of increment levels varies according to the price of the underlying security. In general, higher-priced stocks are assigned greater increments.

When exchange-traded options are initially listed, the strike prices are set close to the current price of the underlying security. Generally, three strike prices at one of the designated increment levels are established. The first is established at the closest-available strike price to the current price of the underlying security, and the remaining two are established at the next-available strikes above and below that strike. As summarized in Figure 2-2, depending on the price of the stock, the difference in strike prices is generally in $2, $5, and $10 increments.

Expiration Date.   The expiration date is the date on which an option and the right to exercise it cease to exist. The third Friday of the expiration month is the last day that options of the expiring month can be traded or exercised. The options of that expiration month expire on the following day (Saturday). Generally, options that are .75 of a dollar or more in the money are automatically exercised by the Options Clearing Corporation (OCC).

Expiration Cycle

Although you might suspect that options would be standardized with consecutive expiration months (for example, January, February, and March),

Figure 2-2   *Strike increments and strike price assignments.*

Strike Increments and Strike Price Assignments

- 2-1/2 point strike increments are used when the current price of the underlying security is less than $25, (and the strike must be a multiple of 2-1/2, e.g. 17-1/2). Therefore, if new options were added when a stock was trading at $18, the strikes added would have exercise prices of 15, 17.50, and 20. [NOTE: Some large cap issues trading above $25 will have listed 2-1/2 strike increments when the current price of the underlying security is less than $50.]

- 5 point strike increments are assigned when the current price of the underlying security is between $25–$200 (and the strike must be a multiple of 5, e.g. 60 or 75).

- 10 point strike increments are used when the current price of the underlying security is trading over $200 (and the strike must be a multiple of 10, e.g. 290).

NOTE:

- New strikes are added when the underlying security rises above the highest strike or drops below the lowest strike.
- New strikes are added when stock splits occur. Some may include options with odd fractions (e.g. 3/8, 5/8), depending on the split ratio (e.g. 1 for 2, 1 for 3 . . .).

expiration months fall into cycles. This system was established to provide an orderly and liquid marketplace, because a large multitude of strikes would make the options less liquid. Therefore, although in the course of a year options will expire during each calendar month for a given stock, generally four outstanding expiration months are available for an underlying security at any given time.

The first two of these months, referred to as the near-term months, will be the calendar months with the next two upcoming expiration dates. (Remember that expiration takes place on the third Friday of the month.) For example, if we are in early January, the near-term months would be January and February—while if we were later in January (that is, after expiration), the near-term months would be February and March. The remaining two months, referred to as the far-term months, will vary based on the expiration cycle for a particular stock. Expiration cycles are designed so that options will be listed to coincide with the release of the underlying company's earnings. In addition to enabling investors to protect their stock holdings in the event that the underlying company releases poor earnings, this arrangement provides the opportunity for earnings speculation.

The three expiration cycles include the following:

• The January cycle: January—April—July—October
• The February cycle: February—May—August—November
• The March cycle: March—June—September—December

Here is an example. After December expiration (but on or before January expiration), the following option months would be trading for each cycle:

1. The January cycle would include the following months:
   January—February—April—July
2. The February cycle would include the following months:
   January—February—May—August
3. The March cycle would include the following months:
   January—February—March—June

Notice how all three cycles have the same two near-term months while the far-term months vary. Refer to Appendix D in this book for a comprehensive list of expiration cycles.

NOTE

If you exercise an option early and there is still time value attached to the option (the price of the option less its intrinsic value), you will lose that time value. We will cover these concepts in future sections of this book.

The holder or writer of any option contract can close out his or her open position at any time prior to expiration by purchasing the option or by selling it.

Unit of Trade/Contract Size

The unit of trade, or contract size, represents the number of shares of stock that are linked to an option contract. One option contract generally represents 100 shares of the underlying stock. Therefore, if the holder of one call option were to exercise his or her option to buy the underlying stock for the stated per-share amount (exercise price), he or she would then own 100 shares of the underlying company's stock and would no longer have an open option position. Therefore, one unit equals one option contract, which equals 100 shares.

Remember, although one option contract generally represents 100 shares, options are quoted on a per-share basis.

Here is another example of unit of trade/contract size. XYZ stock is trading $44/share. If the XYZ July 45 call is trading for $1, then the aggregate premium for a single option contract would be $100 ($1 $\times$ 100 = $100) plus commissions.

Although one option contract usually represents 100 shares, there are exceptions to the rule. If, for example, a company's stock splits after an option has been listed, both the option's exercise price and the number of shares covered are adjusted accordingly. An example of how an options exchange deals with a stock split is illustrated in Figure 2-3.

Option Styles

Two current styles of options exist: American and European. Nobel Laureate Paul Samuelson coined these labels in his groundbreaking 1965 article on warrants. These styles reflect the different needs of investors. Importantly, the terms American and European have nothing to do with where these options contracts (or their underlying securities) are traded. For example, most options that are listed on European exchanges are American-style options.

European-style options are option contracts that you can exercise only during a specified time (typically one day prior to expiration). European exercise is common for many cash-based index options. Large institutional traders who are hedging (a transaction undertaken to reduce the risk of another transaction) their stock positions by using index options want some assurance that the options will not be exercised early—leaving them vulnerable to market exposure.

American-style options are option contracts that you can exercise at any time (up to and including the expiration date of the option). Most exchange-traded options are American style. Because of the flexibility that American-style options give, they are generally more valuable than European-style options. This statement is true for two reasons. First, the holder of an American-style call option might want to exercise the option early in order to convert the position into a long stock position and thereby collect the dividend issued by the underlying company. The purchaser of this call is willing to pay more for this added opportunity, whereas the call writer (seller) requires more to cover the possibility of losing the dividend by being forced to sell the stock when the option is exercised early.

Figure 2-3 *Unit of trade and stock splits.*

EXAMPLE: Unit of Trade and Stock Splits

XYZ announces a 3-for-2 stock split. XYZ option series will be adjusted to reflect this 3-for-2 stock split on Wednesday, March 29, 2000. For each outstanding XYZ series, dividing the existing exercise price by the split ratio (1.5) and rounding to the nearest eighth of a point will reduce the exercise price. Then the option symbol will change to AYZ. The contract unit of each adjusted AYZ series will be increased to 150 shares, and the contract multiplier will change to 150, i.e., 1 point of premium or strike\price will equal $150. [Any existing FLEX series will be adjusted in a similar manner to the standardized option.] No new months will be listed for AYZ options.

Adjusted Exercise Prices:

EXISTING SERIES   ADJUSTED SERIES

100 Shares   150 Shares

MONTH/STRIKE		CALLS	PUTS	MONTH/STRIKE		CALLS	PUTS
Apr	65	XYZ	XYZ	*become>* Apr	43 3/8	AYZ	AYZ
Apr	70	XYZ	XYZ	*become>* Apr	46 5/8	AYZ	AYZ
Apr	75	XYZ	XYZ	*become>* Apr	50	AYZ	AYZ
Apr	80	XYZ	XYZ	*become>* Apr	53 3/8	AYZ	AYZ
Apr	85	XYZ	XYZ	*become>* Apr	56 5/8	AYZ	AYZ
Apr	90	XYZ	XYZ	*become>* Apr	60	AYZ	AYZ
Apr	95	XYZ	XYZ	*become>* Apr	63 3/8	AYZ	AYZ

To facilitate the maintenance of a fair and orderly options market, new XYZ series with a contract unit of 100 shares will be introduced on Friday, March 31, 2000. The XYZ series will be added for April, May, June, and September expirations at exercise prices nearest the money.

Note:

• The position and exercise limits following this stock split will be any combination of AYZ and XYZ option contracts on the same side of the market not to exceed 9,000,000 shares of the underlying security through September 16, 2000. Following the September 2000 expiration, the position and exercise limits will revert to the standard limit of 60,000 contracts.

• It is important to contact the options exchanges and/or your broker to check the effects of the stock split on your options holdings. The option exchange web sites will contain all information on stock splits and the corresponding options adjustments.

Secondly, the early exercise of puts enables a trader to convert long puts into short stock. This feature ensures that he or she will be able to either avoid long stock interest or collect on short stock interest.

Option Styles: LEAPS and FLEX Options

Some options are not the standard of the industry. We will discuss LEAPS© and FLEX©, two commonly traded options that fall into this category, in the following paragraphs.

LEAPS©. Although they might last as long as seven months, options generally expire within five months or less. *Long-Term Equity Anticipation Securities* (LEAPS©) represent a variation of standard option contracts. In

1990, with the development of LEAPS©, investors were offered the opportunity to trade a longer-term option with an expiration date up to three years into the future. Therefore, as with regular equity options, the owner (or holder) of a LEAP© call has the right to purchase (or sell, in the case of a put) a predetermined amount of the underlying stock (unit of trade/contract size) at a predetermined price (strike price) for a specified period of time. For LEAPS©, the specified period can be up to three years into the future.

LEAPS© give traders and investors the capability to trade for the long-term without making an outright stock purchase. In particular, LEAPS© puts can be used to hedge an existing stock position, therefore providing protection in the event of a substantial decline in the underlying stock for a longer period of time than regular short-term options. Along with the advantage of being able to trade for the long term, one of the benefits of trading LEAPS© is that time decay (the erosion of the time-value portion of the option price) moves at a much slower rate than shorter-term options. In other words, LEAPS© hold their time value longer, which is an important benefit for investors.

You can distinguish LEAPS© by their unique option symbols that enable investors to distinguish them from other options that are currently available on a particular stock. LEAPS© symbols begin with either L, W, Z, or V, depending on the number of years in the future until expiration. Figure 2-4 illustrates the ease at which a LEAP can be distinguished from near-term option simply by referring to options symbol.

As time passes and LEAPS© have fewer than nine months remaining until expiration, they are renamed and become an ordinary option on the underlying security.

There are some disadvantages to trading LEAPS©. Due to the large cash outlay (you pay more for the added time value) and a larger bid-to-offer spread, LEAPS© tend to be more illiquid than front-month (near-term) options, making it more difficult to close an existing LEAPS© position. In addition, LEAPS© are more sensitive to changes in interest rates because of the amount of time until expiration (known as Rho risk).

Figure 2-4   *LEAP© symbols.*

Example:

Stock Symbol	Expiration Date	Option Symbol	Strike Information
XYZ	Standard Option expires January 2001	XYZ	January 50 Call
XYZ	LEAPS° Option expiring January 2002	LYZ	January 50 Call
XYZ	LEAPS° Option expiring January 2003	ZYZ	January 50 Call

Like any interest rate-sensitive financial, a change in interest rates has a much greater effect on a long-term instrument than it does on a short-term one.

In addition, an investor will find that there is a notable difference between the prices of LEAPS© call and put options. This difference, known as the cost of carry, is a result of the long and short interest. For example, when a trader has a long stock position, he or she either pays an interest rate for the borrowed funds used to purchase the stock or must forego interest that would have been earned on the cash used to fund the purchase. When a trader has a short stock position, he or she receives cash in his or her account for selling the stock and will be paid interest for the funds in the account. Because option traders hedge their positions by using stock and the stock must be held for the life of the option, interest rates greatly affect the options. As interest rates go up, the price of the calls increases and the price of the puts decreases. In addition, as the interest rates go down, the price of the calls decreases and the price of the puts increases. Therefore, as interest rates change, the price of the options changes to reflect the cost of carry. As far as LEAPS© are concerned, then, the longer to expiration the greater the effect on the cost of carry. Cost of carry and Rho risk are discussed further in Chapter 7, "The Greeks."

As with the near-term options, the expiration date for LEAPS© is the Saturday following the third Friday of the expiration month. All LEAPS© contracts expire in the month of January. LEAPS© are subject to American-style exercise. In other words, the holder has the right to exercise the options on any trading day prior to expiration. We will discuss LEAPS© strategies in the strategies sections of this book.

FLEX® Options.   In spite of standardization within the options industry, the need for customization continues. Large professional and independent traders have special needs requiring the flexibility of customized option contracts. Therefore, in 1993, the four U.S. option exchanges developed a new product: *Flexible Exchange Index* (FLEX®) options, which enable investors to customize key contract terms (including expiration date, exercise style, and exercise price). FLEX® options have been expanded from index options to listed equity options by creating E-FLEX® options (Equity Flexible Exchange options). E-FLEX© options also enable investors to custom design their contract specifications in order to fit their investment portfolio strategy. Due to the large financial requirements associated with opening a FLEX® or E-FLEX® option position, generally only specialized traders and large institutions use FLEX® or E-FLEX® options as a means to protect their index and/or equity positions.

To create a FLEX® or E-FLEX® option, the customer must submit to his or her broker a *Request for Quote* (RFQ). An exchange representative then quotes the FLEX® or E-FLEX® option in the corresponding options trading pit where the standard options are traded. The exchange then contacts the brokerage firm to deliver the FLEX® or E-FLEX® quote. The two-sided quote is disseminated with a minimum quote size of 250 contracts. The RFQ is disseminated as an administrative text message over the *Options Price Reporting Authority* (OPRA). This message contains all of the FLEX® or E-FLEX® terms. Each FLEX® or E-FLEX® quote will have a 2 to 20 minute response time known as the *Request Response Time* (RRT). This RRT enables all members who are on-floor and off-floor to respond to the FLEX® or E-FLEX® quote. At the end of the RRT, the *best bid and offer* (BBO) is reported to the customer who has the option of accepting all or part of the BBO, seeks to improve the BBO, or wants to reject the entire BBO. If the customer accepts, then the contract is traded.

Option Class

Having defined some of the basic attributes of options, we are now able to address what makes up an option class. An option class is the term used to refer to options that share the following characteristics:

1. Type (either call or put)
2. Style (either American, European, or FLEX)
3. Underlying security
4. Contract size/unit of trade (for example, covering the same amount of the underlying security)

Here is an example:

CPQ MAR 30 CALLS

CPQ MAR 35 CALLS

CPQ APR 30 CALLS

CPQ APR 35 CALLS

These Compaq Computers calls are all of the same option class. We know that they are the same type because they are all calls, and they are the same style because they are American style. Finally, they are all derivatives of the same underlying security, CPQ stock. Therefore, all CPQ calls would make up an option class.

The ability to refer to a class of options is essential when implementing complicated option strategies. If the investor is looking to speculate or insure his or her portfolio, he or she needs to know exactly what the components of the option class represent. For example, in the case of a stock split, there will be two sets of call option classes: one representing the pre-split shares and another representing the post-split shares. In this case, the unit of trade/contract size of the option class has changed. The amount of underlying stock that a pre-split (old) option represents can be drastically different from that of a post-split (new) option. The investor who needs options for a specific amount of the underlying stock must know how much of the underlying stock the option that he or she is trading represents. Similarly, if the investor needs the capability to exercise an option early, he or she needs to know that the style component of the option class is American and not European. Most importantly, if the investor is looking for down-side protection for his or her long stock position, he or she needs to be aware of the type of option being purchased. Incorrectly buying a call instead of a put can be a costly mistake.

Reading Options Quotes

Due to the overwhelming number of stock options listed, it is impossible to list them all in the newspaper. Consequently, newspapers tend to list the most actively traded options of the day and/or the options that have the least amount of time remaining to expiration. Remember, the newspaper provides historical information, so not all options are listed. Additionally, if an option is not listed on a particular day, it does not mean that it expires or is delisted (options that are no longer listed on an exchange for trading). Rather, it might simply mean that it was not one of the most actively traded options issues.

The Internet has made it easy to view trading information on all options online. Many online data providers disseminate free end-of-day option bid and offers, the trading day's last sale and/or closing price, volume of trade, and sometimes the open interest (the amount of current open positions in a particular option series). For a fee, the active trader can subscribe to a quote service that provides real-time stock and options quotes. Figure 2-5 is an example of a quote that an may come across on-line.

Bid/Ask. Quotes are broadcast to the public, reflecting the best (highest) price that someone is willing to pay for an asset and the best (lowest) price at which someone is willing to sell. The bid is the disseminated price at which exchanges indicate that options can be sold, and it is the best available price that the purchaser is willing to pay. The ask is the disseminated price at which exchanges indicate that options can be bought and the lowest price at which the seller is willing to sell. A buyer can purchase an option or stock by paying the ask price, or offer.

Daily Volume. Daily volume indicates the total number of options contracts that are traded during the trading day in a particular series. If the broker sells 102 XYZ Apr 40 calls to the market makers in the crowd and nothing else trades in that series for the remainder of the day, the daily volume will be 102 contracts.

Open Interest (OI). OI is a measure of the number of outstanding (open) option contracts. Importantly, then, the open-interest volume should not be confused with the daily or total volume at which a particular series traded during the day. When an investor is purchasing (or selling) an option contract that he or she does not already own (or has not

Figure 2-5 *Option quotes.*

C-OI	BID	OFFER	VOL	STRIKE	VOL	BID	OFFER	P-OI
209	4 3/8	4 1/2	50	**APR 35**	30	1/4	3/8	361
5.94K	1 1/8	1 3/8	102	**APR 40**	400	1 3/4	2	2.73K

already bought), he or she is said to be opening a position. This transaction increases the open-interest volume. When an investor sells a contract that he or she already owns or purchases a contract that he or she is already short, he or she is said to be closing a position. The open-interest will decrease by this amount.

You can best understand open interest by thinking of options as inventory. If a trader and/or investor has an inventory of options, these options are considered open and are recorded as part of the open-interest. Therefore, open interest can and will increase and decrease as investors and traders increase and decrease their options inventory. Open interest will also decrease if you exercise an option. An exercised option ceases to exist, because the investor has elected to close the position in order to receive or deliver stock. For example, if an investor were to buy five XYZ Apr 50 calls that he or she does not already own, then he or she would have an open interest of five contacts. The OCC keeps track of the total number of contracts that are opening trades. Once the five XYZ Apr 50 calls are liquidated (sold) and he or she no longer owns them, the open interest decreases by five.

Last Sale versus Closing Price.   Many investors confuse last sale with closing price. The last sale is a reflection of the last transaction between the buyer and seller. The last sale could be days or even months old at a price that is substantially different from the current bid and offer. Given this definition, the last sale certainly does not reflect where an option can be bought or sold at any given time. On the other hand, the closing price of an option is the closest price to the bid or offer of the last sale (or the mean when there is no last sale). The closing price, then, is a closer reflection than the last sale of where the option could be bought or sold at the close of the day. An example of option markets on IBM is presented in Figure 2-6. Note that the calls are displayed on the left side of the window, while the puts are displayed on the right.

Figure 2-6   *IBM options quote page.*

CALLS							PUTS					
LAST	HIGH	LOW	VOL	BID	ASK	SYMBOL	BID	ASK	HIGH	LOW	VOL	LAST
23 1/2	23 1/2	23 1/2	2	23	24	IBMAUG100	3/16	1/4	5/16	3/16	13	5/16
25 1/8				18 1/4	19	IBMAUG105	3/8	7/16	3/8	1/4	223	3/8
16	16	16	10	13 5/8	14 3/8	IBMAUG110	3/4	13/16	7/8	11/16	68	11/16
11 3/8	11 3/8	9 7/8	65	9 7/8	10 3/8	IBMAUG115	1 9/16	1 5/8	1 5/8	1 5/16	177	1 1/2
7	8	6 1/4	313	6 1/4	6 3/4	IBMAUG120	3	3 1/4	3 3/8	2 9/16	418	3
4	5	3 3/4	902	4	4 1/8	IBMAUG125	5 3/8	5 5/8	5 5/8	4 5/8	391	5 1/2
2 3/8	2 7/8	2	4120	2 1/4	2 3/8	IBMAUG130	8 1/2	8 7/8	8 3/4	7 1/4	246	8 3/4
1 3/16	1 1/2	1 1/8	1012	1 3/16	1 1/4	IBMAUG135	12 1/4	13	13	10 7/8	29	11 3/8
11/16	3/4	1/2	401	5/8	3/4	IBMAUG140	16 3/4	17 1/2	17 3/8	17 3/8	2	17 3/8
3/8	7/16	1/4	181	5/16	3/8	IBMAUG145	21 1/2	22 1/2				20 1/2
3/16	1/4	3/16	128	3/16	1/4	IBMAUG150	26 1/2	27 1/2				25 1/4
1/16	1/16	1/16	60	1/16	1/8	IBMAUG155	31 1/2	32 1/2				

Quiz

1. What are the two types of options?

2. The established price at which the purchase (in the case of a call) or sale (in the case of a put) of the underlying security will occur upon exercise of the option contract is known as the _____.

3. The date on which the right to exercise an option ceases to exist is known as the _____ and generally falls on the _____ of the month.

4. One stock option generally represents _____ shares of the underlying security.

5. The seller of an option is referred to as the option _____.

6. The owner of a(n) _____ option has purchased the right to sell the underlying asset for the designated strike price for a specified period.

7. What are the two styles of options?

8. Options that have more than one year until expiration are typically referred to as a(n) _____.

9. The measure of the number of outstanding option contracts is the _____.

10. The seller of a(n) _____ is obligated to purchase the underlying security in case of assignment.

Please refer to Appendix I for quiz answers.

Chapter 3

Building Blocks

Introduction

Having reviewed the basics of option characteristics, we are now aware that we have a number of investment choices: stock, calls on the stock, and puts on the stock. For each of these, we can initiate a position either by purchase (referred to as a long position) or by sale (referred to as a short position), thus giving us six different initiating strategies:

- Long stock
- Short stock
- Long call
- Short call
- Long put
- Short put

These tools are what we can use to construct all option-based strategies. By combining these building blocks, the individual investor can create strategies ranging from basic to complex. Mastery of each of the individual building blocks is essential for understanding how they work in combination. Therefore, we will now look at each of these six alternatives in some detail.

Retail investors are already familiar with one of these building blocks: long stock. With an understanding of the other five building blocks, the investor will have the ability to create positions that are best suited to capitalize off any market outlook. The only limit to creating positions is the investor's creativity. Once you master the six building blocks, the possibilities are endless.

Long Stock

Long stock is the most common position among investors. After analyzing the fundamentals of a company and deducing that the company's product, its revenue model, and current market conditions reflect the likelihood of positive growth, the retail investor purchases the stock as an investment in that company. Over a period of time, if the investor's analysis proves correct, the stock value increases—rendering a profit. In this case, the investor who purchases stock with his or her own capital is said to be long stock.

Here is an example. An investor who has no position in XYZ purchases 100 shares of XYZ at $50 per share. The investor is now long 100 shares of XYZ. Figure 3-1 shows the profit and loss associated with the outright ownership of stock.

Figure 3-1 *Black line = long 100 share of stock for $50/share.*

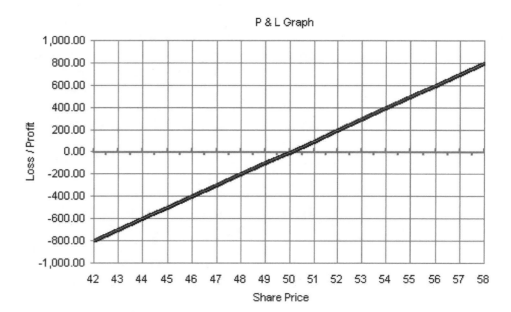

The profit in this case is unlimited. This position will profit as the stock increases in value. Each $1 increase in the market price of the stock will result in $100 worth of profit.

The loss in this example is limited. This position will generate a loss as the stock declines in price. The risk is limited only because the stock can only decrease to zero. Each $1 decrease in the market price of the stock will result in $100 worth of loss.

The outlook on this stock is bullish.

Short Stock

Being long stock is a bullish strategy, meaning that you believe there will be a rise in the market price. What if the stock is not performing positively, however? What if it is declining in price? Or, what if the investor believes that the stock is highly overvalued and is ready for a significant price pullback? Is the investor simply out of luck?

Stock that is in a downward trend (decreasing in value) is referred to as behaving bearishly. Similarly, an investor who has a pessimistic outlook on a stock is referred to as being bearish. The bearish trader can take advantage of an anticipated declining market by selling a stock short. In other words, he or she will sell a stock that he or she does not currently own. In this case, the brokerage firm lends the investor a certain number of stock shares at a particular price under the condition that the investor has capital in his or her account in order to cover the cost of the stock being borrowed. With the stock in hand, the investor now has the ability to capitalize off what he or she is speculating to be a downward move in the stock. The investor sells the borrowed stock in the marketplace at its existing price and waits until the price decreases. Once the stock price declines, the investor buys the stock back in the open market at the lower price. He or she is then able to return the stock to the brokerage firm while capturing the profit. To be sure, by selling stock short, a retail investor can take advantage of a declining market. There is always a risk that the stock that has been sold short will increase in price, however. This situation could force the investor to purchase the stock back at a higher price, resulting in a loss. If the investor is correct, however, the stock will decrease in price and he or she can buy the stock back from the open market in order to capture profit.

Here is an example. An investor who has no position in XYZ borrows 100 shares from his broker and sells it for $50 per share. Figure 3-2 shows the profits and losses associated with the short sale of a security. In this case, the profit is limited to the amount collected for the stock and risk is unlimited.

The profit in this situation is limited. This position will profit as the stock declines in value. Each $1 decrease in the market price of the stock will result in $100 worth of profit.

The loss in this case is unlimited. This position will lose money as the stock rises in value. Each $1 increase in the market price of the stock will result in $100 worth of loss. There is also the risk of stock being demanded back by the brokerage firm.

The outlook on this stock is bearish.

Figure 3-2   *Black line = short 100 shares of stock at $50/share.*

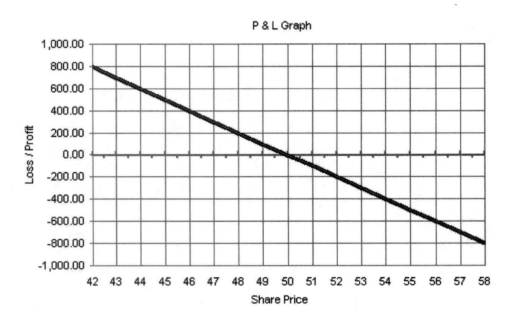

Long Call

The buyer (holder) of a call has as much profit potential as the owner of the underlying stock but has significantly limited the risk of loss. Because of the limited capital used in controlling a large interest, the long call position is a leveraged position. The risk involved is the total amount paid for the call.

A long call position is used when the trader is bullish on the underlying security and is an alternative to long stock.

Here is an example. XYZ stock is trading at $50 per share, and the XYZ July 50 call is trading at $2. An investor purchases one XYZ July 50 call for $200. Figure 3-3 shows the profits and losses associated with ownership of a call option. The profit potential to the upside is similar to that of long stock, whereas the risk is limited to the purchase price of the option.

The profit in this case is unlimited. When measured upon expiration of the option, each $1 increase in the price of the stock higher than $52 ($50 strike price of the option plus $2 paid for the option) results in $100 worth of profit. The profit from a long call will always be less than the profit from the same amount of long stock as represented by the option because of the time premium paid for the option. In this case, the profit from long stock would be $200 higher than the profit derived from the option.

The loss in this situation is limited to the amount paid to purchase the option. When measured upon expiration of the option, if the stock is trading at $50 or lower, the option will expire worthless—and the entire

Figure 3-3   *Black line = long 1 July 50 call for $2 at expiration.*
Thin gray line = long 1 July 50 call for $2 (100×$2=$200) with
21 days to expiration.

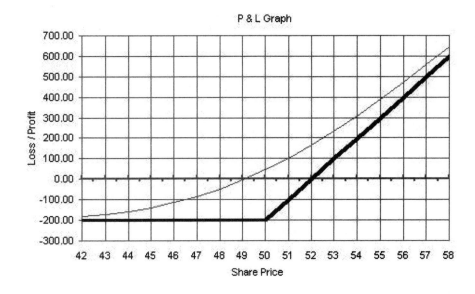

investment in the option will be lost. There will be a partial loss if the stock is trading between $50 and $52 upon expiration of the option.

The outlook on this stock is bullish.

Short Call

The seller (writer) of a short call has as much loss potential as the short seller of stock but faces much less potential for gain. The retail investor will need to meet capital requirements in order to transact this position. He or she will also need to have cash in the account in order to cover the short call position or to own the underlying security. The short call is frequently combined with long stock. This strategy is called a covered call or a buy-write and is covered in detail in Chapter 8, "Trading Strategies."

Here is an example. XYZ is trading at $50 per share, and the XYZ July 50 call is trading at $2. One XYZ July 50 call is sold for $200. Figure 3-4 illustrates the risks and losses associated with the sale of a call option. The profit potential is limited to the amount collected for the sale of the option and the risk is unlimited.

The profit in this situation is limited. The total profit to the option seller is the $2, or $2 × 100 = $200. When measured upon expiration of the option, if the stock is trading at $50 or lower, the option will expire worthless and the entire premium received is retained. There will be a

Figure 3-4   *Black line = short 1 July 50 call for $2 ($2×100 = $200) at expiration.*
Thin gray line = short 1 July 50 call for $2 ($2×100 = $200) with 21 days to expiration.

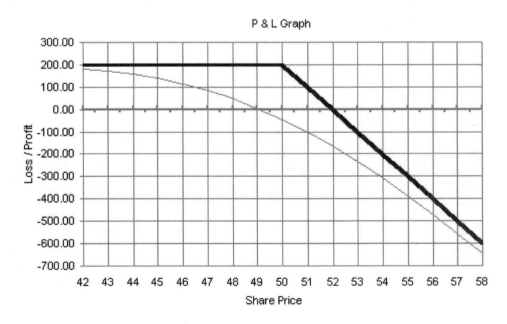

lesser gain if the stock is trading between $50 and $52 upon expiration of the option.

The loss here is unlimited. When measured upon expiration of the option, each $1 increase in the price of the stock higher than $52 ($50 strike price of the option plus the $2 received for the option) will result in $100 worth of loss.

The outlook on this stock is neutral/bearish.

Long Put

A long put position is used when the trader is bearish on the underlying security. The buyer/holder of a put carries the profit potential of a short stock position but has a significantly limited risk of loss. There are no margin requirements for a long put position, and the risk is the total amount purchased for the put. Also, for those who do not trade on margin, selling stock short is not an available option. Therefore, a long put is the exclusive vehicle for speculating on a decline in the price of the underlying stock.

Here is an example. XYZ is trading at $50 per share, and the XYZ July 50 put is trading at $2. One XYZ July 50 put is purchased for $200. The profit and loss associated with the purchase of a put is illustrated in Figure 3-5. The profit potential is considered to be unlimited, although the

Figure 3-5 *Black line = long 1 July 50 put for $2 ($2×100=$200) at expiration.*
Thin gray line = long 1 July 50 put for $2 ($2×100=$200) with 21 days to expiration.

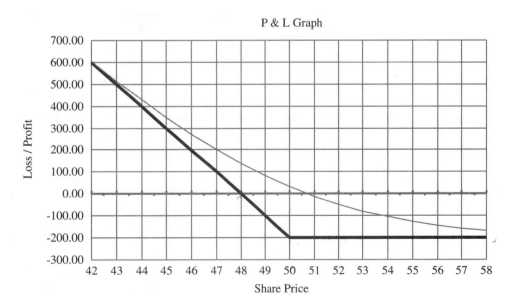

P & L Graph

underlying can only go to zero, and the loss is limited to the purchase price of the option.

The profit in this instance is limited. The profit potential of the long put is limited only because the value of the underlying stock can only decline to zero. When measured upon expiration of the option, each $1 decrease in the price of the stock lower than $48 ($50 strike price of the option minus the $2 paid for the option) will result in $100 worth of profit. The profit from a long put will always be less than the profit that would have been earned by selling the same amount of stock short, covered by the option contract due to the time premium paid for the long put.

The loss here is limited to the amount paid in order to purchase the option. When measured upon expiration of the option, if the stock is trading at $50 or higher, the option will expire worthless—and the entire investment in the option will be lost. There will be a smaller loss if the stock is trading between $48 and $50 upon expiration of the option.

The outlook on this stock is bearish.

The buyer (holder) of a put has much of the profit potential of a short stock position but has significantly limited the risk of loss. No margin is required for this position. The risk is the total amount purchased for the put.

Short Put

The seller (writer) of a put has as much of the same loss potential as a long stock position but has much less potential for gain. The retail trader or investor is required to meet capital requirements for this transaction (in other words, he or she will need to have cash in the account as security against the short put). This requirement is referred to as a cash-covered put, which is similar to a covered call (discussed in the strategy section of this book). Cash in the account covers the short put.

Here is an example. XYZ is trading at $50 per share, and the XYZ July 50 put is trading at $2. One XYZ July 50 put is sold for $200. Figure 3-6 illustrates the profits and losses associated with the sale of a put. As with the outright sale of any option, the profit potential is limited to the amount collected for the sale of the option and the risk is unlimited, or in this case limited as the underlying can only go to zero.

The profit here is limited to the amount received upon sale of the option.

When measured upon expiration of the option, if the stock is trading at $50 or higher, the option will expire worthless and the entire premium received will be retained. There will be a lesser gain if the stock is trading between $48 and $50 upon expiration of the option.

The loss here is unlimited. When measured upon expiration of the option, each $1 decrease in the price of the stock lower than $48 ($50 strike price of the option minus the $2 received for the option) will result

Figure 3-6   *Black line = shot 1 July 50 put for $2 ($2×100=$200) at*
              expiration.
              Thin gray line = short 1 July 50 put for $2 ($2×100=$200) with
              21 days to expiration.

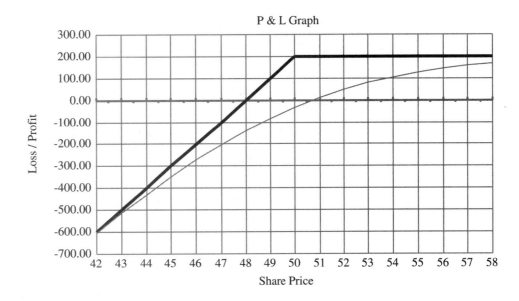

in $100 worth of loss. There will be a smaller loss if the stock is trading
between $48 and $50 upon expiration of the option.

The outlook on this stock is neutral/bullish.

Graphing an Option Position

Although options provide a unique opportunity for capitalizing on movement in the marketplace with a relatively small investment, as with all
trading there is risk. A trader must be aware of the risks associated with
an options position. Knowing where risk lies enables a trader to manage
a position effectively by minimizing loss and increasing profits. Graphing
an options position gives a trader a visual representation of his or her
position's risk and an awareness of when and how to act.

As you can see from the graphs in this chapter, the profit/loss graph for
a long stock and a long call have something in common: both show profits
to the up side. The graph for the call position, however, reveals that the
down-side risk is limited compared to the unlimited risk in the long stock
position. In fact, long call risk is limited to the total premium paid for the
call (only the premium can be lost). The risk to the long stock is unlimited,
because the stock could decline to zero. As the stock increases in value, the
call begins to increase—eventually increasing dollar for dollar with the
stock. Keep in mind, though, the difference in using the much smaller
amount of capital for buying a call versus buying the stock outright.

Looking at the long put graph, we can see that puts have similar characteristics to short stock because both increase in value as the underlying stock declines in price. The risk to the put holder, however, is limited to the purchase price of the option. The short stock position has unlimited risk. After all, as the stock increases in price, the short stock position will lose dollar for dollar. Most individual investors do not have the capital to sell stock short. The put gives the investor a similar short position without the short-stock risk.

All of the preceding profit/loss graphs are portrayed at option expiration. Expiration profit/loss graphs are particularly useful, because they reflect the maximum risk of the position.

We have shown you the expiration profit/loss graphs for the six building blocks. There is a methodology to producing such graphs, regardless of the number of options in the position, and we will introduce this method to you now. To graph the profit/loss as of expiration for any position that contains option(s), you must perform the following actions:

*   Determine the profit or loss of the position with the stock closing at each options exercise price.
*   Select two stock prices: one that is higher than the highest exercise price and one that is lower than the lowest exercise price. Determine the profit or loss for each.
*   Connect the dots, keeping in mind that the graph might bend at each strike price.
*   The x-axis is the stock price.
*   The y-axis is the profit/loss line.

Figure 3-7 illustrates that an option has been purchased. Whenever the line is in the negative, below the breakeven, this indicates that the trade has produced a debit to the account.

Figure 3-7   *Gray line = indicates that an option has been purchased for $2 ($2×100=$200), as the line begins as a deficit.*

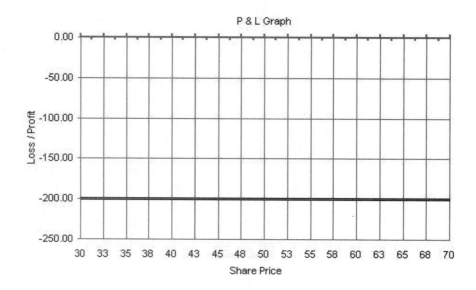

Figure 3-8 *Black line = long 1 50 level call for $2 ($2×100=$200) at expiration.*
Thin gray line = long 1 50 level call for $2 ($2×100=$200) with 21 days to expiration.

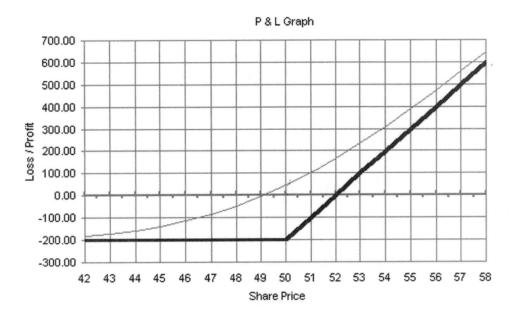

In this example, the *y*-axis (the profit/loss) shows a deficit of $200—indicating that an option has been purchased. A line starting in the positive area of the profit/loss axis indicates that an option has been sold and that money has been collected for the trade. Figure 3-8 illlustrates that the option begins to become profitable as the underlying increases in value and begins to move thru the strike price. Once the purchase price plus the strike price of the option is reached, the position is at the breakeven line. Anything above the purchase price plus the strike price is a profit.

In this example, we see that the $200 has gone toward the purchase of a call with a strike price of $50. The line will begin to bend at the strike price. As the option reaches the break-even price of $52 (the strike price plus the premium paid for the option), the position gains in value. At the break-even price ($52), the option begins to realize a profit. The dark line indicates the option upon expiration. The light line indicates how the position will look with time remaining to expiration.

Quiz

1. If you are bearish on the market, you might _____ the stock.
2. A short stock position has _____ risk.
3. The buyer of a _____ has as much of the profit potential as the owner of the underlying stock but has significantly limited the risk of loss.

4. The purchase of a call will result in a (deficit/credit) to the trader's account.

5. A long put position gives the holder the (right/obligation) to sell the underlying security for a specified amount until the expiration of the option.

6. A _____ call position has unlimited risk.

7. The graph of a long Apr 50 call will bend at the _____ strike.

8. A long put position will increase in value as the underlying security _____ in price.

9. A _____ graph helps a trader visualize the risk/reward associated with a position.

10. The risk involved with the purchase of an option is the _____ price of the option.

11. Graph the following position: long 2 March 50 level calls for $3 ($3 × 100 = $300) upon expiration.

Please refer to Appendix I in this book for quiz answers.

Chapter 4

Pricing Options

Introduction

One of the first questions that options beginners usually ask is, "How can I tell if an option is fairly priced?" To answer this question, we should start by distinguishing between the price and value of an option. You must always evaluate an option in order to determine whether it is fairly priced. A market maker's evaluation of the option fixes the bid or ask price. Whether you choose to buy or sell the option at that price depends on your relative evaluations of the option.

In this chapter, we will take you through the process that is necessary for evaluating an option. To that end, we will review the variables that contribute to an option's value. We will begin by introducing the concepts of in-the-money (ITM), at-the-money (ATM), and out-of-the-money (OTM) options. Then, we can examine in detail the factors that directly impact the listed price of an option.

Option Status Relative to the Underlying Stock

ITM

A call option is said to be ITM when the underlying stock is trading for more than the option's strike price. By contrast, a put option is ITM when the underlying stock is trading for less than the option's strike price. When the strike price of a call option is less than the current price of the underlying security, the call holder can exercise the option and effectively acquire the underlying stock for less than the current market price. On the other hand, the put holder can exercise the put in order to sell the underlying stock for more than its current market price. For example, if XYZ is trading at $53, an April 50 call is considered ITM by $3—while the April 55 put is considered $2 ITM. Note that the value of an option is at its greatest when it is ITM.

ATM

An option is said to be ATM when the underlying stock is trading at the same level as the option strike price. In this case, the investor stands to neither gain nor lose on the option (that is, over and above the initial capital outlays). For example, the XYZ April 50 call and put will both be trading ATM when XYZ is trading at $50. Although technically an option is ATM only when the underlying stock is trading at exactly the strike price, whenever the underlying stock is trading close to a strike price, the common practice is to refer to the options at that strike as ATM options.

Figure 4-1   *In, at and out-of-the-money options.*

CALLS	XYZ Apr	PUTS
ITM	45	OTM
ATM	50	ATM
OTM	55	ITM

OTM

A call option is said to be OTM when the underlying stock is trading for less than the option's strike price. A put option, by contrast, is OTM when the underlying stock is trading for more than the option's strike price. The value of an option is at its lowest when it is OTM.

Therefore, in the case of a call, if the strike of a call is more than the current price of the underlying security, then the call is said to be OTM because the holder has the right to purchase stock at a higher price than the underlying stock's current price. For example, when XYZ is trading at $48, the April 50 call is said to be OTM by $2.

Similarly, if the strike price of a put is less than the current price of the underlying security, the put is said to be OTM. You have the right to sell the underlying stock for the put option for less than the value at which the stock is trading in the marketplace. Therefore, if XYZ is trading at $48, the April 50 put will be ITM by $2. But if XYZ increases to $53, the April 50 put will now be OTM by $3 (and, correspondingly, the April 50 call will be ITM by $3).

For an overview, suppose that XYZ is trading at $50 a share. The various April calls and puts shown next would be in, at, or out-of-the-money as follows: Figure 4-1 is an example of option strike prices where the underlying is trading $50/share. As the underlying price fluctuates the options will fluctuate from being in, at, and out-of-the-money.

Factors Affecting the Price of an Option

The general context for discussing an option's price is always the current price of the underlying security. Here, we refer to the intrinsic value of an option, which corresponds to the amount that an option is said to be ITM. (Note that only ITM options have intrinsic value. Fortunately, we do not need any computer programs to calculate intrinsic value; rather, we only need a simple subtraction formula.) Figure 4-2 illustrates the formula used to determine the intrinsic value of an in-the-money option.

As we can see, then, the intrinsic value of an ITM depends upon the relationship of the option's strike to the current price of the underlying

Figure 4-2 *Intrinsic value calculations.*

FORMULA: In-The-Money/ Call Intrinsic Value

Current Stock Price − Strike Price = Call Intrinsic Value

Example: XYZ is trading at $62.

The intrinsic value of the Mar 55 call is $7.   ($62 − 55 = $7)

FORMULA: In-The-Money Put Intrinsic Value

Strike Price − Current Stock Price = Put Intrinsic Value

Example: XYZ is trading at $13.

The intrinsic value of the Apr 15 put is $2. ($15 − 13 = $2)

---

security. Because the option's strike price is a constant, the intrinsic value of an option will fluctuate dollar for dollar with any price change of the underlying security (as long as the option remains ITM). As soon as the price of the underlying security moves below a call option's strike price or above a put option's strike price, that option would become ATM or OTM and would have no intrinsic value. To summarize:

1. The intrinsic value of an option is the amount that an option is ITM.
2. OTM and ATM options have no intrinsic value.

Extrinsic Value

Although intrinsic value plays a fundamental role in determining the price of an option, it alone is not responsible for the overall pricing of the option. In fact, intrinsic value is only one component of the price of an option. Stock options have both intrinsic and extrinsic value. The price of an option is the sum of its intrinsic and extrinsic values.

The extrinsic value of an option is that part of its price that is determined by certain variables other than the price of the underlying security and the strike price. These variables are as follows:

1. Time to expiration
2. Interest rates
3. Volatility
4. Dividends of the underlying security (if applicable)

We will examine the impact of each of these variables on option pricing separately. First, however, let's look at the simple formula for identifying extrinsic value. Figure 4-3 is an example of the formula used to determine the extrinsic value of an option.

Before proceeding, we should give you a few words about terminology. In the industry, extrinsic value is frequently referred to in a number of ways (such as time value, time premium, or premium value). Informally, this concept is often referred to as the juice or fluff of the option. From this point forward, we will use the term time premium interchangeably with extrinsic value. But although we are using the word *time premium*, we should keep in mind that extrinsic value is influenced by more than just time until expiration. To complicate matters a bit more, an option's overall (or total) price—its intrinsic and extrinsic values combined—is frequently referred to in the industry as the option's premium. In this book, when we refer to an option's premium, we are speaking about the overall price of the option. When we talk about the time premium, on the other hand, we refer to the extrinsic value of a particular option.

Having reviewed these basic formulas, we can now gain some insight as to how the time to expiration, interest rates, and volatility impact the price of an option. In the following example, consider how differing input variables will affect the price outcome for options that are listed for two different stocks.

Figure 4-3 *Call and put extrinsic value formulas.*

FORMULA: Call Extrinsic Value
Call Option Price − Call Intrinsic Value = Call Premium Value
Example: XYZ is trading at $23.
The XYZ Sep 20 call is trading at $4.
Intrinsic Value is $3.
Premium = $1 (option price of $4 – intrinsic value $3)

FORMULA: Put Extrinsic Value
Put Option Price − Put Intrinsic Value = Put Premium Value
Example: XYZ is trading at $44.
The XYZ Dec 45 put is trading at $3.
Intrinsic Value is $1.
Premium = $2 (option price of $3 – intrinsic value $1)

If an option has no intrinsic value then its total value must consists of extrinsic value.
Example: XYZ is trading at $23.
The XYZ Sep 25 call is trading at $1 1/4.
Extrinsic Value is $1 1/4.

Example: XYZ is trading at $55
The XYZ Dec 50 put is trading at $2.
Extrinsic Value is $2.

Assume the following:

1. Stocks ABC and XYZ are both trading at $52.
2. ABC is an Internet company.
3. XYZ is a well-established, traditional retailer.
4. April options have 30 days until expiration.
5. May options have 58 days until expiration.
6. You are interested in purchasing stock in both ABC and XYZ.

Consider the role of interest rates and the time to expiration when comparing the purchase of April 40 calls on both ABC and XYZ to buying stock:

1. By buying the stock, you pay $52 per share now. If you purchase the April 40 call, you defer payment of the $40 per share exercise price until you exercise the option. In the meantime, you can invest this $40 per share and earn interest. The amount of interest earned depends on the time until exercise and the interest rate that you will be paid on the funds. This economic benefit has a value that will be reflected in the price of the option. We need to make two important observations here:

   a. Benefit is the same for ABC and XYZ. This benefit is measured solely by the amount of money involved ($40 per share in this case), the interest rate, and the time until expiration. Therefore, the benefit would be the same whether you were considering an investment in ABC or XYZ.

   b. The more time until exercise, the larger the economic benefit. You could earn more interest—in fact, approximately twice the amount—by delaying exercise until May. Thus, the price of the May 40 calls will include a larger fee for the right to earn interest by investing the amount needed to exercise the calls until option exercise.

2. In this example, consider the role of volatility and time to expiration:

   a. If the stock plunges to $30 prior to April expiration (the anticipated time that you would exercise your call), you would lose $22 per share if the stock were purchased (but only the price of the call if you acquired that instead). This reduction in your risk has a value that will also be reflected in the price of the option.

   b. The benefit is different for ABC and XYZ. You would probably assess that the risk of this significant price move prior to April expiration is greater for ABC than for XYZ and would therefore be willing to pay more for this risk protection in the case of ABC than XYZ. Surely the seller of the April 40 calls would charge more for assuming this risk of a large move in the price of the stock prior to April option expiration in the case of ABC than for XYZ. For this reason, the price of the ABC April 40 call will likely be greater than the price of the XYZ April 40 call.

    c. The more time until exercise, the greater the risk to the seller. For the same, obvious reason that the premium on a 60-day health insurance policy for an individual is greater than the premium on the same policy for the same individual if the term is only 30 days, the price of the May 40 calls in ABC will include a larger amount that is attributable to the risk that the stock price will move away from $40 by May expiration than the Apr 40 calls by April expiration.

Without attempting to calculate the fair value of the benefits offered by the April 40 calls over the immediate purchase of the stock, it should now be clear that the factors of time, interest rate, and anticipated stock price volatility all impact the price of an option. We will now turn our attention to methods that are available for quantifying the value of these and other factors in order to address the question posed at the beginning of this chapter: "How can I tell if an option is fairly priced?"

Pricing Models: An Overview

As mentioned earlier in this book, widespread use of options did not occur until there was a widely accepted approach to determining the value of options. This goal was achieved with the introduction of the Black-Scholes pricing model in 1972–1973. As one of the first pricing models, Black-Scholes is now considered inferior to more recent pricing models (such as Cox-Rubinstein's binomial option pricing model). The Black-Scholes model, although faster on a computer due to less-complex calculations, did not take into consideration American-style options (that is, options that enable early exercise). You can find an option-pricing calculator online at www.marketcompass.com, or you can purchase them separately as software from a variety of sources.

We return now to the function of our models. What we refer to as the *theoretical value* of an option is the value determined by our particular pricing model by using the six factors previously mentioned:

1. The price of the underlying stock
2. The option's strike or exercise price
3. The time until expiration of the option
4. The applicable interest rate
5. The anticipated volatility of the price movement of the underlying security
6. Dividends (where applicable)

Entering values for the six (five if the company does not issue dividends) required inputs into a pricing model will generate a theoretical value for an option. A detailed discussion of how the various pricing models work is beyond the scope of this book, and in the opinion of the authors, this discussion is unnecessary for all but the most hard-core market professionals. What is useful is a general discussion of how the pricing formulas determine theoretical, or fair value and how the six factors affect an options price. Furthermore, because each variable (except for the strike price) is susceptible to change, you must be able to interpret the values generated by the pricing model in order to understand how an option price might react.

Although pricing models differ somewhat in the way in which they assess data, they all essentially work the same way. Pricing models propose a series of possible prices for the underlying security, assign a probability to each price, and use this information to calculate the expected return (expected value) as measured at expiration of an option that is purchased with a particular exercise price. From this point, the model adjusts for any applicable carrying costs (interest rate related) and determines a theoretically fair value for the option. Your job, then, is to input the information that you gather into the pricing model, acquire the probability-generated fair value of the option, and find a bid/offer in the market place that will enable you to establish an edge on that fair value.

Consider, for example, the odds that are associated with a game of roulette. In roulette, the player attempts to pick one of the 38 slots on which the ball will land. If the player chooses the correct slot, he or she will win $36. For this opportunity, the casino charges $1. Each one of the 38 slots has an equal probability of hitting. The expected return on such a bet played time after time is calculated by dividing the amount that is capable of being won ($36) by the amount of probable outcomes (38). In other words, we have 36/38 = .95. The resulting, expected return of the bet is $.95; therefore, the fair value is $.95. In other words, a player who pays $.95 to play will break even over time. Hence, a player who pays less than $.95 to play is getting a good deal—one that should produce a profit over time. Paying more than $.95 to play is overpaying, which invariably will result in losses over time. Casinos charge $1 to play because they understand the mathematics of expected return.

Pricing Model Variables

Having reviewed the logic of a pricing model and the procedures that are necessary for using one, we now turn to the specific variables that you will need to identify in order to set the pricing model in motion.

Underlying Stock Price.   Obviously, the price of the underlying stock is important for establishing the value of an option. Understanding how future changes in the price might affect the value of an option will be a significant factor in determining whether a particular option is an appropriate investment choice, given the expectations that you might have for the performance of the underlying security. We will discuss this aspect of the pricing models in detail in our discussion of market risk. For now, however, the Figure 4-4 indicates how a $1 change in the price of the

Figure 4-4   *Underlying prices effects on options prices.*

Underlying Price		
Stock Price: 50	**Stock Price: 49**	**Stock Price: 51**
Strike Price: 45	Strike Price: 45	Strike Price: 45
Days to Expiration: 365 (1yr)	Days to Expiration: 365 (1 yr.)	Days to Expiration: 365 (1 yr.)
Interest Rate: 6%	Interest Rate: 6%	Interest Rate: 6%
Volatility: 32	Volatility: 32	Volatility: 32
Dividend: none	Dividend: none	Dividend: none
Call Option Value: 10.43	**Call Option Value: 9.73**	**Call Option Value: 11.18**
Put Option Value: 2.98	**Put Option Value: 3.29**	**Put Option Value: 2.70**

underlying security—with all other variables remaining constant—affects the theoretical value of the 45 calls and 45 puts.

Strike/Exercise Price.   The exercise price is fixed throughout the life of the option and will not change. Only in the case of a stock split would a change to this value occur, and even so, this change would have no effect on the theoretical value of an option.

Time until Expiration.   An option's price is directly related to the amount of time until the option's expiration. When trading options, time equals opportunity. Therefore, the more time that is attached to an option, the greater its chance of finishing ITM. Consequently, a buyer is willing to pay more for the added opportunity afforded by time on the option. Consequently, the option seller will demand more for the added risk that additional time requires him or her to assume. All else being equal, then, an option that has more time is more valuable to an investor and will therefore trade at a premium (as opposed to an option that has less time remaining). Time until expiration is an important factor in determining the next two factors affecting time premium: interest rates and volatility.

For now, remember the following:

1. An option's expiration date is fixed for the life of the option and will not change.
2. Options that have a distant expiration date trade at a premium relative to those that are approaching expiration.
3. As each day passes, the time to expiration decreases and the theoretical value of the option erodes, thereby giving the option its status as a wasting asset.

Figure 4-5 illustrates the effect of time on an options value; as time to expiration decreases, all other factors remaining constant, the value of the option decreases.

Interest Rates.   Interest rates also will affect the price of an option. Over a given period, interest is earned on a credit balance in a trader's

Figure 4-5 *Time to expiration and option prices.*

Time to Expiration		
Stock Price: 50	Stock Price: 50	Stock Price: 50
Strike Price: 45	Strike Price: 45	Strike Price: 45
Days to Expiration: 365 (1yr)	**Days to Expiration: 182 (6 mo.)**	**Days to Expiration: 90 (3 mos.)**
Interest Rate: 6%	Interest Rate: 6%	Interest Rate: 6%
Volatility: 32	Volatility: 32	Volatility: 32
Dividend: none	Dividend: none	Dividend: none
Call Option Value: 10.43	**Call Option Value: 8.12**	**Call Option Value: 6.63**
Put Option Value: 2.98	**Put Option Value: 1.85**	**Put Option Value: .99**

account and is paid on a debit balance. The resulting cost/credit of carrying the position must be considered when evaluating an option's fair value. Consider, for instance, that a trader pays interest on a long position (options that are bought and owned) and will receive interest on a short position (selling options that one does not own). Correspondingly, because the purchase or sale of options and stock will result in a debit or credit to an investor/trader's account, the carrying costs associated with a debit (or the interest earned on any credit balances) will affect the overall value of an option. This process is a function of the effect of interest rates over the life of the option.

To discuss the effect of interest comprehensively, we need to introduce the concept of hedging—something that we will discuss in much greater detail in a future chapter. For now, though, consider what would happen if a trader acquired a stock position in order to hedge the directional risk associated with an option transaction. In this case, as interest rates rise, the value of a call will increase. The long (or short) stock position associated with the sale (or purchase) of a call will create a debit (or credit) to the trader's account (on which he or she will pay or collect interest). Conversely, as interest rates rise, the value of the put will decrease. This situation is again because of the stock position that is used to hedge the risk associated with the option transaction. When a put is purchased (or sold), a trader will purchase (or sell) the underlying stock as a hedge in order to reduce his or her directional exposure. The stock that is purchased (or sold) creates a debit (or credit) to the trader's account (for which he or she pays or receives interest). This cost is referred to as the cost of carry (the difference between the cost of financing the purchase of an asset and the asset's cash yield), and interest rates directly impact this cost.

Not surprisingly, the time until expiration also plays an important role in relation to interest rates. The longer the life of the option, the greater the influence that a change in interest rates will have on the option's valuation. For your information, the interest rate that we use for assessing the value of an option is usually based on a risk-free asset (which is an asset whose future return is known with certainty, such as a 90-day, U.S. Treasury bill or a U.S. Treasury bond for long-term options).

Figure 4-6 *Interest rates and option prices.*

Interest Rates		
Stock Price: 50	Stock Price: 50	Stock Price: 50
Strike Price: 45	Strike Price: 45	Strike Price: 45
Days to Expiration: 365 (1yr)	Days to Expiration: 365 (1yr)	Days to Expiration: 365 (1yr)
Interest Rate: 6%	**Interest Rate: 5%**	**Interest Rate: 7%**
Volatility: 32	Volatility: 32	Volatility: 32
Dividend: none	Dividend: none	Dividend: none
Call Option Value: 10.43	**Call Option Value: 10.158**	**Call Option Value: 10.70**
Put Option Value: 2.98	**Put Option Value: 3.10**	**Put Option Value: 2.86**

Remember, then, that all other factors being equal:

1. The higher the interest rate, the higher the call price and the lower the put price.
2. The lower the interest rate, the lower the call price and the higher the put price.
3. The degree to which a change in interest rates impacts the theoretical value of an option is directly correlated to the amount of time until expiration.

The effects of change in interest rates on an options value is shown in Figure 4-6, we can see from this illustration that as interest rates increase the value of the call increases and the value of put decreases. Conversely, as interest rates decrease the value of the call decreases and the value of the put increases.

Volatility. Volatility is a measure of the speed and magnitude at which the underlying security's price changes (expressed in a percentage). This factor significantly impacts the price of an option, because it measures not only the likelihood that the option will expire ITM or OTM relative to its strike price, but in the case of ITM finishes, how deeply ITM it might end up at expiration. All other factors being equal, options that have a highly volatile underlying security will be sold at a higher premium than options that have a relatively less-volatile underlying security.

The volatility measure that is most commonly used for pricing options is a whole number, which actually represents the standard deviation associated with a percentage in change from the median price (assuming a log normal distribution of prices as measured at expiration). The median price is the break-even price at expiration, including the cost of financing the purchase of the stock through expiration. For example, suppose that a stock was trading at $100, that interest rates were at 6 percent, and that the stock had a volatility of 36 (assuming that an option has 365 days to go until expiration). For an investment in the stock to break even after one year, the stock would need to be trading at $106 in order to compensate for the $6 of interest per share ($100 financed at 6 percent for one year). The volatility of 36 would mean that approximately 68 percent of the time, the price one year later would fall between the ranges of 106 ± 38 (36 percent of 106). Approximately 95 percent of the time, then, the price would fall between the ranges of 106 ± 76 (72 percent of 106).

The appropriate measure of volatility to use as the input for your pricing model is the one that would most closely reflect the actual future movement of the underlying security. Let's refer to this measure as the future volatility. Absent a crystal ball, however, future volatility is unknown. Therefore, most traders review the performance of the stock in the past (historic volatility), factor in any special circumstances that are reasonably anticipated prior to expiration, and come up with a forecast volatility that is really their best guess as to future volatility. You should note that there is not just one measure of historic volatility; rather, historic volatility can be calculated over any time period that you choose. Generally, historical volatility over both a short term (1–2 months) and a longer term (one year or more) are examined and a judgment is made as to how to weigh them when forecasting future volatility. As you can see, volatility assessment can be a highly subjective process that requires considerable skill of behalf of the trader or market maker. No guarantee of accuracy can be offered, because volatility is never truly knowable until the expiration of the option. For this reason, you should remember that in the area of volatility, pricing options is as much an art as it is a science. Because of its importance to option pricing, we will be discussing volatility in detail in an upcoming chapter.

Note how relatively small changes in volatility assumptions can have a dramatic effect on an options price, as the following chart indicates. Figure 4-7 illustrates the effects of volatility on an options value. As the volatility decreases from 32 to 22 the value of the options, both calls and puts, decrease. As the volatility increases from 22 to 42 the value of the options increase. Increases volatility adds increased opportunity and increased risk therefore a higher volatility warrants a higher premium. Conversely, as volatility decreases opportunity and risk decrease and thereby the option premium will decrease.

Figure 4-7   *Volatility and option prices.*

Volatility 32	− 10 point	+ 10 point
Stock Price: 50	Stock Price: 50	Stock Price: 50
Strike Price: 45	Strike Price: 45	Strike Price: 45
Days to Expiration: 365 (1yr)	Days to Expiration: 365 (1yr)	Days to Expiration: 365 (1yr)
Interest Rate: 6%	Interest Rate: 6%	Interest Rate: 6%
Volatility: 32	**Volatility: 22**	**Volatility: 42**
Dividend: none	Dividend: none	Dividend: none
Call Option Value: 10.43	**Call Option Value: 8.96**	**Call Option Value: 12.12**
Put Option Value: 2.98	**Put Option Value: 1.44**	**Put Option Value: 4.69**

Dividends. A dividend, when applicable, is a portion of a company's profits that is paid back to its shareholders. A company issues dividends as a reward for investing in the company and as an incentive to investors. The company determines the amount of the dividend, the issue dates, and any increases or decreases in the dividend amount. Generally, dividends are paid from one to four times annually, and the amount of the dividend is quoted on a per-share basis. Therefore, a quarterly dividend of $.25 would pay the holder of 100 shares $25 per quarter.

Dividends that are paid to the shareholder of the underlying company directly affect an option's theoretical value. A trader who owns a dividend-yielding stock will pay the costs associated with owning the stock; however, these carrying costs are offset by the dividend received. Hence, receiving the dividend makes stock ownership more desirable as the interest that the long stockholder pays is reduced by the dividend that is received. Call ownership, on the other hand, is less desirable—because the holder of the call will not receive any dividends. Conversely, puts will increase in value relative to dividends, because the alternative to owning a put is to have a short stock position in the underlying stock. The short seller is required to pay the dividend to the owner from whom he or she borrowed the stock, thereby negating the interest received for a short stock position and making the long put position more attractive. Remember, then, the following concepts:

1. An increase in the dividend of the underlying security results in lower call prices and higher put prices.
2. A decrease in the dividend will increase the value of the call and decrease the value of the put.

In addition, the longer the life of the option, the greater the influence of anticipated dividends. For example, the near-term option premium might not reflect any dividends, because no dividends can be paid prior to expiration. Conversely, the long-term option premium might reflect a great number of dividends (for example, a two-year LEAP© option might include a dividend payment each quarter for the next two years). In summary, the higher the dividend, the greater the discount in the call premium and the higher the premium of the puts. As the amount of a dividend changes, the call and put premium will adjust accordingly. Figure 4-8 illustrates the effect of a dividend on a

Figure 4-8 *Dividends and option prices.*

Dividends		
Stock Price: 50	Stock Price: 50	Stock Price: 50
Strike Price: 45	Strike Price: 45	Strike Price: 45
Days to Expiration: 365	Days to Expiration: 365	Days to Expiration: 365
Interest Rate: 6%	Interest Rate: 6%	Interest Rate: 6%
Volatility: 32	Volatility: 32	Volatility: 32
Dividend: .25/qtr	**Dividend: .10/qtr**	**Dividend: none**
Call Option Value: 9. 88	**Call Option Value: 10.21**	**Call Option Value: 10.43**
Put Option Value: 3. 34	**Put Option Value: 3.12**	**Put Option Value: 2.98**

options value. As shown, the value of a call (put) will decrease (increase) as the dividend goes from $.10/qtr. to $.25/qtr. Conversely, as the dividend is cut from $.10 to zero the value of the call (put) increases (decreases).

NOTE

Note that on a stock's ex-dividend date, which is the date on which a dividend-paying stock is trading without the right to receive the next payable dividend through ownership of the stock, the stock is decreased by the amount of the dividend. For example, if XYZ is trading at $51 per share and pays a dividend of $1 per year (or $.25 quarterly), then the value of the stock will be discounted by $.25 on the ex-dividend date and will now have a price of $50.75 per share.

In sum, pricing models not only help you understand how options are priced, but they have also become an almost indispensable tool for assessing the risk/reward profile of any options strategy. They enable the prediction of how prices will change as market conditions change. This knowledge gives you the crucial advantage when analyzing and comparing various option positions. There are times when it is to an investor's advantage to exercise an option early, Figure 4-9 illustrates the concept.

Figure 4-9 *The early exercise of options.*

Early Exercise:

The significance of knowing an option's time premium is especially important when the investor or trader considers exercise of an option before its expiration date. If an investor exercises an option early, s/he will lose any premium attached to that option. Unless there is a corresponding benefit to early exercise which exceeds the lost premium, early exercise is likely a mistake. Nevertheless, as discussed in the Option Style section there are reasons to exercise early as an individual investor. In addition, a professional trader *may* exercise options early for a number of reasons, including long/short stock positions, dividend plays and interest rates to name a few.

Lets look at why you would not exercise an option early simply from the option premium standpoint:
XYZ is trading at $31.

The investor purchases the MAR 30 Call, giving the investor the right to purchase stock at anytime up to the date of expiration for $30/share. The investor pays $3 ($3 X 100 = $300) for the MAR 30 Call. We can calculate the intrinsic value and premium quite easily.

Stock Price ($31) − Strike Price ($30) = Intrinsic Value ($1).

Option Price ($3) − Intrinsic Value ($1) = Premium ($2)

The stock now has increased to $38.

The MAR 30 Call is currently trading $9.

Figure 4-9 *The early exercise of options (Continued).*

Note that the investor's MAR 30 call has increased in price not only $8 but $9.

Stock Price ($38) − Strike Price ($30) = Intrinsic Value ($8)

Initial Option Purchase Price ($3) − Current Intrinsic Value ($8) = $5

The investor has two options. He or she can either exercise the option early or sell the option. Our understanding about the extrinsic value of time until expiration allows us to see that selling the option at this point will create a greater net profit than if the investor were to exercise.

The investor can **exercise the option early**. If so his/her net profit will be $5 × 100 = $500. The investor pays 30 for the stock while it is currently trading 38. It looks as though the investor has made 8 dollars, but we still have not added in the cost of the option that was purchased for 3 dollars. The investor has only made 5 dollars. Current stock price ($38) − Strike Price ($30) = $8 – Option Price ($3) = $5 (Current stock price − strike price − option price). Notice that the $1 of premium that was part of the option price was lost by exercising the option early.

By comparison, if the investor were to **sell the option**, she/he would gain a net profit of $6 × 100 = $600. The investor sells the option at its current price of $9. The investor has effectively collected not only the intrinsic value of $8, but was also able to capture the premium of $1. The investor has made a profit of $6 dollars: 9 − 3 = 6 (Current option price − initial purchase price). As you can see being able to calculate the option's premium is an important factor.

Theoretical Value versus the Marketplace

In the introduction to this chapter, we highlighted the difference between an option's price and its value. Now that we have overviewed the pricing variables and pricing models, we would like to return to describing this distinction.

Of the inputs that the pricing models require in order to calculate a theoretical price for an option, all but one are known. The current price of the underlying security, the option's exercise price, the number of days until expiration, the applicable interest rate, and the date(s) and amount(s) of dividends (if applicable) are all givens. This situation leaves volatility as the one unknown. We know that the market provides a current price for each option. If this market price differs from your theoretical value, we have either one or two situations: you have incorrectly inputted one or more of the known factors, or the market is using different volatility input. After double checking your fixed inputs and determining that they were correct, you will be left with only the conclusion that your volatility expectation differs from that of the market. This volatility assumption that is implicit in the market's pricing of an option is referred to as the

Figure 4-10   *Theoretical volatilites versus implied volatilites.*

Theoretical Volatility: 32	Implied Volatility: 22	Implied Volatility: 42
Stock Price: 50	Stock Price: 50	Stock Price: 50
Strike Price: 45	Strike Price: 45	Strike Price: 45
Days to Expiration: 365 (1yr)	Days to Expiration: 365 (1yr)	Days to Expiration: 365 (1yr)
Interest Rate: 6%	Interest Rate: 6%	Interest Rate: 6%
Volatility: 32	Volatility: 22	Volatility: 42
Dividend: none	Dividend: none	Dividend: none
Call Option Value: 10.44	Call Option Price: 8.94	Call Option Price: 12.12
Put Option Value: 3.00	Put Option Price: 1.44	Put Option Price: 4.69

option's implied volatility and it is critically important data to the serious options trader or investor. (Readily available formulas have been developed to determine what volatility assumption is implied by the market price of the option.) The difference between the theoretical value of an option and its current market price is your benchmark for determining which options are overpriced and which are underpriced. Consequently, this difference can be quite substantial. Figure 4-10 illustrates the difference between theoretical and actual volatilites.

Based on your assumption of 32 volatility in the stock over the next year, you calculate the value of the calls and puts to be $10.44 and $3, respectively. The second column presents a situation in which the market price of these options are $8.94 for the calls and $1.44 for the puts, resulting in an implied volatility of 22. By contrast, the third column represents market prices for the calls and puts that are well in excess of your theoretical value, reflecting an implied volatility of 42. If you were considering a strategy that involved purchasing these options, you would be much more inclined to make the purchase if they appeared to be underpriced rather than overpriced. If you were considering a strategy that involved selling these options, then you would be much more inclined to sell the overpriced options than the underpriced ones.

Summary

Having an understanding of the variables that determine the value of an option and knowing how changes in these variables affect an options valuation enables a trader to take advantage of price discrepancies in the marketplace. This foundational knowledge is paramount to understanding the risk/reward aspects of options trading. A general summary of these changes is shown in Figure 4-11.

Figure 4-11 *Changing market conditions and theoretical value.*

Changing Market Conditions and Theoretical Value	Call Value	Puts Value
Underlying Increases In Value	Increases	Decreases
Underlying Decreases In Value	Decreases	Increases
Time To Expiration Decreases	Decreases	Decreases
Dividends Increase	Decreases	Increases
Dividend Decreases	Increases	Decreases
Volatility Increases	Increases	Increases
Volatility Decreases	Decreases	Decreases
Interest Rates Increase	Increases	Decreases
Interest Rates Decrease	Decreases	Increases

In this chapter, we have become familiar with the following concepts:

1. The variables that contribute to the price of an option
2. How these variables are entered into a mathematical pricing model
3. How theoretical value is a calculation of the probable break-even point for an option contract, based on specific information provided
4. The importance of determining the volatility implied by the market's pricing of an option

With this information under our belts, we will venture into the depths of volatility. Although an understanding of the mathematical formulation of volatility is not a requisite for understanding how volatility will affect the price of an option, it is useful information nonetheless.

Quiz

1. A call option is said to be _____-the-money when the underlying security is trading for more than the option's strike price.
2. A put option is _____-the-money when the strike price is less than the current price of the underlying security.
3. The amount that an option is ITM is referred to as the _____ value.
4. Strike price − current stock price = _____ intrinsic value.

5. The price of an option is the sum of its _____ and _____ values.

6. Name two variables that influence the extrinsic value of an option.

7. The fair or theoretical value of an option can be calculated by using a(n) _____.

8. What are the six factors that are used to determine the price of an option?

9. The greater the amount of time remaining until an option's expiration, the _____ the time premium.

10. The higher the interest rates, the _____ the value of calls.

11. _____ is a measure of the speed and magnitude at which the underlying security's price changes.

12. The portions of a company's profits that are paid back to its shareholders are the _____.

13. The value of a stock will be discounted by the amount of the dividend on the _____ date.

14. As the underlying security increases in value, the value of call (with all other variables remaining constant) will _____ in value.

15. OTM and ATM options have no_____ value.

Please refer to the Appendix I in this book for quiz answers.

Chapter 5

Option Volatility

Introduction

As we saw in the previous chapter, the one real variable that enters into a pricing model is volatility. All of the other inputs—stock price, option strike price, days until expiration, applicable interest rates, and dividends—are essentially readily determinable. The validity of a pricing model's output depends on the accuracy of all input amounts, but the quality of the volatility input plays an important role. As the saying goes, "Garbage in, garbage out." But what is the appropriate measure of volatility that we should use? There are, in fact, a handful of ways in which we can measure volatility.

The ideal volatility input for a pricing model would be the one that most closely reflects the actual future movement of the underlying security. Let's refer to this input as the future volatility. Absent a crystal ball, however, we do not know the future volatility. Therefore, most traders turn (for good measure) to the performance of the stock in the past, which we call the historical volatility. Next, the trader will factor into the historical volatility any special circumstances that he or she anticipates prior to expiration. This foresight enables the trader to generate a forecast volatility, which is essentially the trader's best guess at future volatility. Armed with his or her forecast volatility, the trader is then able to draw a comparison between the volatility indicated by the market price of the option and the volatility determined by this market (referred to as the implied volatility). Let's examine these measures more closely.

Measures of Volatility

Historical volatility, as its name implies, is a measure of actual price changes in an underlying issue over a specific period in the past. Through the statistical analysis of historical data, a trader attempts to predict the future volatility of the underlying issue. You should note, however, that there is not just one measure of historic volatility. You can calculate historic volatility over any time period that you choose. The trader will have to decide which period(s) he or she wants to analyze: a week, a month, or a year. In addition, he or she must also ask which price comparisons (closing price to closing price, opening price to opening price, or the daily high/low range) upon which he or she should base volatility assessments. Different price comparisons will calculate different volatilities. Generally, the trader calculates historical volatilities over both a short term (one to two months) and a long term and then decides how to weight each calculation when forecasting future volatility.

Expected/forecast volatility is what a trader attempts to predict based upon his or her informed and/or educated speculation. More specifically, forecast volatility is an estimate of the volatility of the underlying issue for a specific period in the future. For most traders, the starting point of volatility forecasting is a review of one or more historical volatilities. Knowing that news events move markets, the trader adds to the equation his or her assessment of how anticipated news events will affect volatility. For example, volatility usually rises in the period just prior to a quarterly earnings announcement. If the company is the subject of a government investigation or is involved in major litigation, you should not ignore the possibility of news involving a major development. For these reasons, volatility assessment is a highly subjective process that offers no guarantee of accuracy.

Implied volatility is the marketplace's assessment of the future volatility of the underlying issue. This implied volatility measures the level of volatility that is implicitly assumed within the current market price of the option. You could also consider implied volatility as a measure of the market consensus of expected volatility of the underlying stock. Implied volatility can be derived from running a pricing model backwards. In other words, the trader can enter the current market price of an option into a pricing model along with the underlying price, strike price, time until expiration, interest rate, and any applicable dividends. When he or she then runs the model, then, it will solve for the unknown—the volatility that the marketplace is using to price the option. This number represents the implied volatility.

Implied volatility might or might not be equal to the future volatility assumption of an underlying issue. When the volatility assumption that we are using to determine the theoretical value of an option differs from the volatility that marketplace is using to determine the value of an option, we are able to enter all of the data into the pricing (as we have done below). We exclude the volatility assumption and enter the theoretical value that we have previously solved for in order to determine what volatility the marketplace is giving the option, Figure 5-1 summarizes this.

In this example, we see that the marketplace has placed a higher value on the March 40 call than on the trader who generated an informed

Figure 5-1   *Implied versus forecast volatility.*

IMPLIED vs. FORECAST VOLATILITY			
XYZ is trading $42/share.			
MAR 40 calls are trading 5 7/8 in the marketplace:			
Pricing Model Inputs to determine theoretical value:		Pricing Model Inputs to determine implied volatility:	
Underlying:	42	Underlying:	$42
Volatility assumption:	**40**	**Volatility:**	**Unknown**
Interest Rate:	6%	Interest Rate:	6%
Dividend:	0	Dividend:	0
Strike price:	40	Strike price:	40
Days to Expiration:	91	Days to Expiration:	91
Option Price:	**Unknown**	**Option Price:**	**5 7/8**
Output:		**Output:**	
Theoretical Value:	**4 3/4**	**Marketplace Volatility:**	**55**

volatility prediction based on current movement in the underlying, historical volatility and an expectation of market sentiment. What explains this divergence? Generally, this disparity anticipation of news might result in a large move in the price of the underlying issue (whether that move is up or down).

Factors Influencing Implied Volatility

When assessing the market's implied volatility, you must realize how variations in supply and demand might also require market makers to change the volatility variable in order to ensure liquid markets. In these circumstances, the customer brings his or her anticipation of a change in price to the market and buys or sells accordingly. The market maker recognizes the importance of responding to or capitalizing on these changes. The market maker is not changing volatility on an option contract based on his expectation of a news event; rather, he or she is changing volatility based on the public's expectation of an event that will possibly affect the value of an option.

Depending on how a particular option exchange is structured, market makers and/or a specialist are charged with providing liquidity to the markets. For each option on each stock for which they make the market, these floor traders establish two prices: the bid and the offer. The bid is the price at which they will purchase that option, and the offer (sometimes referred to as the ask or asking price) is the price at which they will sell that option. The difference between the bid and offer prices, known as the spread, is limited in size by regulation. When supply and demand for options are in balance (that is, when there are approximately as many buyers as there are sellers), market makers act as middlemen—collecting the spread as they buy at the bid price from the sellers and sell at the offer price to the buyers. At these times, they collect their profit without assuming much risk.

These conditions are infrequent, however, due to a typically one-sided order flow in option markets. Usually, most customers want to either purchase options or sell options. If all of the customers are purchasing options, the option market makers are selling. We refer to this situation as one-sided order flow. In a two-sided order flow situation, customers are buying *and* selling. Two-sided order flow is generally more common in larger issues that have greater volume. Again, for most option market makers, however, two-sided order flow is rare.

Given a typically one-sided market, market makers are obligated (albeit reluctantly) to create the balance. In other words, when there are more sellers, the market makers become buyers. Then, market makers are like merchants who have an inventory of products that are not selling. Also, because of their role, the market makers must continue to buy. When this situation happens, they invariably lower their prices for the option. They will continue to lower their prices as long as the imbalance continues.

When there are more buyers, the floor traders accumulate not only inventory but also risk. Under these circumstances, floor traders will increase their prices in an effort to reduce further buying or to provide a larger cushion against their increased risk. At these times of imbalance between option demand and supply, an option's implied volatility can vary dramatically from any notion of a reasonable forecast volatility. The market is not really adjusting volatility; rather, it is adjusting prices in order to reflect changed market conditions. Volatility, however, is the pricing variable that absorbs this change.

In terms of the increase in demand for options, consider the increased demand during earnings months when investors enter the options marketplace in order to speculate on the earnings of a particular underlying issue. As large buy orders continue to enter the trading pit, the floor traders continually increase the price (as explained earlier). This price increase produces an increase in the implied volatility. Continued buying by the public under these circumstances means that the public is willing to pay more for the perceived opportunity of making money on a large earnings move in the underlying issue. Other events that might increase the demand for options include takeover rumors, earnings releases, and other news announcements.

Conversely, if there is a large supply of a particular class or type of option, prices will decrease resulting from a corresponding decrease in the volatility variable. After the earnings have been announced, for example, option-implied volatility will generally revert to more normal levels as orders come in to sell options. The unknown is now known, and the speculators are now selling the options that they purchased. Clearly, the old adage, "Buy the rumor, sell the news" is true when evaluating volatility. The excess demand now becomes the source of an excess supply. Again, the increased selling will cause the floor traders to lower their prices by a decrease in volatility, this effect is illustrated in Figures 5-2 and 5-3.

The Importance of Implied Volatility

Implied volatility is your benchmark not only for determining which options are overpriced and which are underpriced, but also for determining how much they are out of line. These differences can be substantial. Consider Figure 5-4, which illustrates the effects of varying volatilities. In this example, implied volatility is shown to be both 10 points above and below the theoretical assessment of 32.

Based on your assumption of 32 volatility in the stock over the next year, you calculate the value of the 45 level calls and puts to be $10.44 and $3, respectively. The second column presents a situation in which the market prices of these options are $8.94 for the calls and $1.44 for the

Figure 5-2   *Earnings: effect on option volatility.*

EARNINGS: Effect on Option Volatility		
Before Earnings with expectation of upcoming announcement, **XYZ** is trading $42.		
MAR 40 calls are valued 4 3/4		
Inputs:	Underlying	42
	Volatility	**40**
	Interest Rate	6%
	Dividend	0
	Strike price	40
	Days to Expiration	91
	Option Theoretical Value:	4 3/4

Figure 5-3   *Option value after earnings.*

After Earnings:		
XYZ is trading 42.		
MAR 40 calls are valued 3 1/4		
Inputs:		
	Underlying	42
	Volatility	**20**
	Interest Rate	6%
	Dividend	0
	Strike price	40
	Days to Expiration	90
	Option Theoretical Value:	3 1/4
With a drop in volatility and all else remaining equal, the new option value will be considerably less than it was directly prior to earnings announcements.		

puts, resulting in an implied volatility of 22. Thus, by your assessment, the calls are undervalued by $1.50 and the puts are undervalued by $1.56. By contrast, the third column represents market prices for the calls at $1.68 more than you think that they are worth and market prices for the puts at $1.69 overpriced, reflecting an implied volatility of 42.

Understanding the differences between implied and forecast volatility is critical for the serious options investor or trader. This knowledge is the basis for selecting the most appropriate option position to implement. For any market expectation that you might have (such as bullish, bearish, or neutral), there will be several strategies available to exploit that expec-

Figure 5-4   *Option values at varying volatilities.*

Theoretical Volatility: 32	Implied Volatility: 22	Implied Volatility: 42
Stock Price: 50	Stock Price: 50	Stock Price: 50
Strike Price: 45	Strike Price: 45	Strike Price: 45
Days to Expiration: 365 (1yr)	Days to Expiration: 365 (1yr)	Days to Expiration: 365 (1yr)
Interest Rate: 6%	Interest Rate: 6%	Interest Rate: 6%
Volatility: 32	**Volatility: 22**	**Volatility: 42**
Dividend: none	Dividend: none	Dividend: none
Call Option Value: 10.44	**Call Option Price: 8.94**	**Call Option Price: 12.12**
Put Option Value: 3.00	**Put Option Price: 1.44**	**Put Option Price: 4.69**

tation with limited risk. In evaluating these alternatives, you will find a strategy that involves purchasing options more appealing if those options appear to be underpriced, just as a strategy for selling options would be more appealing if the options appeared to be overpriced. Similarly, you would not want to use these strategies under conditions where underpriced options were being sold or overpriced options needed to be purchased. We will cover investing and trading strategies using options in great detail later in this book.

Volatility's Impact on the Pricing Model

We discussed the relationship of volatility to the value of an option in general terms. In so doing, we have learned the following:

1. Volatility is a significant factor in pricing an option.
2. Theoretical pricing through the use of pricing models is sensitive to small changes in volatility inputs.
3. Increased volatility translates to higher option prices, with the reverse being true for decreased volatility.

That said, a rigorous examination of the detailed mathematics of the various pricing models is beyond the scope of this book. In the judgment of the authors, this knowledge is unnecessary for gaining useful mastery of the concepts involved. Needless to say, some familiarity with these models is useful. We will now turn our attention to the following issues:

1. How pricing models account for price movement in the underlying issue
2. How volatility is expressed and what that expression represents
3. How the models use that information to establish an option's theoretical price

Pricing Models and Price Movement

Pricing models generally make the assumption that consecutive price changes are random (that the next price of the underlying trades will either be unchanged or up or down, without any bias as to direction). If we graphed where prices might be as of a future date (along the x-axis or horizontal axis) versus the likelihood of the stock trading at each of those possible prices (along the y-axis or vertical axis), we would come up with a bell-shaped curve (a normal distribution curve). Figure 5-5 illustrates a normal distribution curve.

Normal distribution is a probability distribution that describes the behavior of many events. Pricing models use this knowledge to describe the probable occurrences of stock-price fluctuations. You should note that the pricing models actually tend to use a slightly skewed variation of normal distribution (called lognormal distribution). Use of the normal distribution herein will simplify the discussion while still conveying the essential concepts and relationships involved between pricing models and volatility. The normal distribution, or bell-shaped curve, is symmetrical about its mean price and has the property of the values that are most likely to occur closer to the mean value than those that are less likely to occur.

We can describe a normal distribution by using two characteristics: the mean and the standard deviation.

Mean

The arithmetic mean, generally referred to as the average, is the sum of all of the occurrences divided by the number of occurrences. For example, given the following XYZ closing prices over a two-week period, the mean

Figure 5-5 *Normal distribution of price changes.*

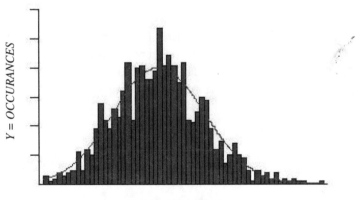

Y = OCCURANCES

X = PRICE CHANGE

Figure 5-6   *The mean of varying closing stock prices.*

Date:	12/3	12/4	12/5	12/6	12/7	12/10	12/11	12/12	12/13	12/14	12/17	12/18
Closing Price:	48	50.75	51	51.25	50.75	51.50	52	52.75	51.25	50.75	51.25	54

= 615.25 / 12 = **51.27 (the mean).**

would be 51.27. Figure 5-6 is an example of closing prices over a 12-day period and how these prices determine the mean price.

Note that most of the closing prices (data) are close to the mean price (51.27), while there are only a few at one extreme or the other (48 or 54). This bunching of most-likely outcomes near the mean is an important characteristic of a normal distribution and is measured by each distribution's standard deviation.

Standard Deviation

Standard deviation, which we can also describe as the mean of the mean, is a statistic that describes mathematically how potential outcomes are distributed from the mean of a normal distribution. By definition

1. Approximately 68.3 percent of all outcomes will be within ± 1 standard deviation from the mean.
2. Approximately 95.4 percent of all outcomes will fall within ± 2 standard deviations from the mean.
3. Approximately 99.7 percent of all outcomes will fall within ± 3 standard deviations from the mean.

For example, if the price distribution of Stock XYZ is described by a normal distribution with a mean of 20 and a standard deviation of 3, this situation would be characterized as follows:

1. A bell-shaped curve centered at 20
2. 68.3 percent of all outcomes would fall within the range of 17 ± 23 (20 − 3) to (20 + 3).
3. 95.4 percent of all outcomes would fall within the range of 14 ± 26 (20 − 6) to (20 + 6).
4. 99.7 percent of all outcomes would fall within the range of 11 ± 29 (20 − 9) to (20 + 9).

If the price distribution of Stock ABC is described by a normal distribution with a mean of 20 and a standard deviation of 5, we would characterize this situation as follows:

1. A bell-shaped curve centered at 20
2. 68.3 percent of all outcomes would fall within the range of 15 ± 25.

Figure 5-7 *Low volatility stock and high volatility stock.*

XYZ
Low Volatility Stock

ABC
High Volatility Stock

3. 95.4 percent of all outcomes would fall within the range of 10 ± 30.
4. 99.7 percent of all outcomes would fall within the range of 5 ± 35.

Figure 5-7 illustrates normal distribution graphs of XYZ, a non-volatile stock, and ABC, a more volatile stock.

The height of the normal distribution at any stock price measures the relative probability, or frequency, that the stock will be trading at that value at the time in question. Therefore, the relative flatness of ABC's normal distribution compared to that of XYZ means that it is much more likely that XYZ will be trading at one of the possible prices near the mean than ABC. Conversely, ABC is much more likely to reach prices away from the mean than XYZ is. Thus, ABC has a tendency to move much farther in price much faster than XYZ, making it a more volatile stock. A higher standard deviation translates to a more volatile stock.

Volatility, Standard Deviation, and Mean

Let's assume that Stock XYZ is currently trading at $100, that interest rates are at 6 percent, and that we are told that XYZ's volatility is 36. What do these numbers tell us? The number 36 is the standard deviation of the normal price distribution expected one year from today. This number is expressed as a percentage of the mean price also as measured a year from today. That mean price represents the stock price that will be necessary if the investor is to break even when the net cost of financing the purchase of the stock for a year is factored into the equation.

For example, under our current assumptions, it would cost $6 in interest charges to finance the full cost of the $100 purchase price at 6 percent for one year. If this stock did not pay dividends, the stock would need to be trading at $106 one year from now in order to compensate for the $6 of interest charges incurred. You should note that if the stock paid a dividend, the $6 interest charge would need to be reduced by the amount of dividends to be received over the next year. For example, if the stock paid dividends totaling $2.50 during the course of the year, the break-even price (and thus, the mean price) of the distribution would be $103.50

($100 plus $6 interest to be paid minus the $2.50 dividend to be received). The volatility of 36 would mean that the prices one year from now should fall in a normal distribution with a mean of $106 and a standard deviation of 38.16 (36 percent of 106). This situation would mean that approximately 68 percent of the time, the price of the stock one year from now would fall within the range of 68 to 144 (106 ± 38) and approximately 95 percent of the time would fall within the range of 30 to 182 (106 ± 76).

Although this example helps us understand volatility in relation to stock, we must keep in mind that when we deal with options, it is not always practical to use a 12-month period when making volatility assumptions. If an option has three months until expiration, it is not particularly helpful to know in what range the expected price will fall 12 months from now. Is it possible, then, to determine what a 40 annual volatility translates to in predicted stock price movement over a shorter period?

The answer is yes. We can use the following formula to compute volatility for a shorter period of time (daily, weekly, monthly, and so on). Divide the annual volatility by the square root of the number of trading periods in a year. For example, if XYZ is trading at 100 with an annual volatility of 10 percent and we want to determine its daily volatility, we need to divide the annual volatility (10 percent) by the square root of the number of trading periods in a year (256). The square root of the number of trading days in one year is 16 (16 × 16 = 256). There is no trading on weekends or holidays; therefore, these days do not apply, because prices cannot change on these days). Now, we divide 10 percent by 16, which equals five-eighths percent. At this point, we can conclude that the daily standard deviation for a one-day period is $5/_8$ percent × 100 (XYZ's price) = .625. XYZ is expected to move within a range of .625 ± two trading days out of three, 1.25 ± 19 trading days out of 20, and more than 1.25 ± only one day out of 20 trading days.

Let's look at this example of annual volatility divided by the square root of the number of trading periods in a year:

$$\text{Monthly volatility} = \frac{\text{annual volatility}}{\text{square root of 12}}$$

$$\text{Weekly volatility} = \frac{\text{annual volatility}}{\text{square root of 52}}$$

$$\text{Daily volatility} = \frac{\text{annual volatility}}{\text{square root of 256*}}$$

Pricing Models and Option Theoretical Value

Given all required inputs (particularly volatility), the various pricing models can then assess the probability (the likelihood, if you will) that a

*Excluding holidays and weekends

Figure 5-8   *The expected return of rolling the dice.*

Sum of dice	2	3	4	5	6	7	8	9	10	11	12
Number of occurrences*	1	2	3	4	5	6	5	4	3	2	1
Total payoff for that sum	$2	$6	$12	$20	$30	$42	$40	$36	$30	$22	$12

Let x:y represent the result of a roll of the dice, with the value x representing the number rolled on the first die and y representing the number rolled on the second die. There are then 36 different outcomes, ranging from 1:1 to 1:2 . . . to 6:6. Six of these outcomes add up to a roll of seven. These are 1:6,2:5,3:4,4:3,5:2, and 6:1. Five of these outcomes add up to a roll of six. These are 1:5,2:4,3:3,4:2, and 5:1. There is only one way to roll a 2, 1:1, and so on for each potential sum.

stock will reach a certain price by an option's expiration. This feature enables the pricing model to calculate the average amount that the investment would be worth upon expiration of the option. This average return is commonly referred to as the expected return. Expected return is an important concept, so let's look at it more closely.

Consider a game in which you roll two dice and you get back a dollar amount that is equal to the sum of the dice. For example, if you roll a 5:1, you get $6 (5 + 1). Let's calculate the expected return from playing this game. There are 36 different outcomes from rolling two dice. Each of these outcomes is equally likely. The expected results from rolling the dice 36 times are summarized in Figure 5-8.

For all 36 outcomes, the total payoff would be $252 (2 + 6 + 12 + 20 + 30 + 42 + 40 + 36 + 30 + 22 + 12). By dividing this total by 36, the number of outcomes, we get the average or expected return of $7 for each time the game is played. If it cost you $6 to play this game, you would be getting a bargain. If it cost you $8, on the other hand, you would be overpaying. Finally, if the game cost you $7, this price would be considered fair value.

This example is a simplified model for how the pricing calculators establish the fair value of an option:

1. Using the volatility input to calculate the probabilities of various investment outcomes as of an option's expiration
2. Computing the resulting expected return
3. Adjusting the expected return for various costs associated with purchasing and holding the option contract until expiration, then considering that adjusted expected return to be the fair value of the option.

Expected return is an important consideration when determining whether an option is a viable purchase. Figures 5-9 and 5-10 help to illustrate the concept of expected return. In each example, the trader makes assumptions on where the underlying will be at expiration and determines the likelihood of the underlying security will finish at a specific price.

Let's look at some simplified examples involving options.

Stock XYZ (example Number 2) is more likely to increase enough in price for its May 55 call to finish ITM than is Stock ABC (example

Figure 5-9 *Example of expected return.*

Example #1

Assumptions: It is mid-April. Stock ABC is trading at $50. Based on *expected volatility,* we calculate that the probability that ABC will close at 55 or below May option expiration is 80% and that of the remaining 20% of the time, the average value that ABC will close at May option expiration is $58.

What is the expected return on purchasing the May 55 call? If this exact situation occurred 100 times, our probability calculations indicate that the May 55 call would finish worthless 80 times (that is what an 80% chance of finishing at or below $55 at May expiration means), and the total return from the remaining 20 times would be $60 (20 finishes above $55 with an average option value of $3 per each occurrence). By dividing the aggregate return of $60 by 100 (the number of times the investment was made), we get $.60, the average or *expected return* you would anticipate getting back from a single investment in the option. If you only expect to get back $.60 each time you purchase the option, you probably wouldn't pay more than $.60 for it. Ignoring any other costs (commission, etc.), the fair value for the May 55 call would be $.60.

Figure 5-10 *Example of expected return.*

Example #2

Assumptions: It is mid-April. Stock XYZ is trading at $50. Based on *expected volatility* , we calculate that the probability that XYZ will close at 55 or below May option expiration is 60%, and that of the remaining 40% of the time, the average value that XYZ will close at May option expiration is $62.

What is the expected return on purchasing the May 55 call? If this exact situation occurred 100 times, our probability calculations indicate that the May 55 call would finish worthless 60 times, and the total return from the remaining 40 times would be $280 (40 finishes above $55 with an average option value of $7 at expiration per each occurrence). This would result in an average return of $2.80 each time you made the investment. Again ignoring any other costs (commission, etc.), the fair value for the May 55 call would then also be $2.80.

Number 1). Without attempting to quantify that difference for now, we say that XYZ is more volatile than ABC. As a result of that increased volatility, not only is the XYZ May 55 call more likely to finish ITM than the ABC May 55 call (40 percent of the time for XYZ versus only 20 percent of the time for ABC), but when it does finish ITM, it will do so more greatly than the ABC May 55 call. Thus, the increased volatility has a double-barreled impact on the value of the option: it increases both the probability that it will finish ITM and increases how much that option might be worth. Both increases impact the expected return on an investment in the option (and therefore affect its fair market price).

Summary

The material in this chapter has provided us with the foundation for proceeding into the real world of options trading. After having learned how to do our homework, we can now see how our research fares in the less-than-perfectly-predictable real world. The reality is that market conditions change all the time. As we have learned, changes in volatility in particular can offset our original estimated value for an option. In order to secure our positions against these changes, we need to be on our toes—ready to act in any number of ways in order to respond to change.

Imagine yourself as a tennis player who is returning forehands from a ball machine that is programmed on one setting. Perhaps under these circumstances, you could learn well how to perfect a stroke when returning the ball from that particular spot on the court. In a real tennis match, however, the balls come at you from a number of directions with different speeds and respond to the wind in different ways. You will need to rapidly assess the best strategy for returning the ball in order to win the point. As such, our next step on the options court is to become familiar with how we can measure an option's sensitivity to changes in the variables that are used to determine an option's value.

Quiz

1. Volatility as indicated by the marketplace is known as _____.
2. The _____ is the difference between the bid and offer prices.
3. An increase in volatility _____ the price of calls and puts.
4. Normal distribution is generally described by what two characteristics?
5. Approximately 95.4 percent of all occurrences will fall within _____ standard deviation.
6. The average return is commonly referred to as the _____ return.

7. As volatility decreases, the value of options will generally _____ .

8. _____ volatility = annual volatility / the square root of 52.

9. The phrase, "mean of the mean" can be used to describe _____ .

10. _____ is a measure of actual price changes in an underlying issue over a specific period in the past.

Please refer to the Appendix I in this book for quiz answers.

Chapter 6

Introduction to Synthetics

Introduction

People frequently ask us for the secret money-making strategies that option professionals use. If only such strategies existed. There are no real secrets to using derivatives. There is, however, a fundamental relationship between puts and calls of the same strike and expiration, and many people do not understand this relationship. We will explore this issue by introducing specific examples.

Examples

Assume that XYZ is trading at $50 and the July 50 XYZ calls and puts are each trading at $2. Let's construct the expiration profit and loss graph of a position resulting from the purchase of 100 shares of stock for $50 per share: Figure 6-1 illustrates that a long stock position will increase in value as the stock rises in value and decreases in value as the stock decreases in value.

Now, on the same graph, let's construct a representation of one July 50 put for $2 ($200): Figure 6-2 illustrates the profit and loss of a long put. This position has limited loss on the upside and can theoretically profit until the underlying reaches zero.

Step Number 1. Because the options strike price is $50, we first calculate the position P&L upon expiration—assuming that the stock closes at precisely $50. At a $50 stock price, the stock purchase will break-even

Figure 6-1 *Black line = long 100 shares of stock for $50/share.*

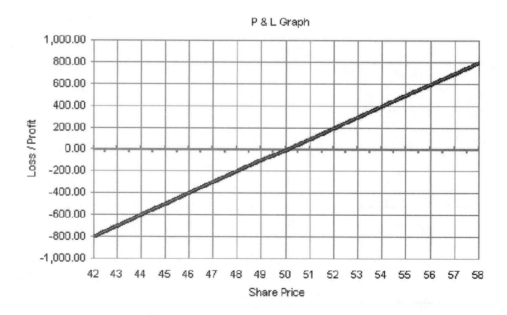

Figure 6-2   *Black line = long 1 50 level put for $2 ($200) at expiration.*
Thin gray line = long 1 50 level put for $2 ($200) with 21 days to
expiration.

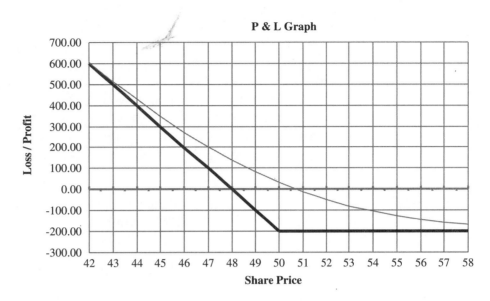

Table 6-1   *P&L Table for Puts and Stock*

Stock Price	46	47	48	49	50	51	52	53	54	55
Stock P&L	-$400	-$300	-$200	-$100	0	$100	$200	$300	$400	$500
Put Cost	-$200	-$200	-$200	-$200	-$200	-$200	-$200	-$200	-$200	-$200
Put Intrinsic	$400	$300	$200	$100	0	0	0	0	0	0
Put P&L	$200	$100	0	-$100	-$200	-$200	$200	-$200	-$200	-$200
Position P&L	-$200	-$200	-$200	-$200	-$200	-$100	0	$100	$200	$300
Note: Put P&L = Put Cost − Put Intrinsic (at expiration)										

while the put purchased for $2 will expire with an intrinsic value of $0
(for a loss of $200). Thus, the aggregate position would lose $200 (break-
even on the stock and lose $200 on the option). Enter these values into a
matrix table that is similar to the Table 6-1.

> **NOTE**
>
> If the position contains options that have different strikes (for example,
> a July 45 call along with a July 50 put), you would determine the P&L
> position twice: once by assuming a stock price at an expiration of $45,
> and again by assuming a stock price of $50.

Step Number 2. Select several stock prices above the options strike
price of $50 (we arbitrarily selected $51, $52, $53, $54, and $55) and several stock prices below $50 (we arbitrarily selected $46, $47, $48, and

$49). Determine the position P&L upon expiration at each selected price, and enter the results in the table.

NOTE

If the position contains options that have several different strikes (for example, a July 45 call along with a July 50 put), you would select several stock prices below $45 (the lowest strike price in the position) and several stock prices above $50 (the highest strike price in the position). Then, you do not have to select any stock prices between $45 and $50. The accompanying Table 6-1 listed some stock price and indicated the value of the put and underlying stock at these prices.

In this example, in order to calculate the position P&L, subtract the stock P&L by the put P&L as follows:

$$\text{Position P\&L} = \text{Stock P\&L} - \text{Put P\&L}$$

Step Number 3.   With the horizontal axis of the graph representing the price of the stock upon expiration and the vertical axis representing the position P&L, place dots on the graph representing the P&L for each stock price selected. Figure 6-3 illustrates the long stock position. Figure 6-4 illustrates the long put position.

Step Number 4.   Connect the dots, remembering that the graph might bend at the stock price (equaling the option's strike price).
    Figure 6-5 illustrates the two graphs combined (the long put in black and the long stock represented by the gray line).

Figure 6-3   *Black line = long 100 shares of stock for $50/share.*

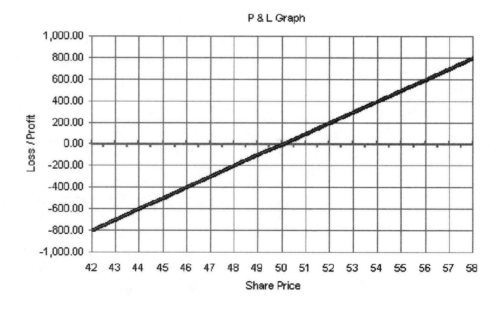

Figure 6-4   *Black line = long 1 50 level put for $2 ($200) at expiration.*
Thin gray line = long 1 50 level put for $2 ($200) with 21 days to expiration.

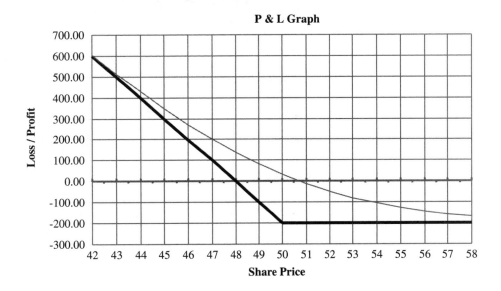

Figure 6-5   *Gray line = short 100 of stock for $50 / share.*
Black line = long 1 50 level put for $2 ($200) at expiration.
Thin gray line = long 1 50 level put for $2 ($200) with 21 days to expiration.

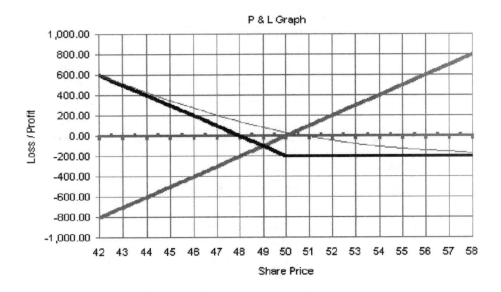

    Now, compare this graph to the graph of the purchase of the July 50 call for $2. Figure 6-6 is the combined P&L of the long stock, long put position.
    The figures have identical profit and loss characteristics. Is this situation a coincidence? The answer is no. If you think about it, they have the same risk/reward profile. Let's see what we have learned. Upon July expiration:

Figure 6-6   *Black line = synthetically long 1 50 call for $2 ($200) at*
expiration.
Thin gray line = synthetically long 1 50 call for $2 ($200) with 21
days to expiration.

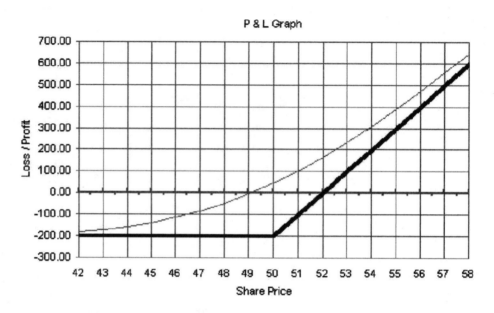

- If the stock closes at $50 per share, the call will expire as worthless
—resulting in a $200 loss. This situation will also happen with the
put-stock combination.
- For each $1 the stock closes above $50 per share, the call will
increase in value by $100. This situation will also occur with the put-
stock combination (with the put remaining worthless).
- The value of the call is unaffected at any stock price below $50 per
share upon expiration. At any such price, the call will be worthless—
resulting in a $200 loss. The put, however, will increase in value by
$100 for every $1 that the stock closes below $50 per share. This sit-
uation, in turn, will completely cancel the loss of $100 for every $1
the stock closes below $50 per share. Note how this situation also
gives the position the same result as if the stock had closed at $50
per share (a $200 loss).

When the investor buys puts in order to protect a long stock position,
he or she is effectively purchasing a long call. In this case, the investor
has synthetically created a long call by purchasing puts. In the industry,
this procedure is referred to as purchasing the call synthetically. Although
both positions produce the same P&L, the purchase of the long call uses
less capital and results in a higher return on investment (ROI) than the
long stock and long put position (which requires purchasing both the
stock and the put). The call purchaser has leveraged his or her position,
and in so doing, he or she has freed up capital to either increase the size
of the position or to make other investments.

Now, consider another example. Suppose that you were to purchase 1
July 50 call and sell 1 July 50 put. Because the prices of the call and put

offset each other, there is no net cost to putting on this position. Upon expiration, if the stock is trading above $50, you will exercise the call option and own 100 shares of XYZ at a net cost of $50 per share. Also, if the stock closes below $50, the holder of the put will exercise it and you will be assigned (which will result in the purchase of 100 shares for $50 per share). In either event, you will end up owning 100 shares of XYZ for $50 per share.

Is this method an alternative way to purchase stock? The answer is yes. Unlike the previous example, this method is not a leveraged alternative—because the short put position will require a margin account. Trading alternatives can be more cost effective than a position in the underlying stock. As you can see yet again, a creative understanding of synthetics is one of the successful market maker's greatest attributes.

These examples illustrate the complementary inter-relationship of calls, puts, and stock. As it turns out, each of our six building blocks can be constructed synthetically. These combinations are known as the synthetic positions.

The six synthetic position formulas are as follows (note that in each formula, each call and put has the same strike price and expiration):

1. Synthetic long stock = long call + short put
2. Synthetic short stock = short call + long put
3. Synthetic long call = long stock + long put
4. Synthetic short call = short stock + short put
5. Synthetic long put = long call + short stock
6. Synthetic short put = short call + long stock

NOTE

Pin risk is an important consideration when trading synthetics. Pin risk is the risk to the seller of an option that at expiration the option will close at the options strike price. When this happens the seller is uncertain as to whether or not the option will be exercised thereby leaving the seller long the underlying, in the case of a put, or short the underlying in the case of a call.

Pricing Synthetics

We have now learned that there are two different ways to acquire a building block. One, we can purchase (sell) the building block directly, or two, we can purchase (sell) it synthetically. Not surprisingly, what determines one choice over the other is the bottom line: cost. In order to determine whether to put a position on directly or synthetically, we need to calculate the price of the synthetic position.

The following information is required to calculate the synthetic position price:

- Current stock price
- Option strike price
- Dividend payment dates and amounts
- Days until option expiration
- Cost to carry the synthetic position (in other words, the applicable interest rate)

Synthetic pricing formulas, then, are as follows:

Synthetic long call price = (+put price + stock price + cost to carry) − strike price

Synthetic long put price = (+call price + strike price − cost to carry) − stock price

Synthetic short call price = (−put price − stock price − cost to carry) + strike price

Synthetic short put price = (−call price − strike price + cost to carry) + stock price

The applicable interest rate varies from broker to broker, and in the case of long stock, the rate depends on whether you have cash available in your account or whether you will borrow the funds from your broker.

An important consideration when trading any position is the cost of carry, which is how much interest is paid for a particular strike until expiration if you are long stock or how much is received for a particular strike until expiration if you are short stock:

Cost to carry = applicable interest rate × strike price × days to expiration/360

Here is an example of pricing options versus synthetic positions. Compare the prices of the long call and long synthetic call in order to determine which would be cheaper to buy. Use a pricing formula to calculate the cost based on the following information as shown in Table 6-2.

Stock price: 52

Interest rate: 6 percent

Table 6-2   *We can purchase the Mar 50 call directly for $4.75. We can purchase the same call synthetically by paying $1.75 for the Mar 50 put and purchasing 100 shares of stock for $52/share.*

CALL	STRIKE	PUT
4.50 – 4.75	MAR 50	1.50 – 1.75

Days until expiration: 60
Volatility: 35

The formula is as follows:

synthetic long call = put + stock.

The pricing formula is as follows:

(Put price + stock price + cost to carry) − strike price = synthetic long call price
(1.75 + 52 + .50) − 50 = 4.25

The cost to carry is .50 or $\frac{1}{2}$, calculated as follows: $.06 \times 50 \times \frac{6}{360} = .50$.
The synthetic call is cheaper than the actual call. The synthetic call, however, will require a larger capital investment because the investor is purchasing stock and puts instead of the call. The tradeoff, then, is effectively paying $.50 less for the calls or using less investment capital.

The Synthetic Triangle

In the beginning, understanding synthetics requires a bit of mental juggling. In time, however, it becomes easier to see how synthetic positions can mirror the effect of a direct option or stock purchase. To this end, we have found that a synthetic triangle serves as a useful memory aid. This is shown in Figure 6-7.

Figure 6-7   *Synthetic triangle.*

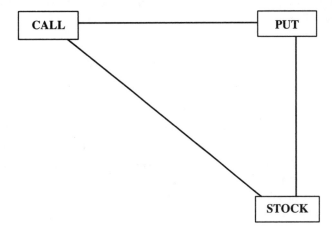

Remember that putting on a building block synthetically always involves a combination of the other types of building blocks. In the case of calls, this process involves using puts and stock. In the case of puts, this process means using calls and stock. In the case of stock, this process involves puts and calls. The three rules of the synthetic triangle are as follows:

1. Completion of one (leg) corner of the triangle = 1 building block (directional risk).
2. Completion of any two (legs) corners of the triangle = synthetic position (directional risk).
3. Completion of all three (legs) corners of the triangle = conversion/reversal (eliminating directional risk).

> **NOTE**
>
> When puts and stock are combined to create a synthetic call, they are always either both bought or both sold. (Puts and stock are always traded from the same side to create a hedge or synthetic call). When calls are combined with either puts or stock in order to create a stock or put position synthetically, if the call is purchased, then the other leg is sold and vice-versa (calls are always traded from the opposite side to create a hedge or synthetic put or stock).

Conversion/Reversal

Previously (that is, prior to reading this chapter), the only way to close out a long position was to sell it—and the only way to close out a short position was to cover it. Synthetics create a myriad of possibilities, however. The fact that we can initiate a position either directly or through the use of its synthetic equivalent means that we can also effectively close out a long position by selling its synthetic or a short position by acquiring its synthetic. Under these circumstances, the closed-out position takes one of two forms:

$$-\text{Call} + \text{Put} + \text{Stock}$$
$$+\text{Call} - \text{Put} - \text{Stock}$$

In other words, the synthetically closed-out position is essentially no longer subject to directional risk[1]. Changes in the value of the underlying stock will have no effect on the position. When this synthetically closed-out position includes long stock, it is known as a conversion. If it includes short stock, it is called a reversal.

---

[1]Refer to the section concerning conversion/reversal risks in this chapter.

Table 6-3 *Components of Synthetic Positions*

Synthetic (Formula)	Neutralizing Direct	Reversal / Conversion
+ Cn = + P + S	− C	Conversion
+ Pn = + C − S	− P	Reversal
− Cn = − P − S	+ C	Reversal ·
− Pn = − C + S	+ P	Conversion
+ Sn = − C − P	− S	Reversal
− Sn = − C + P	+ S	Conversion

(KEY: C = Call, P = Put, S = Stock, n = Synthetic, + = Long, − = Short)

Table 6-3 summarizes the components of synthetic positions.

Conversion/Reversal and Free Money

In the pricing synthetics section earlier in this chapter, we learned how to calculate the effective cost (never forgetting to include the carrying costs of the synthetic position) of purchasing a building block synthetically. We examined in detail one example where we calculated that purchasing the call synthetically was actually cheaper than purchasing the call directly. In the example, the purchase price for the synthetic call came to 4.25 when we could purchase the call for 4.75 immediately from a market maker (the market quote being 4.50–4.75). Consider what would happen, based on this example, if you purchased the call synthetically and immediately sold it directly for 4.50. Your position would be long 1 Mar 50 Put, Long 100 shares of stock and short one Mar 50 call. Your account would be immediately debited $4,925 (paying $5,200 for 100 shares of stock at $52/share, paying $175 for one Mar 50 put and receiving $450 for selling one Mar 50 call). At expiration, the position will unwind and return $5,000 in cash to your account (if the stock closes above $50/share at expiration the short Mar 50 call will be exercised and your stock will be sold for $50/share. Conversely, if the stock closes below $50/share at expiration you will exercise your Mar 50 put thereby selling your stock for $50/share. Additionally, you would have incurred a cost of carry of $50 ($0.50 per share times 100 shares). Your conversion (because the position involves being long stock) would have locked in a $.25 per share profit ($25 for the entire position, prior to figuring in commissions).

This profit results from the fact that the prices of calls and puts with the same expiration month and strike price are inextricably related. As soon as they become out of alignment, professional traders will attempt to lock in profits by purchasing the cheaper leg and by selling the more expensive one, just as in our example. They will continue to perform this action until the prices return to alignment and until this profit opportunity ceases to be available. This dynamic quickly forces the prices of the puts and call back into synchronicity.

When comparing the prices of calls and puts with the same expiration month and strike price in order to determine whether you can lock in a profit, you need to calculate the net result of putting on both the conversion and the reversal. If either calculation results in a net credit (do not forget to include carrying costs), that credit represents a locked-in profit. Thus, you have two formulas to consider: one for the conversion and the other for the reversal.

Here is the conversion formula:

$$-\text{call} + \text{put} + \text{stock} + \text{cost of carry}$$
$$\text{net credit} = \text{profit}$$
$$\text{net debit} = \text{loss}$$

Here is the formula for reversal:

$$+\text{call} - \text{put} - \text{stock} - \text{cost of carry}$$
$$\text{net credit} = \text{profit}$$
$$\text{net debit} = \text{loss}$$

Conversion/Reversal Risks

Although conversions/reversals are substantially devoid of market risks, they are subject to fluctuation in value due to interest rate changes prior to expiration. They are also subject to uncertainty that is created when the closing stock price upon expiration equals the strike price of the options in the conversion/reversal.

Interest-Rate Risk

Because conversion/reversals include stock (either long or short, carried until expiration), any change in applicable interest rates might have some effect on the overall profitability of the position. When the options are near term and any interest-rate changes are small and gradual, the effect will be small.

Closing at the Strike

When the stock closes at the strike price upon expiration, there is uncertainty about the exact composition of the post-expiration position of the stock. The decision to exercise the option that you are short might be unclear and might be made by someone else, and you will generally not know whether it has been exercised until the next trading day.

For example, consider a conversion involving the March 40 puts and calls. The position would be as follows:

$$+\text{March 40 put} + 100 \text{ shares of stock} - \text{March 40 call}$$

If upon March expiration the stock is trading for $45, you would expect the holder of the March 40 call to exercise the call if he or she owned it—thus acquiring your stock from you. Because you would not exercise your March 40 put (post March expiration), you would have no position in the stock. If at March expiration the stock were trading at $38, your short call would expire worthless and would therefore not be exercised. Instead, you would exercise your March 40 put, thus selling your stock. Again, you would have no post-expiration position.

Compare this situation to a case in which the stock closes at March expiration at $40, however. If you desire to have no post-expiration position in the stock, you will have to guess whether your short call will be exercised. If it will be exercised, resulting in your stock being called away from you, you would choose not to exercise your put. If it will not be exercised, then you would need to exercise your put in order to dispose of your stock.

Unfortunately, you will not learn whether the call has been exercised until the following trading day (generally Monday unless the market is closed on that day), which is well after your deadline for deciding whether or not to exercise your put. This situation is known as pin risk. For those who are uncomfortable with the uncertainty of not knowing what their post-expiration position will look like until the opening on the next trading day, the only solution is to go out to the market just prior to closing on expiration Friday and close out your short option position.

Summary

Trading synthetics and reversal/conversions is a good way to limit the risks associated with trading options. Many times, however, the risks that are associated with an options position far exceed the simple, directional risk associated with the outright purchase or short sale of an individual security or the manageable pin or interest-rate risk associated with a reversal/conversion. Furthermore, it is not enough to simply identify various option risks. The next challenge is to determine how these risks fluctuate in an ever-changing market environment. Risk comes in many forms, after all, and it is essential to understand the type of risk exposure to which a position is vulnerable before we attempt to manage the position. Learning how to identify risks and knowing how stock options will behave under a multitude of conditions represents an option trader's most challenging task. Understandably, the trader wants to quantify his or her position risk, and in the following chapter on the Greeks, we will learn how to identify the various risks and how to calculate them.

Quiz

1. Long call + short put = _____.
2. Short call + long put = _____.
3. Long stock + long put = _____.
4. Short stock + short put = _____.
5. Long call + short stock = _____.
6. Short call + long stock = _____.
7. _____ = applicable interest rate × strike price × days until expiration / 360

Synthetic pricing formulas are as follows:

8. _____ = (+put price + stock price + cost to carry) − strike price
9. _____ = (+call price + strike price − cost to carry) − stock price
10. _____ = (−put price − stock price − cost to carry) + strike price
11. _____ = (−call price − strike price + cost to carry) + stock price
12. A _____ consists of short stock + short put + long call.
13. A _____ consists of long stock + long put + short call.
14. _____ and _____ risk are the risks associated with a reversal/conversion.

Please refer to the Appendix I in this book for quiz answers.

Chapter 7

The Greeks

Introduction

Purchasing a stock has an obvious risk/reward profile. If the stock goes up, you make money. If it goes down, you lose money. The reverse is true if you sell a stock short. We refer to this loss exposure as directional risk (refer to Graph 7-1). Furthermore, the amount of the profit or loss is easy to anticipate. If you purchase 100 shares of XYZ, for each $1 increase in price the position increases in value by $100, and for each $1 reduction in price, the position loses $100 in value. If you sell 100 shares of stock short, for each $1 decrease in price you will make $100, and you will lose $100 for each $1 increase in price.

By contrast, determining the risk/reward profile of an option position is much more complicated. As we have seen, an option's value can be affected by a change in any one of these five variables:

- Stock price
- Time until expiration
- Volatility
- Interest rate
- Amount and timing of dividends

When two or more of these inputs changes, the changes can either act to offset each other in whole or in part or can work in concert to magnify either the increase or decrease in price. The situation is further complicated when options are used in combination.

Graph 7-1   *Directional risk.*
            Black line = long 100 share of stock for $50/share

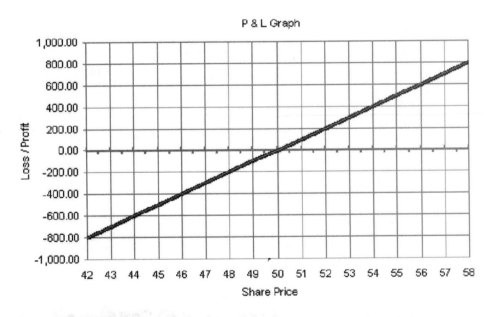

Fortunately, there are analytical tools available to simplify the analysis of option positions. These tools are commonly referred to collectively as the Greeks and individually as delta, theta, gamma, rho, vega, and omega. Individually, they each measure some aspect of an option position's market risk/reward profile. This statement is true whether the position is a simple one involving one or perhaps a few different options or an extremely complicated position (such as a professional floor trader who has scores of different option contracts—some of which are long and some of which are short—and who may have a long or short position in the underlying asset). Collectively, the Greeks provide the practiced trader with a comprehensive assessment of a position's risk/reward profile. Not only will the trader have an accurate picture of which market conditions will enhance the value of the position and which will subject it to a loss of value, but the trader will be in a position to determine what adjustments are appropriate in order to reflect the trader's current expectations concerning the stock. The trader can also reduce exposure to one or more aspects of market risk.

The Greeks

The various Greeks, the variables with which they are associated, and a short introductory definition of each are summarized in Figure 7-1.

This chapter not only explores how the Greeks affect option pricing individually but also describes how they affect option pricing in combination. With the availability of option-analytical software, it is neither

Figure 7-1 *The Greeks.*

Greek	Associated with Option Variable	Definition
Delta	Exercise/Strike Price & Underlying Price	The relationship between a change in the price of the underlying and the price of the option
Gamma	Exercise/Strike Price & Underlying Price	The measurement of how quickly delta changes as the price of the underlying changes.
Theta	Time to Expiration	The measurement of the rate at which an option's time premium diminishes as time passes.
Rho	Interest Rates	The measurement of how a change in interest rates will affect the value of the option.
Vega	Volatility	The measurement of how a change in implied volatility will affect the value of the option.
Omega	Exercise/Strike Price & Underlying Price	Measures the leverage of an option

necessary nor particularly useful for you to learn the mathematical formulas involved. What is important, however, is that you grasp conceptually the insight that these tools provide. This knowledge will help you identify your risks and respond to them appropriately.

Let's start our inquiry by examining the impact of price movement of the underlying asset on an option's theoretical value. We will isolate the impact of change in price of the underlying asset by keeping the other inputs constant while varying the price of the stock. Consider Stock ABC that has a volatility of 50. Using an interest rate of 5 percent, assume that the company does not issue a dividend. A table of the theoretical values of the 60-level calls and puts with 30 days to go until their expiration is shown in Table 7-1.

This table highlights two important aspects of the relationship between the price of an option and the price of the underlying stock:

Table 7-1   *Theoretical Value of the Calls and Puts*

	60 - level call		60 - level put	
Stock Price	theoretical value	Call price change for $1 increase in stock price	theoretical value	Put price change for $1 increase in stock price
50	$.41	+$.13	$10.25	−$.87
51	$.54	+$.17	$9.38	−$.83
52	$.71	+$.21	$8.55	−$.79
53	$.92	+$.25	$7.76	−$.75
54	$1.17	+$.29	$7.01	−$.71
55	$1.46	+$.33	$6.30	−$.67
56	$1.79	+$.38	$5.63	−$.62
57	$2.17	+$.43	$5.01	−$.57
58	$2.60	+$.47	$4.44	−$.53
59	$3.07	+$.51	$3.91	−$.49
60	$3.58	+$.56	$3.42	−$.44
61	$4.14	+$.60	$2.98	−$.40
62	$4.74	+$.64	$2.58	−$.36
63	$5.38	+$.68	$2.22	−$.32
64	$6.06	+$.72	$1.90	−$.28
65	$6.78	+$.76	$1.62	−$.24
66	$7.54	+$.80	$1.38	−$.20
67	$8.34	+$.83	$1.18	−$.17
68	$9.17	+$.85	$1.01	−$.15
69	$10.02	+$.87	$.86	−$.13
70	$10.89	+$.89	$0.73	− $.11

1. As the price of ABC increases, the price of the 60-level call also increases—while the price of the corresponding put decreases. With the stock at $50, the theoretical values of the call and put are $.41 and $10.25, respectively. By the time the price of the stock reaches $55, for example, the theoretical value of the call has risen to $1.46. The put's theoretical value has declined to $6.23.

2. As the price of ABC increases, the price of the call increases while the price of the put decreases. With the stock at $50, a $1 increase in the stock theoretically produces a $.14 increase in the price of the 60-level call and a $.87 decrease in the price of the corresponding put. The call increases in price by $.29 when the stock increases from $54 to $55 and by $.80 when the stock increases from $66 to $67. Correspondingly, the put declines by $.72 when the stock goes from $54 to $55 but only by $.21 as the stock increases from $66 to $67.

The relationship between the change in the price of a stock and the corresponding change in the price of an option is referred to as the option's **delta.**

Delta

The delta is the most widely known of the Greeks and is an extremely important gauge of any option strategy. Delta measures how sensitive an option's price is to change in the value of the underlying stock. There are two particularly useful ways to look at delta: the measure of how much the option's price will change compared to a change in the price of the underlying asset, and the approximate probability that the option will finish ITM. We will explore both of these perspectives in some detail.

Related Change. An option's delta is the ratio of the change in its theoretical value to a small change in the price of the underlying stock. More commonly (but marginally less precise), delta is defined as how much an option's price changes for every $1 change in the price of the stock. A positive delta means that an option's price moves in the same direction as price movement in the underlying asset. An option that has a positive delta will increase in value as the underlying asset increases in value and will decrease in value as the price of the underlying asset decreases. Conversely, a negative delta reflects the fact that an option's price moves in the opposite direction from the price movement in the underlying asset. An option that has a negative delta will decrease in value as the underlying asset increases and will increase in value as the underlying asset decreases. Because a long call and short put increase in value as the underlying asset increases (in other words, their value rises and falls along with the underlying asset), they have a positive delta. Conversely, both a long put and a short call have negative deltas, because their values decrease as the underlying asset increases in price and increase when the stock price declines. Going back to the table presented earlier in this chapter, with ABC stock trading at $50, the fact that the 60-level call's price would theoretically increase by $.13 when the stock price increased $1 to reach $51 indicates a delta of .13. In comparison, the delta of the 60-level put with the stock trading at $50 would be $-.87$. Because one equity option contract generally represents options on 100 shares of the underlying asset, the delta is most commonly expressed as the aggregate change in price of the option contract for a $1 change in the underlying asset. In other words, the delta for one option is multiplied by 100 (the number of shares represented by one contract). Under this approach, the 60-level call with ABC trading at $50 would have a delta of 13, not .13. From now on, we will refer to option deltas by using this aggregate designation.

Many option strategies and positions include holdings in the underlying asset, which can be long or short. When you are determining the delta for a complicated position that includes a combination of options and/or positions in the underlying asset, the aggregate delta of the entire position is most relevant. Using the same ratio definition of the delta as for options, the delta of one share of long stock is $+1$, while the delta of one share of short stock is -1. Therefore, if a position included 1,000 shares of stock, this stock would contribute 1,000 deltas to the aggregate position delta. On the other hand, if the position included a short of 1,000 shares, this short position would contribute $-1,000$ deltas to the aggregate position delta. In summary

If the holding is:	It will contribute the following:
Long underlying security	Positive delta
Short underlying security	Negative delta
Long call	Positive delta
Short call	Negative delta
Long put	Negative delta
Short put	Positive delta

Although you can calculate an option's delta precisely by using an option-pricing model, many experienced option traders approximate option deltas by using the following rules of thumb:

- An ATM option typically has a delta of about $+50$ for calls and -50 for puts.
- With the stock trading at or near a strike price, give the nearest ITM options a delta of 75 and the next-closest ITM options a delta of 90. Then, estimate the deltas of all other ITM options to be 100.
- With the stock trading at or near a strike price, give the nearest OTM options a delta of 25 and the next-closest OTM options a delta of 10. All other OTM options should receive a zero delta.

Table 7-2 *Determining Options Deltas*

Option Strike Price	Call Delta	Put Delta
45	+100	0
50	+90	−10
55	+75	−25
60	+50	−50
65	+25	−75
70	+10	−90
75	0	−100

For example, if XYZ were trading at $60, we would approximate option deltas as shown in Table 7-2.

As you learned in the previous chapter, being long a call and short a put with the same strike and expiration is the equivalent of being long 100 shares of the underlying asset (synthetic long stock). Because long 100 shares always represent an aggregate 100 deltas, combining the deltas of the long call and the short put with the same strike price and expiration date must also always equal 100. Similarly, the aggregate delta of a short call, long put position with the same strike price and expiration date will be −100, the equivalent of being short 100 shares of the underlying asset. This example highlights an important relationship between the deltas of puts and calls with the same strike price and expiration date. If you know one, you can easily determine the other. For example, if the March 60 call has a delta of +38, the delta of the March 60 put is −62.

Probability of an ITM Finish upon Expiration

An easy way to think of delta is as the probability that the option will finish ITM upon expiration. The ATM calls and puts each have a 50-50 (or 50 percent) chance of finishing ITM upon expiration and both carry an approximate delta of 50. The ITM calls and puts have a much greater chance of finishing ITM upon expiration than their ATM counterparts—with a deeper ITM call or put having a higher likelihood of finishing ITM than one that is less ITM. Their deltas reflect those respective probabilities. The OTM options have the least percentage chance of finishing ITM—and not surprisingly, their small deltas reflect this decreased probability.

Delta and Time

The time until expiration impacts an option's delta. Considering delta as the probability of finishing ITM makes it easier to understand this effect. This thought leads to the following relationship:

- The delta for an ITM option will move towards 100 as time expiration decreases. The likelihood of the option staying ITM increases as the time until expiration decreases.
- The delta of an ATM option will remain at 50, because it still has a 50-50 chance of finishing ITM.
- The delta of an OTM option will move towards zero as expiration approaches, because the likelihood of the option finishing ITM decreases as the time until expiration decreases.

Tables 7-3 through 7-5 show examples of delta and time until expiration.
As we can see from these examples, strike prices at differing expiration dates have different deltas. Hence, as the time until expiration increases, the probability that the underlying asset will move towards or

Table 7-3 *Options with One Month Remaining*

XYZ   24 days to expiration

Option	Call Delta Δ	Put Delta Δ	Combined Delta
Jan 45	85	−15	100
Jan 50	60	−40	100
Jan 55	20	−80	100

Table 7-4 *Options with One Week Remaining*

XYZ   7 days to expiration

Option	Call Delta Δ	Put Delta Δ	Combined Delta
Jan 45	99	−1	100
Jan 50	80	−20	100
Jan 55	5	−95	100

Table 7-5 *Options with One Day Remaining*

XYZ   1 day to expiration (expiration Friday)

Option	Call Delta Δ	Put Delta Δ	Combined Delta
Jan 45	100	0	100
Jan 50	100	0	100
Jan 55	0	−100	100

away from a particular strike increases. Therefore, the delta of the long-term ITM call will decrease, reflecting the decreased probability that the option will finish ITM. The delta of the ATM call, still having a 50 percent chance of finishing ITM, will remain the same. The delta of the OTM calls will increase because there is a greater probability that the underlying asset can move towards the strike and that the option will finish ITM. The more time and the less certainty—and in the world of derivative products—six months to one year can seem a lifetime. The uncertainty of the stock price in the future is reflected in the options deltas.

Some examples of delta and different expiration months are shown in Tables 7-6 through 7-8.

These examples enable us to observe the varying deltas of particular expiration months. You should realize that not only do deltas in each individual month change as the time until expiration decreases, but options

Table 7-6 *Examples of Delta and Different Expiration in January*

XYZ 51   **January Expiration**

Option	Call T.V.	Delta Δ	Put T.V.	Delta Δ	Combined Delta
JAN 45	6 5/8	85	5/8	−15	100
JAN 50	2 1/4	60	1 1/4	−40	100
JAN 55	3/4	20	4 3/4	−80	100

Table 7-7 *Examples of Delta and Different Expiration in February*

XYZ 51   **February Expiration**

Option	Call T.V.	Delta Δ	Put T.V.	Delta Δ	Combined Delta
FEB 45	7	82	1 1/8	−18	100
FEB 50	3 1/8	55	2 1/4	−45	100
FEB 55	1 1/4	30	5 3/8	−70	100

Table 7-8 *Examples of Delta and Different Expiration in May*

XYZ 51   **May Expiration**

Option	Call T.V.	Delta Δ	Put T.V.	Delta Δ	Combined Delta
MAY 45	7 3/4	73	1 7/8	−27	100
MAY 50	4 1/4	50	3 3/8	−50	100
MAY 55	2 1/8	35	6 1/8	−65	100

that have the same strike price and differing expiration months also have different deltas. The expected price upon expiration for each individual month varies depending on a multitude of factors. For example, volatility might be higher in the month in which earnings will be released because there is increased speculation, or perhaps there is a perceived change in interest rates or general market uncertainty. Changes in time until expiration not only affect an option's delta, but they also affect the theoretical value of an option and therefore present a risk.

The Trouble with Deltas

Remember that the technical definition of the delta is the ratio of the change in an option's price for a small change in the price of the underlying asset. Combine this fact with the observation noted earlier in this chapter that an option's delta will change as the price of the underlying asset changes. This situation leads to the important point that the current delta is not necessarily a good measure of what effect a significant change in price of the underlying asset will have on the value of the position.

Consider the following example. ABC is trading at $50, and the March 50 ABC calls are trading for $2. Let's assume that you purchase 10 March 50 calls for $2,000 and sell short 500 shares of ABC, whereas I do exactly the reverse (sell short 10 March 50 calls and buy 500 shares of ABC). The aggregate delta of your position is zero (+50 delta for each of the 10 calls, for a total call delta of +500 and −500 delta for the 500 shares of short stock). My position also has zero delta (−50 delta for each of the 10 calls, for a total call delta of −500 and +500 delta for the 500 shares of ABC stock that I purchased). Therefore, based on our deltas, we both have positions that appear neither bullish nor bearish. Let's examine these positions after a dramatic move in ABCs price (for convenience, we will assume that after the price move, all options are worth their intrinsic value).

Here is situation number 1. The next day, a takeover of ABC is announced, and ABC is suddenly trading at $75. The March 50 calls are worth $25 each. Your calls have increased in value by $23—from $2 to $25 —for a profit of $23,000 ($23 per option × 100 options per contract × 10 contracts), while your short stock position has lost $12,500 (loss of $25 per share × 500 shares). Your net position has earned a $10,500 profit. Because I have the exact opposite position, I have lost $10,500.

Here is situation number 2. Overnight, the company announces that it has been cooking its books and that earnings have been substantially over-reported. The next morning, the stock opens at $25. Your calls are now worthless, resulting in a loss of $2,000. You have made $12,500 on the 500 shares that you sold short at $50, however, so your aggregate position has made you $10,500. Again, I have lost the amount that you made.

You and I both had delta-neutral positions. Your position responded favorably to a large move in the stock in either direction, however, while my position responded poorly. This example highlights why relying on delta alone in order to assess directional risk is ill advised. Gamma is the measure of how one's position will respond to price movement in the underlying asset.

Gamma

The fact that an option's delta changes as the underlying asset changes in price should be obvious to you by now. We empirically discovered this concept earlier in this chapter when we examined how the theoretical price of the ABC 60-level calls and puts changed as the price of the underlying asset moved from $50 to $70 (with all other pricing inputs remaining the same). Common sense tells us that this situation is true. With ATM calls having a delta of around 50, if the delta did not change as the price of the underlying asset changed, then the delta of the call would remain around 50. This delta would remain even if the underlying asset increased substantially so that the option became deep ITM or if the underlying asset had lost so much market value that the option became far OTM. We know that in the former case, the delta would increase to near 100—and in the latter case, it would decrease to near zero. Thus, there is no question: As the price of the underlying asset changes, the delta of an option will also change.

Gamma is the ratio of the change of an option's delta to a small change in the price of the underlying stock. Similarly to the definition of delta, gamma is more commonly (but marginally less precisely) defined as how much an option's delta changes for every $1 change in the price of the stock. A positive gamma means that an option's delta increases as the underlying asset increases in value and decreases as the price of the underlying asset decreases. Conversely, the delta of an option that has a negative gamma will decrease as the underlying asset increases and it will increase as the underlying asset decreases. Because the deltas of both a long call and a long put increase as the underlying asset increases (the deltas of the long put are negative numbers), the price of the underlying asset increases and the delta moves towards zero. This situation represents an increase in the delta, and they both have a positive gamma. Conversely, both the short put and short call have a negative gamma, because their deltas decrease as the underlying asset increases in price and increase when the stock price declines.

Gamma is expressed as a number between zero and one for both calls and puts. Therefore, if a call option's delta is .50 and its gamma is .08, a one-point increase in the underlying asset will theoretically result in a delta increase of .08 (to .58). Similarly, if the underlying asset decreases in value, the delta of the option will decrease by .08 for a one-point decrease. As in the case of delta, an option's gamma is most commonly expressed as the aggregate change in delta for the option contract for each $1 change in the underlying asset (in other words, the gamma for one option multiplied by 100, which is the number of shares of stock represented by one contract). Under this approach, the gamma would not be expressed as .08; rather, we would express it as 8. From now on, we will refer to option gamma by using this aggregate designation (see Figure 7-2).

In the first example, the call option has a delta of +53, which increases to +65 as the underlying asset increases by one point. Note that

Figure 7-2   *Option gamma.*

Option Gamma/Delta		
Stock Price: 50	Stock Price: 51	Stock Price: 49
Strike Price: 50	Strike Price: 50	Strike Price: 50
Days to Expiration: 14 (2 wks.)	**Days to Expiration: 14 (2 wks.)**	**Days to Expiration: 14 (2 wks.)**
Interest Rate: 6%	Interest Rate: 6%	Interest Rate: 6%
Volatility: 32	Volatility: 32	Volatility: 32
Dividend: none	Dividend: none	Dividend: none
Call Gamma: 12	**Call Gamma: 11**	**Call Gamma: 11**
Put Gamma: 12	**Put Gamma: 11**	**Put Gamma: 11**
Call Delta: +53	**Call Delta: +65**	**Call Delta: +41**
Put Delta: −47	**Put Delta: −35**	**Put Delta: −59**

Figure 7-3   *Deltas and gammas.*

If the holding is:	It will contribute:
Long Underlying Security	**No Gamma**
Short Underlying Security	**No Gamma**
Long Call	**Positive Gamma**
Short Call	**Negative Gamma**
Long Put	**Positive Gamma**
Short Put	**Negative Gamma**

the increase in the delta of +12 is the option's gamma. The put increases from a delta of −47 to a delta of −35 (−35 is greater than −47), which is again an increase in the amount of the gamma. Instead, if the underlying asset decreased in price from $50 to $49 and the delta of both the call and the put decreased by the amount of the gamma (+12), the call delta would become +41 and the put delta would become −59.

As mentioned previously, the delta of stock does not change; long stock always has a delta of 1; and short stock always has a delta of −1. Thus, stock has no gamma. Therefore, although stock will contribute either positive or negative deltas to a position, it will never contribute gamma.

This information is summarized in Figure 7-3.

Gamma measures how quickly the delta of the option changes. For those of you who are mathematically inclined, it is the second derivative of an option's price in relation to the price of the underlying asset, which we sometimes refer to as the acceleration of the option's price to its underlying asset. The greater the gamma, the faster the delta will change.

When an option is deep ITM, its delta will be close to 100 and will not be much affected by a small change in the price of the underlying asset.

The change will still leave the option deep ITM. Thus, the gamma of a deep, ITM option is nearly zero. The same is true for a far OTM option. For example, with XYZ trading $60 per share, the 30-level call will be so far ITM that a one-point change in the underlying asset will not affect the delta of 100. The corresponding 30-level put will be so far OTM that it will also have a zero delta, because a one-point move in the underlying asset will have no effect on the option's theoretical value. Both deep ITM and far OTM options have little or no gamma.

Conceptually, you might find this relationship easier to understand when you relate it to the notion of percentage chance that the option will finish ITM. If the ATM call and put have a delta of 50 and a gamma of 10 (calls and puts of the same strike and expiration month have the same gamma), then as the underlying asset rises by one point, the call delta will increase to 60. This situation reflects the fact that the call option now has a greater chance of finishing ITM than the put option, whose delta has moved from −50 to −40, thereby reflecting a decreasing probability of the put finishing ITM.

The pricing models tell us that the deltas of the ATM options are the most sensitive to small changes in the price of the stock, and therefore, the ATM options have the greatest gamma. This statement is consistent with the delta rule of thumb that we mentioned earlier in this chapter. An ATM option will tend to have a delta of approximately 50; the nearest ITM strike price will have a delta of about 75; and the nearest OTM strike will have a delta of about 25. In other words, of the entire amount of 50 delta that the delta can change from the ATM value of 50 to either the deep ITM maximum of 100 delta or the far OTM delta of zero, fully half of that move occurs between the ATM strike price and the next-closest strike.

Consider the following example (also see Table 7-9):

Stock price:	$50
Volatility:	30
Dividend:	none
Interest rate:	5 percent
Days until expiration:	90

This example indicates that the gamma is greatest when the underlying price is at an option's strike price and decreases as the underlying asset moves away from the option's strike price. When an option is ATM,

Table 7-9 *Option gammas*

Strike	25	30	35	40	45	50	55	60	65	70	75
Call Gamma	0.00	0.00	.20	1.37	3.68	5.29	4.76	3.03	1.48	.59	.20
Put Gamma	0.00	0.00	.20	1.37	3.68	5.29	4.76	3.03	1.48	.59	.20

the option's theoretical value is most sensitive to changes in the price of the underlying asset. As the underlying asset moves away from the strike price, the gamma of both the calls and puts decreases as their extrinsic value is less responsive to movement in the underlying asset. When the underlying asset is trading at the 50-level strike price, the gamma is the greatest. A one-point change in the price of the underlying asset will have a greater impact on the delta then the ITM or OTM option.

Table 7-9 also highlights the fact that puts and calls with the same strike price and expiration date have the same gamma. Although this statement might not seem obvious, it is true. Remember from the previous chapter that the combination of a put option with a given strike price and expiration date and 100 shares of stock in the underlying asset is the equivalent of purchasing the call with the same strike price and expiration date. If the call has a certain gamma, then the synthetic call must have the same gamma. Because the gamma of the stock is zero, this situation can only result if the put has the same gamma as the stock. Only the pricing models bear this relationship out.

Gamma and Time

As the time until expiration decreases, the gamma of the ATM options increases—and the gamma of the ITM or OTM options decreases. Conceptually, we can understand this idea by again referring to the probability of the option finishing ITM upon expiration. As the expiration date approaches, the probability that the ITM option will finish ITM increases. Therefore, the option will behave more and more like the underlying asset itself (remember that an ITM option will become a position in the underlying asset upon expiration). The delta of the ITM option will move towards ± 100 as time moves forward and will be less sensitive to small changes in the price of the underlying asset. The same statement holds true for the OTM options. As the time until expiration decreases, the probability that the option will finish ITM decreases. The option's delta will approach zero, and movement in the underlying asset will have a diminishing effect on the option's delta (approaching zero impact). As the time until expiration approaches, consider what will happen to the delta of the ATM options as the option moves slightly ITM or OTM. At the ITM price, the option will have a greater delta than if it had more time left to reflect the increasing likelihood that it will finish ITM. At the OTM price, the option will have a smaller delta due to the increasing probability that it will finish OTM. In either event, the ATM delta will change more dramatically than it would have with a longer time until expiration. This increased change in the delta means an increased gamma (see Figure 7-4). Figure 7-4 illustrates the effects of time on an options gammas and deltas.

We can see from this example that a decrease in time until expiration increases the gamma of the ATM and decreases the ITM strikes.

Theta

An option's price has two components: its intrinsic value and its extrinsic value, or time premium. Upon expiration, an option has no time premium.

Figure 7-4 *Time to expiration and gamma/delta values.*

Option Gamma and time to expiration								
Stock Price: 50			Stock Price: 50			Stock Price: 50		
Strike Price: 50			Strike Price: 50			Strike Price: 50		
Days to Expiration: 90 (3 mos.)			**Days to Expiration: 30 (1 mo.)**			**Days to Expiration: 7 (1 wk.)**		
Interest Rate: 6%			Interest Rate: 6%			Interest Rate: 6%		
Volatility: 32			Volatility: 32			Volatility: 32		
Dividend: none			Dividend: none			Dividend: none		
Strike Price:	**50**	**45**	**55**	**Strike Price:**	**50**	**45**	**55**	**Strike Price:**	**50**	**45**	**55**
Call Gamma:	5	3	5	**Call Gamma:**	8	3	6	**Call Gamma:**	17	1	3
Put Gamma:	5	3	5	**Put Gamma:**	8	3	6	**Put Gamma:**	17	1	3
Call Delta:	+56	+79	+32	**Call Delta:**	+55	+89	+16	**Call Delta:**	+51	99	1
Put Delta:	−44	−21	−68	**Put Delta:**	−45	−11	−84	**Put Delta:**	−49	−1	−99

An ITM option will go to parity, having only intrinsic value, and neither OTM nor ATM options will have intrinsic value and will therefore expire as worthless. Thus, options are referred to as wasting assets because their time premium loses value over time. Theta is the measure of how much value an option's price will diminish over time. Theta is usually expressed as the amount that is lost per day, with all other factors influencing the option's price remaining constant.

For example, if an option has a theta of .0625, it will theoretically lose 6.25 cents in value per day—assuming no other changes in the market. Thus, an option that has a theta of .0625, which is valued at 2⁷/₈ on Friday's close, will be worth 2³/₄ on Monday morning when the market opens. The option lost 12.5 cents over the weekend (6.25 cents each day) while the market was closed.

By convention, the theta of an option is represented as a negative number in order to reflect that the option is losing theoretical value. When an option is sold short, as far as the seller is concerned, the decay of that option's time premium is a benefit. Therefore, the holder of an option has a negative theta from that option (while the seller has a positive theta).

Several observations about theta are as follows (see Figure 7-5):

- ATM options have the greatest time premium and thus the greatest theta.
- The time decay for ATM options is not linear. Their theta accelerates as expiration approaches.
- The more ITM or OTM that an option gets, the closer its theta decays in a straight line.

As a general rule, options that have a negative theta have a positive gamma (and vice versa). The theta/gamma combination gives the trader valuable information concerning the risks of holding the position over

Figure 7-5 *Options lose value as expiration approaches.*

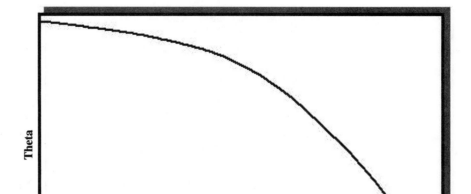

time. Owning gamma means that a position benefits from movement. Negative theta means that your position loses money if the underlying asset does not move. If you are long gamma/short theta, the risk of your position is measured by your theta and your reward is measured by the gamma. If you are short gamma/long theta, your risk is measured by your gamma and your reward is measured by your theta. This situation represents the eternal tension between purchasing options and selling them short.

Rho

Rho measures the sensitivity of option prices to changes in interest rates. An option's rho is the amount that its value will theoretically change for a 1 percent change in interest rate. Rho is a positive number for calls and a negative number for puts. In other words, calls increase in price and puts decrease in price as interest rates rise, and calls decrease in price and puts increase in price as interest rates fall.

Why is this situation so? Without attempting to give a technical explanation, we will say that this relationship makes perfect sense if you treat calls as an alternative to buying stock and puts as an alternative to selling stock short. If you have a cash balance in your trading account, it will earn interest. If it is used to purchase stock, those funds will no longer earn interest. The smaller cash outlay required to purchase a call enables the remaining cash balance to earn interest. During periods of higher interest rates, a cash balance would earn more interest than at lower interest rates, thus creating a greater benefit from retaining that cash balance. This situation makes the call relatively more attractive. Conversely, selling stock short creates a credit balance in your account, which earns interest. Higher interest rates mean an increasing benefit from that short stock credit balance. This situation makes puts less attractive than they had been for a lower interest rate, which translates to a reduced market value. When interest rates decline, the dynamic reverses itself. Puts become more valuable, and calls become less valuable.

The interest rate is usually considered the least-significant pricing-model input. An option's price is generally much more sensitive to the other Greeks (delta, gamma, vega, and theta) than to rho. Furthermore, interest rates tend to change slowly and in small increments. For these reasons, most traders tend to ignore this measure of risk when assessing positions.

Long-term options have greater rhos than short-term options. All else being equal, the greater the amount of time that an option has until expiration, the greater the effect of a change in interest rates. Therefore, LEAPS are much more interest rate sensitive than shorter-term options. This statement is highlighted by the example shown in Figure 7-6.

A rho of .24 for the option that has one year until expiration means that a one-point rise in interest rates (in this case, from 6 percent to 7 percent) would theoretically result in a 24-cent increase in the price of the call. By contrast, the impact on the price of the option that has three months left until expiration would only be a .06 increase. If the increase in interest rate were a more realistic .25 percent, then the impact on the one-year options price would be .06, and the impact on the three-month option would be 1.5 cents.

Vega

We learned that volatility is an important determinant of an option's value. Vega is the measurement of the sensitivity of an option's price to a change in its implied volatility. Specifically, vega is the change in an option's theoretical value resulting from a one percentage point change in its volatility. If an option has a vega of .10, its theoretical price will increase by 10 cents for a one percentage point increase in its volatility.

Figure 7-6 *LEAPS are more interest rate sensitive than shorter-term options.*

Example: Rho and Time to Expiration		
Stock Price: 50	Stock Price: 50	Stock Price: 50
Strike Price: 50	Strike Price: 50	Strike Price: 50
Days to Expiration: 365 (1 yr.)	Days to Expiration: 182 (6 mos.)	Days to Expiration: 90 (3 mos.)
Interest Rate: 6%	Interest Rate: 6%	Interest Rate: 6%
Volatility: 32	Volatility: 32	Volatility: 32
Dividend: none	Dividend: none	Dividend: none
Call Rho: .24	**Call Rho: .12**	**Call Rho: .06**
Put Rho: −.16	**Put Rho: −0.088**	**Put Rho: −.046**

What measure of volatility should we use, however? In Chapter 5, "Option Volatility," we examined three measures of volatility: historical volatility (the measure of volatility in the past), forecast volatility (our estimate of volatility for the future), and implied volatility (the market's current assessment). Remember that vega is one aspect of our risk/reward profile. As such, vega assesses what the impact of change from current conditions might be. Implied volatility is the current condition. Thus, vega is measured by using the current implied volatility of the option.

We discussed volatility extensively in Chapter 5. The importance of vega and what we are focusing on here is measuring how responsive the profit and loss profile of a position will be to changes in the implied volatilities of its component options, whether there is only one option or many. For this purpose, the following attributes of vega are important:

- When comparing options with the same expiration month, vega is generally greatest in terms of total dollar change in price in the ATM strike. In Table 7-10, note that the ATM options and the 60-level calls and puts each have the largest vega of their respective types at .07 cents. As implied volatility increases, the option's extrinsic value will increase by .07 cents for each point volatility increases. Conversely, as volatility decreases, the option's extrinsic value will decrease by .07 cents for each one-point decrease.
- OTM options—especially those that have strikes that are nearest to ATM—will have greater percentage changes in theoretical value for each one-point move in the underlying asset's volatility than ATM. A vega of .07 cents represents a 3.2 percent change in the price of the 60-level call and a change of 3.65 percent in the price of the 60-level

Table 7-10   *Vega's Attributes*

XYZ: Trading at $60 Days to Expiration: 30 Volatility: 30

Option	Call Theo Value	Call Vega	Put Theo Value	Put Vega
40	$20.20	$0.00	$0.00	$0.00
50	$10.27	$0.01	$0.02	$0.01
55	$5.63	$0.04	$0.37	$0.04
60	$2.19	$0.07	$1.92	$0.07
65	$0.57	$0.05	$5.34	$0.05
70	$0.09	$0.02	$10.00	$0.00
80	$0.00	$0.00	$20.00	$0.00

call. By comparison, vega produces an 8.8 percent change in the price of the 65-level call, a 23.3 percent change in the 70-level call, an 11.2 percent change in the 55-level put, and a 50 percent change in the value of the 50-level put.

- Vega decreases as the strikes become more deeply ITM or OTM. The value of these deep options is not affected by changes in volatility nearly as much as the ATM strike.

Vega and Time

The more time until expiration, the more uncertainty as to where the stock price will be upon expiration. This unknown represents an increased opportunity for the purchaser of an option and correspondingly more risk for the seller. This situation results in a higher price for the option. It therefore makes sense that a given change in volatility will have more impact on an option that has a greater time until expiration than one that has less time until expiration. This situation would translate to a larger vega for options that have the same strike but that have longer remaining life. This situation is the case, as shown in Table 7-11.

Table 7-11   *Vega and Time*

XYZ: Trading at $52 Days to Expiration: 30 Volatility: 30

Option Strike	Call Vega	Put Vega
45	.013	.013
50	.051	.051
55	.051	.051
60	.018	.018

XYZ: Trading at $52 Days to Expiration: 90 Volatility: 30

Option Strike	Call Vega	Put Vega
45	.055	.055
50	.094	.094
55	.101	.101
60	.076	.076

XYZ: Trading at $52 Days to Expiration: 180 Volatility: 30

Option Strike	Call Vega	Put Vega
45	.095	.095
50	.133	.133
55	.146	.146
60	.133	.133

Summary

As we have seen, determining the risk/reward profile of a position including options is more complicated than a position involving only stock. For example, if you are long 100 shares of stock, you will remain long 100 shares until you sell those shares or buy more. If you are long 100 deltas (the options equivalent of long 100 shares), your deltas might very well change if the price changes, if the implied volatility changes, or if time passes. The value of option positions is also affected by decay (theta), either positively or negatively. Thus, understanding the Greeks not only individually but how they impact each other is fundamental for successfully managing the risks involved with trading options. In an effort to put these concepts into more focus, the next chapter will give you a peek as to how experienced traders assess risk/reward by using the Greeks in a real-world situation.

Quiz

1. The relationship between a change in the price of the underlying asset and the price of the option is referred to as the options _____.

2. Rho is a measurement of how a change in _____ will affect the value of the position.

3. _____ measures the leverage of an option.

4. ITM options have delta approaching _____ for calls and ____ for puts.

5. The delta of an _____ option will move towards zero, because the likelihood of the option finishing in the money decreases as time decreases.

6. _____ is commonly referred to the curvature of an option.

7. Rho is a _____ number for calls and a negative number for puts.

8. Vega tends to be greater for _____ options and less for _____ options and _____ options.

9. As the time until expiration increases, vega _____; as the time until expiration decreases, vega _____.

10. A _____ delta position benefits from an increase in the price of the underlying asset.

11. An options delta increases by the amount of the _____ when the underlying asset increases by one point.

12. As a value, _____ helps a trader to determine the effects of time on his or her overall option position.

13. If a call option delta is .50 and its gamma is .08, then a one-point increase in the underlying asset will result in an increase of ____ to the delta, which will increase to ____.

14. An ATM option typically has a delta of about ____ for calls and ____ for puts.

15. A long call and a short put both have a _____ delta (choose between positive or negative).

16. Complete the following delta table:

Option	Call Delta Δ	Put Delta Δ	Combined Delta
Jan 45		−15	
Jan 50	60		
Jan 55		−80	100

17. ABC is trading $60 per share, and the July 60 calls are trading for $2.50. You purchase five calls for a total of $1,500 and would like to hedge the position as delta neutral. What do you do?

18. You purchase 150 ATM calls for $3.25 that have a theta of .025 cents. How much will you lose over the weekend?

19. Your option position is short 1,500 gamma, and the stock opens down $1. Assuming that you went home delta neutral, how would you have to adjust your position on the opening in order to remain delta neutral?

20. XYZ goes ex-dividend (.25), and you are long 15 deep ITM front-month options that are trading at $16.50. Do you make or lose money?

Please refer to the Appendix I in this book for quiz answers.

Chapter 8

Position Trading

Introduction

The evolution of the option pricing theory, the development of analytical methods (such as the Greeks) in order to assess complicated positions, and the ready availability of high-speed personal computers that can perform real-time analyses have all led to the development of a new approach to investing: position trading. Position trading utilizes an arsenal of different tools (calls, puts, and stock) in order to exploit the stock market. Unlike traditional stock investors who employ the sole strategy of picking stocks that they hope will increase in price, the position trader has the ability to profit from a wide variety of market expectations. Most hedge funds, market makers, firm traders, and professional off-floor traders generally position trade.

As we saw in the preceding chapter, the purchase and/or short sale of option contracts creates a position that has a multi-dimensional risk/reward exposure in contrast to the straight-forward, directional risk associated with the purchase or short sale of stock. As we will see in the following chapter, there will generally be several position-trading strategies available for a particular market expectation. Therefore, anyone who is contemplating the exploitation of a particular market expectation with a position trade should first identify potential candidates and then consider the risks and rewards associated with each.

To help our readers through this process, we offer one approach. This approach is designed to help the trader consider all reasonable alternatives, then make an informed decision as to whether a particular approach is actually an appropriate strategy. This determination also helps the trader decide which risks he or she is willing to assume at what trade-off for potential profits. Fill in the blanks and answer the questions as follows:

1. There is the potential to make money because _____.
   Possible answers include the following:

   a. this stock should rise in price
   b. this stock should decline in price
   c. this stock is stuck in a trading range
   d. this stock is poised for a big move (up, down, or in either direction)
   e. the implied volatility of the options is too low
   f. the implied volatility of the options is too high

2. The ways to exploit this opportunity are _____, _____, and _____. For example, if the answer to the previous question was that you expected the price of the stock to rise, answers to this question would include the following:

   a. buying stock
   b. buying calls
   c. selling puts

Note that in a particular situation, there might be fewer than or more than three answers.

3. For each of the answers to Step Number 2, (a) what are the risks involved with each, and (b) how might you reduce or eliminate those risks? For example, if the answer to the previous question was "buying calls," then the response to part (a) of this question would include the following:

   a. If the stock does not move up past the strike of the calls, the entire investment would be lost.

   b. The actual break-even point is the strike price of the calls increased by the time premium paid for them.

   The response to part (b) would then include the following:

   a. Sell a call(s) with a higher strike in order to defray the cost of the lower strike calls.

3. When comparing strategies, consider the consequences of unwinding positions prior to expiration and focusing on short options. For example, when comparing the naked purchase of stock versus the combination of buying stock and selling an OTM call against it, if the stock did increase in price to a level where the trader was ready to take a profit prior to expiration, unwinding of the combination position would require the repurchase of the short call. This call might have increased in value, thus reducing the profit for this alternative below that of the naked stock purchase.

Once the trader has identified the different ways to possibly capitalize on a perceived opportunity, he or she can then compare the choices and make an informed decision. When making the comparison, we strongly suggest constructing profit and loss graphs for each.

You should note that there is not necessarily one correct strategy. Different traders could reasonably consider the same issues and decide upon different strategies. The right answer for you will depend on the strength of your expectation and your tolerance for risk, among other factors. The important point is to make an informed decision. We will now examine one specific market expectation resulting from a particular market situation from two perspectives: one, how it might be analyzed and then exploited by an experienced off-floor position trader; and two, how the market maker who fills the trader's orders might respond. We will follow this explanation with a general discussion of position trading.

Before we get started, we would like to say a few introductory words about the position of market maker. The floor trader (or market maker, as he or she is officially known) is the party with whom you actually trade when your options order is filled. For each stock in his or her trading area (or pit, as it is commonly referred to in the industry), the market maker must list both bid and offer prices for each outstanding option contract. When a customer or professional trader can pick his spots (that is, determine when and which options to either buy or sell), the market maker must trade whenever the public wants to and must trade whichever option the public requests. If a customer wants to purchase the XYZ July 80 call, the market maker sells the July 80 call to him or her. If a customer wants to sell the XYZ July 80 call, the market maker is the buyer. The market maker is thus in the business of assuming risk. Like an insurance company, if the market maker cannot manage his or her risk effectively, he or she will not be a market maker for long. Successful market makers are therefore effective risk managers.

Panic Sell-Off Expectation: The Bounce

Imagine that it is late June, with 21 days until July options expiration, and the market as a whole has sold off. Stock XYZ has gone along for the ride, its price plunging from $55 to the current $48. The off-floor position trader believes that the market has been experiencing a temporary panic and that XYZ will be back to the $55 level soon after the panic subsides.

Here are the current prices of the July XYZ options (see Table 8-1). Remember that the options can be sold on the bid and purchased on the offer prices.

Let's use the suggested approach.

Step Number 1. There is the potential to make money, because the price of the stock should soon increase from $48 back to $55.

Step Number 2. The ways to exploit this opportunity are a) buying stock, b) buying calls, and c) selling puts.

Step Number 3. Exploring each opportunity

A. Buying stock

1. The risk of buying stock is that the stock will continue to decline in price—perhaps substantially.
2. You can ameliorate this risk by purchasing a put. The cost of the put can be subsidized by selling an OTM call. Because the trader

Table 8-1　*Current Prices of the July XYZ Options*

Call Bid Price	Call Offer Price	Option Strike	Put Bid Price	Put Offer Price
8 3/8	8 5/8	40	1/4	3/8
4 1/2	4 3/4	45	1 1/4	1 1/2
1 7/8	2 1/8	50	3 1/2	3 3/4
5/8	3/4	55	7 1/4	7 1/2

is only looking for the stock to recover its previous $55 price, either the July 50 or 55 call would be a logical choice. Which put should you use: July 40, July 45, or July 50?

3. The ITM July 50 put, which would forfeit its $2 of intrinsic value if the stock increased in price, would not be a good choice given the trader's expectation for such an increase.

4. The OTM July 45 put would limit potential loss to the $3 difference between the current price of $48 and $45, which is the put's exercise price increased by the net premium paid in order to establish the position (the cost of the July 45 put reduced by any premium received if a call is sold). This put would be the best choice.

5. The OTM July 40 put would not provide protection until the stock sold off below $40.

B. Buying calls

1. The risk of buying calls is that the position does not become profitable until the stock rises to a price above the sum of the strike and the time premium paid for the call. Because the trader is looking to profit from a move from $48 to $55, this situation would seem to eliminate the July 50 call (which would not even break even upon expiration until the stock reached $51⅞).

2. The July 45 call is mostly intrinsic value and would protect against the stock falling in price below $45. The cost of the time premium component of the price of the July 45 call could be subsidized by the sale of the July 55 call. If this combination—purchasing the July 45 call and selling the July 55 call—seems similar to the combination of purchasing stock, purchasing the July 45 put, and selling the July 55 call discussed earlier, you are right. This transaction is essentially the same. Remember that the synthetic way to purchase a call is to purchase the put and stock so that purchasing the July 45 put and stock is purchasing the July 45 call synthetically.

C. Selling puts

1. Remember that the synthetic equivalent to selling a put is to purchase stock and sell the call of the same strike price and exercise. Thus, the analysis here would be the same as for purchasing stock and selling calls (in this case, either the July 50 or July 55 call).

2. Refer to the discussion about purchasing stock.

Alternatives. The trader is anticipating a bounce from $48 back towards the stock's previous level of $55. The trader is not anticipating a rally above $55. The candidates would appear to be as follows:

- Alternative 1
  - Buy 100 shares of XYZ at $48
- Alternative 2
  - Buy one July 45 call
  - Or buy 100 shares of XYZ at $48 and buy one July 45 put (synthetic equivalent)

- Alternative 3
    - Sell one July 50 put
    - Or buy 100 shares of XYZ at $48 and sell one July 50 call (synthetic equivalent)
- Alternative 4
    - Buy 100 shares of XYZ at $48, buy one July 45 put, and sell one July 50 call
    - Or buy one July 45 call and sell one July 50 call
    - Or buy one July 45 put and sell one July 50 put
- Alternative 5
    - Sell one July 55 put
    - Or buy 100 shares of XYZ at $48, and sell one July 55 call (synthetic equivalent)
- Alternative 6
    - Buy 100 shares of XYZ at $48, buy one July 45 put, and sell one July 55 call
    - Or buy one July 45 call and sell one July 55 call
    - Or buy one July 45 put and sell one July 55 put

Let's review the profit and loss graphs of each (Figures 8-1 through 8-6).
Given the trader's expectation of a recovery to the $55 level, alternatives Number 3 and Number 4 might be excluded because they put too much of a cap on the position's up-side potential if the position were held to expiration. Also, position unwinding would further reduce profits because the short calls were increasing in value as the stock price was rising.

Figure 8-1   *Alternative 1.*
             Long stock.
             Black line = long 100 shares of stock for $48.

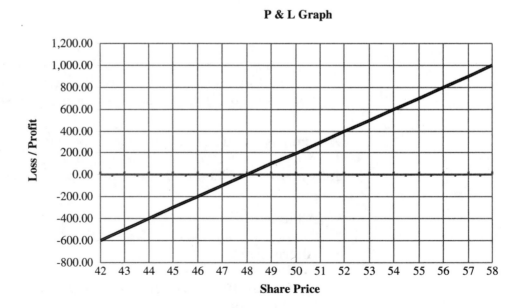

Figure 8-2 *Alternative 2.*
Long puts and stock.
Black line = long 100 shares of stock for $48 and long 1 July 45 put for 1 ¹/₂ at expiration.
Thin gray line = long 100 shares of stock for $48 and long 1 July 45 put for 1 ¹/₂ with 21 days to expiration.

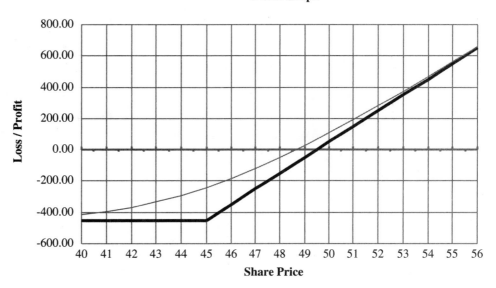

Figure 8-3 *Alternative 3.*
Long stock and short call.
Black line = long 100 shares of stock for $48 and short 1 July 50 call at 1 ⁷/₈ at expiration.
Thin gray line = long 100 shares of stock for $48 and short 1 July 50 call at 1 ⁷/₈ with 21 days to expiration.

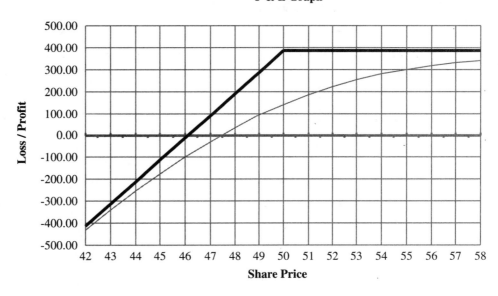

Figure 8-4   *Alternative 4.*
             Long put and stock and short call.
             Black line = long 100 shares of stock for $48 and short 1 July 50
             call at 1 ⁷/₈ and long 1 July 45 put for 1 ¹/₂ at expiration.
             Thin gray line = position with 21 days to expiration.

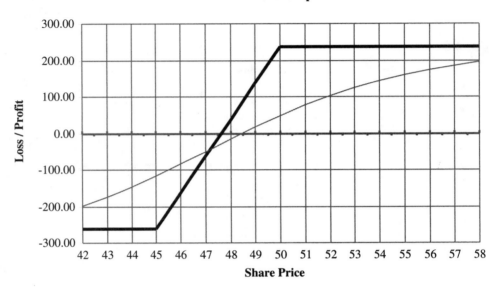

P & L Graph

Figure 8-5   *Aternative 5.*
             Long stock and short call.
             Black line = long 100 shares of stock for $48 and short 1 July 55
             call at ⁵/₈.
             Thing gray line = position with 21 days to expiration.

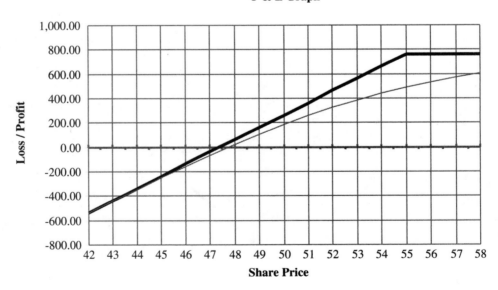

P & L Graph

Figure 8-6 *Alternative 6.*
Long stock, short call and long put.
Black line = long 100 shares of stock for $48 and short 1 July 55
call at ⁵/₈ and long 1 July 45 put for 1 ¹/₂ at expiration.
Thin gray line = position with 21 days to expiration.

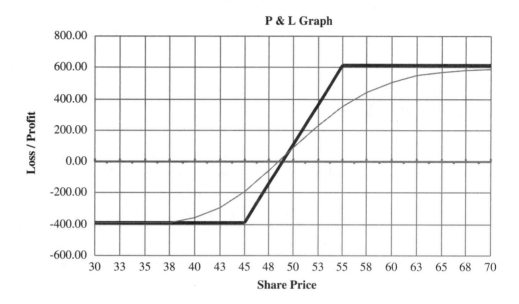

Alternative Number 5 would seem less favorable than alternative Number 1, because the initial credit of ⁵/₈ received for selling the July 55 call is small, and the cost of repurchasing the call prior to expiration if the stock did rebound sharply could be substantially greater than that. For similar reasons, alternative Number 2 would appear to be superior to alternative Number 6. Thus, the choice would likely come down to alternatives Number 1 or Number 2. Most traders would likely select one of the two versions of alternative Number 2 for the following reasons:

- Margin—The margin requirement for purchasing the July 45 call is the cost of the call. By comparison, the margin requirement for purchasing XYZ stock at $48 plus the July 45 put (or the stock alone) would be substantially higher. This situation would enable the trader to purchase several July 45 calls in which, for example, he or she could only acquire 100 shares of stock.
- Flexibility—The stock and put combination would offer several advantages over the naked purchase of the stock:
  - Waiting for confirmation—If the stock does rally, the put can be sold while it retains significant value.
- Down-side alternatives are as follows:
  - If the stock continues to decline and the trader decides to liquidate the position, the gain in value of the put will partially offset the loss of the stock. The trader knows that in most cases, as stock price declines (especially in these market-wide sell-offs), volatility

increases. This situation would mean that the price of the July 45 put would be further increased than it would just by the effect of the decline in stock price.

If the trader decides that the sell-off is not over, the long stock can be sold (remember, selling long stock in a down market is not subject to the up-tick rule), and the put is retained as the investment vehicle.

Market Maker

Assume that the off-floor trader decided to implement alternative Number 6 by purchasing 1,000 shares of XYZ, purchasing 10 July 45 puts, and selling 10 July 55 calls. Also assume that the puts and calls come into the trading pit as separate transactions and are separated in time by several minutes. Let's tag along with a market maker in stock XYZ and see how he or she manages the delta, gamma, vega, theta, and rho exposure. We will start with two additional assumptions:

- Our market maker (OMM) has no position in XYZ at the start.
- OMM will fill both orders.
- OMM has no opinion as to the direction of the price of XYZ.

Trade Number 1. The order comes into the crowd, and OMM sells the 10 XYZ July 45 puts for 1 ½. OMM knows the following information* concerning the July 45 puts in XYZ (see Table 8-2).
 OMM's position summary (short 10 July 45 puts) is as follows:

- +300 delta (directional bias to the up side; the position makes money if the stock price increases and loses money if the stock price declines)

Table 8-2 *July 45 Put Values*

Delta/contract	− 30
Gamma/contract	5.00
Vega	.057
Theta	− .023
Rho	− .018

*In the real world, although OMM will probably know the delta of this contract and might know its gamma at the time of the trade, it is unlikely that OMM would have precise information concerning the other Greeks at his or her immediate command.

- −50 gamma (the delta declines as the stock rises, and the delta increases as the stock price declines)
- short vega (the position loses value as volatility increases, and it gains in value as volatility declines)
- long theta (the position benefits from the decay of the option time premium)
- short rho (the position mildly benefits from an increase in interest rates and mildly loses from a decline in interest rates)

OMM's response is as follows. He or she is fully aware that he or she is now long 300 deltas in XYZ. Not wanting to risk that XYZ will decline in price prior to an order to sell July 45 puts coming into the trading pit, which would increase the price of the put and thus generate a loss for OMM, OMM will quickly delta hedge the July 45 put sale. Although OMM's preference would be to purchase puts with offsetting deltas and gammas as a hedge, the clear and immediate priority is a delta hedge before the stock price moves. As a result, OMM will immediately sell 300 shares of XYZ in order to become delta neutral.

Trade Number 2.   With XYZ still trading at $48, the July 55 call order comes into the crowd, and OMM buys 10 XYZ July 55 calls for ⅝. OMM knows the following information* concerning the July 55 calls in XYZ (see Table 8-3).

OMM's position summary (short 10 July 45 puts, long 10 July 55 calls, and short 30 shares of XYZ) is as follows:

- +200 delta (+300 for July 45 puts, −300 for XYZ stock, and +200 for July 55 calls)
- −9 gamma (−50 for July 45 puts and +41 for July 55 calls)
- −10.0 vega ($10 decrease in position value for each one-point increase in volatility; $10 increase for each one-point decrease in volatility)

Table 8-3   *July 45 Call Values*

Delta/contract	20
Gamma/contract	4.10
Vega	.047
Theta	− .022
Rho	− .056

*In the real world, although OMM will probably know the delta of this contract and might know its gamma at the time of the trade, it is unlikely that OMM would have precise information concerning the other Greeks at his or her immediate command.

- +$1.00 theta (position improves $1 per day from decay)
- −.038 rho

OMM's response is as follows. He or she immediately sells 200 shares of XYZ in order to become delta neutral, noticing that his or her position is relatively gamma, vega, and theta neutral. Knowing that gamma changes as stock price changes, however, OMM does the following quick-and-dirty calculation. OMM determines the position if the stock plummets well below $45 (with the calls becoming worthless and the short puts deeply ITM and therefore effectively behaving like long stock, the net position would be +500 shares of XYZ). OMM also determines the position if the stock rises to well above $55 (with the puts becoming worthless and the long calls deeply ITM, therefore effectively behaving like long stock, the net position would be +500 shares of XYZ). Thus, although the position is delta and gamma neutral with the stock at $48, it is definitely not so if the stock were to move dramatically in either direction. We call this situation a risk conversion, meaning that although it appears relatively balanced and essentially delta, gamma, vega, and theta neutral at this stock price, because the options are of different types with different strikes, their gammas and thus their deltas and vegas would become increasingly out of balance as the stock moved toward one of the strikes. This situation would therefore increase the gamma of that option and move it necessarily away from the other strike, thus reducing the gammas of that option. Let's look at the profit and loss graph of this position is illustrated in Figure 8-7.

Figure 8-7 *Profit and loss graph.*
Black line = short 10 July 45 puts, long 10 July 55 calls, short 500/sh. stock at expiration.
Thin gray line = short 10 July 45 puts, long 10 July 55 calls, short 55/sh. with 21 days to expiration.

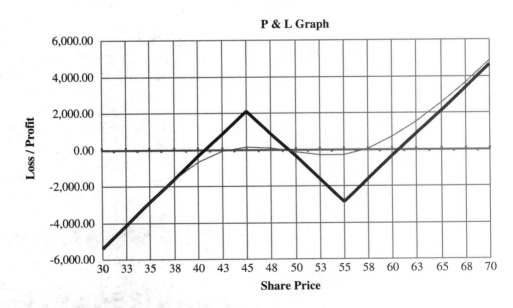

Notice that the thin gray line, which represents profit and loss versus price movement with 21 days until expiration, is relatively flat absent a large down-side gap in price for XYZ. In other words, outside of such a gap, the position is quite stable in the short term—meaning that the market maker can be patient and wait to trade out of the position without the need to adjust the position. If the market maker were concerned about the possibility of a down-side gap, the purchase of 5 July 40 puts would effectively take away that risk.

By contrast, the expiration graph represented by the dark, black line points out that as expiration approaches, if it appears that the stock will finish in the $45–$55 range, the options would be worthless. Also, the position would effectively reduce itself to being short 500 shares of XYZ. If this position is not one with which the market maker was comfortable, he or she would need to monitor this position closely. This position would possibly need to be forcibly liquidated or otherwise adjusted.

General Observations on Position Trading

Position trading is all about tradeoffs. An effective position trader designs a position involving options in combination with stock and/or other options and is fully aware of the risks that the trader is prepared to assume, does not want to assume, and what tradeoff of potential reward to reduce possible risk is acceptable. In the example earlier in this chapter, the trader wanted to profit from an anticipated bounce in the price of a stock but was concerned about the risk that the price of the stock would continue to decline. This desire to retain the up-side benefits of owning stock but to be protected from continuing weakness in the stock's performance could, of course, be realized by purchasing puts along with the stock. But which puts should be purchased? In comparing the July 40, July 45, and July 50 puts as risk protection, the trader would have to balance his or her different amounts of protection against further declines in the price of the stock against his or her impact on profits resulting from the anticipated rise in the price of the stock purchased. The July 40 puts would only reduce profits per share by $3/8$ but would enable a maximum loss of $8 3/8$ per share (stock declines from $48 to $40 or below). The July 45 puts would reduce profits per share by $1.50 versus a maximum loss of $4.50 per share, and the July 50 puts would reduce profits by $3.75 against a maximum loss of $1.75. The trader in our example chose the July 45 puts as representing the best balance between down-side loss protection and the impact of paying that insurance premium on the profits that he or she hoped to make.

The position trader considers risk from four perspectives when analyzing the risk/reward potential of a particular strategy: its immediate directional risk (delta), how directional risk will change as the stock price changes (gamma), the impact of a change in volatility on the position (vega), and the impact of the passage of time on the position (theta). We are intentionally ignoring the impact of changing interest rates (rho), because this factor is usually so insignificant in the real world. Once the trader identifies the risks, he or she can consider the alternatives that are available to offset, or hedge, any undesired risks. The trader achieves this hedging by adding a position that would appreciate in value in circumstances when the original position would lose value, thus offsetting the exposure to the risk of loss. Again, going back to the earlier example, the risk associated with purchasing stock to benefit from the expected bounce is the continued decline in the price of the stock. Purchasing puts that increase in value as the stock price declines, thus offsetting the loss from owning the stock, is an example of a hedge. Selling a call with a higher strike would be a hedge against the risk of losing the entire purchase price of a call with a lower strike price.

Effective hedging is the key to successful position trading. Those who master how different building blocks can be combined to create a desired risk/reward profile are well placed to successfully exploit a wide variety of market conditions. How risk is hedged depends upon the nature of the risk involved. Directional risk is hedged either on a contract-neutral or delta-neutral basis. Other Greek risks are hedged by an approach called spreading. We will now discuss each of these methods.

Directional Risk Hedging

Deltas are a measurement of directional risk. In order to reduce directional risk, the trader must sell or buy a position whose value moves opposite to the value of the original position as the price of the stock moves.

Directional risk hedging is most commonly done on either a contract-neutral basis or a delta-neutral basis.

Delta Neutral versus Contract Neutral

A delta-neutral hedge reduces a position's delta to zero based on the stock's current price at the current time. Market makers tend to be delta-neutral traders. They can make money without taking a directional risk because of the bid-ask spread. For example, if a call option is 1.875 bid at 2.125, the market maker stands ready to both buy the option for $1.875 (total contract price of $187.50) and sell it for $2.125 (total contract price of $212.50). If the market maker sells a contract for $212.50 and then buys it back for $187.50, he makes a $25 profit and has no remaining risk that the price of the contract will fluctuate. Consider what would happen if the option were ATM with a delta of 50 and the price of the stock had decreased by $1 between its purchase by the market maker and the time that an offer to buy it back was received. If the purchase of the call had not been hedged (all other factors being equal), the market for the contract should have changed to 1.375 bid at 1.625 (for an option with a 50 delta, the impact of a $1 decline in the price of the stock would be a $.50 reduction in the price of the option). Selling the option for 1.625 ($162.50) would result in a $25 loss. Compare this situation to hedging the 50 deltas gained by purchasing the call by immediately selling 50 shares of stock at the current price. When the price of the stock declines by $1, the sale of the stock results in a $50 profit. Combined with the call contract loss of $25, a $25 profit results—just the same as if the market for the option had remained unchanged between the option's purchase and subsequent sale. By hedging delta neutral, as long as the price fluctuation of the stock is small, the market maker will ultimately net the $25 profit when the closing transaction occurs. By not trading delta neutral, a market maker would be betting on the direction of the stock.

By contrast, most other position traders usually have a directional bias in the marketplace. They establish a trade because they expect the stock to move either up or down. They are willing to establish a position where they will make money if the stock behaves as they expect, but they do not wish to assume significant risk that the stock will make a large move in the opposite direction. They are making a directional play and want to limit their potential loss if the stock goes dramatically against them. They are not concerned about their position delta. In fact, they have likely constructed the position with a definite directional bias. What they want to do is protect their down-side risk share for share if the stock should move strongly against them. This process involves purchasing or selling enough option contracts that their position would be neutral beyond some point if the stock should move against them. Covering your risk on a share-by-share basis is known as contract-neutral hedging.

We have already seen these approaches in action. Returning to our earlier example once again, the trader purchased 1,000 shares of stock at $48 and 10 July 45 puts. After purchasing the stock and put combination, although the trader was long 700 deltas, the 10 puts would fully protect the 1,000 shares in the event that the stock would drop lower than $45 per share. The purchase of the stock was therefore hedged on a contract-neutral basis. In contrast, the market maker hedged his sale of 10 July 45 puts by selling 300 shares of stock. Although this procedure reduced his position delta to zero, if the stock plunged below $45, his position would continue to lose money as the stock continued to decline. The short sale of 300 shares would only partially offset the continuing losses from the 10 puts, representing 1,000 shares of stock. The market maker used a delta-neutral hedge. Note that the decision of how to hedge directional risk in each case resulted from their respective profit expectations. The trader was willing to accept directional risk on the up side, but with only limited risk on the down side. Therefore, a contract-neutral hedge was the appropriate choice. The market maker wanted to protect the projected profit from the bid-ask spread differential and therefore chose a delta-neutral hedge. As we will see shortly, the market maker's preferred hedge would have been to purchase other puts on a delta-neutral basis. This action would provide three benefits. One, the position would be delta neutral in order to protect the anticipated profit from repurchasing the July 45 puts. Two, the purchase of the other puts created another anticipated profit from their eventual resale. Three, the purchased puts would provide more down-side protection than the stock in the event of a major downward move in the price of the stock.

You *must* keep in mind that as option deltas are affected by both the passage of time and changes in the price of stock, the position delta will fluctuate as these factors come into play. For delta-conscious traders, position delta should be monitored on a regular basis. This advice is emphasized by the following situation.

Stock ABC is currently trading at 62. There are 30 days until March expiration. The investor has the following position.

- Long 2, 500 shares of stock = long 2, 500
- Long 25 March 55 puts with a −22 each (25 × −22) = short 550
- Short 25 March 70 calls with a −18 each (25 × −18) = short 450
- The total net position delta (P) is long 1, 500 (2, 500 − (550 + 450) = 1, 500).

In other words, the position is the equivalent of being long 1,500 shares of stock while stock ABC is trading at or near $62 at this particular time. This situation translates to an anticipated increase in the value of the position of $1, 500 if ABC increases to $63. You *must* note that this situation does *not* translate to the position increasing $1, 500 for each $1 increase in the price of ABC. Let's look at the situation after a significant change in stock price. Stock ABC is currently trading at $87. There are 30 days until March expiration. The investor has the following position:

- Long 2, 500 shares of stock = long 2, 500
- Long 25 March 55 puts with a 5 delta each (25 × −5) = short 125
- Short 25 March 70 calls with an 85 delta each (25 × −85) = short 2,125
- The net delta position (P) is long 250 (2,500 − (125 + 2,125) = 250).

As the stock increased in price, the deltas of the March 55 puts decreased—and those of the March 70 calls increased. The March 70 calls are now $17 ITM with a delta of almost 100.

Let's look at this example again, this time moving forward to the day of expiration (where the stock price remains at the original price). Stock ABC is currently trading at $62. There is one day until March expiration, and the investor has the following position:

- Long 2, 500 shares of stock = long 2,500
- Long 25 March 55 puts (0 each) = 0
- Short 25 March 70 calls (0 each) = 0
- The net delta position (P) is long 2,500 (2,500 − (0 + 0) = 2,500).

We have the same position in each case. Depending on the time until expiration and/or changes in the price of the stock, the position delta can be dramatically different. This example is designed to impress upon you that the position delta (P) is time and price sensitive, just like individual option deltas. Although not highlighted in this example, position delta might also be sensitive to changes in implied volatility.

We offer one final point concerning position deltas and option-price changes in the real world. We must point out that far OTM options, whether they are calls or puts, consistently behave differently than the pricing models would suggest. In the case of puts, they tend to retain a higher value than the models would indicate (based on the implied volatility of the other options with the same expiration). This situation results from a bias towards the demand for these options, reflecting the facts that (1) there is little incentive to assume risk by selling these cheap options, and (2) they retain an attraction to be purchased as disaster protection in case of a crash in a stock. By contrast, people who have long positions in a stock become additional sellers of OTM options, because their positions are already gaining value as the stock increases towards the OTM strikes. It is not uncommon to have a situation where the pricing model assigns an OTM call option a 10 delta, the option is trading for .50, the stock increases in value by $2, and the option price remains unchanged. Many experienced traders ignore or substantially discount farther-out OTM call deltas when calculating their position delta.

Spreading

Spreading is a risk-management strategy that employs options as the hedging instrument, rather than stock. Like stock, options have directional risk (deltas). Unlike stock, options carry gamma, vega, and theta risks as well. Therefore, if a position involves any combination of gamma, vega, and/or theta risk, this risk can be reduced or eliminated by adding one or more options positions. Table 8-4 summarizes the possible hedges

Table 8-4 *Possible Hedges*

Building Block	Hedge	Hedge Delta	Hedge Gamma	Hedge Vega	Hedge Theta
Long Stock positive delta, no gamma, no vega, no theta	Sell Call	Negative	Negative	Negative	Positive
	Sell Stock	Negative	None	None	None
	Buy Put	Negative	Positive	Positive	Negative
Short Stock negative delta, no gamma, no vega, no theta	Buy Call	Positive	Positive	Positive	Negative
	Buy Stock	Positive	None	None	None
	Sell Put	Positive	Negative	Negative	Positive
Long Call positive delta, positive gamma, positive vega, negative theta	Sell Call	Negative	Negative	Negative	Positive
	Buy Put	Negative	Positive	Positive	Negative
	Sell Stock	Negative	None	None	None
Short Call negative delta, negative gamma, negative vega, positive theta	Buy Call	Positive	Positive	Positive	Negative
	Sell Put	Positive	Negative	Negative	Positive
	Buy Stock	Positive	None	None	None
Long Put negative delta, positive gamma, positive vega, negative theta	Sell Put	Positive	Negative	Negative	Positive
	Buy Call	Positive	Positive	Positive	Negative
	Buy Stock	Positive	None	None	None
Short Put positive delta, negative gamma, negative vega, positive theta	Buy Put	Negative	Positive	Positive	Negative
	Sell Call	Negative	Negative	Negative	Positive
	Sell Stock	Negative	None	None	None

and their gamma, vega, and theta impact for each of the six building blocks.

Notice that owning option contracts, be they puts or calls, means that you are adding positive gamma, positive vega, and negative theta. Being short either of these contracts means acquiring negative gamma, negative vega, and positive theta. This statement points out that as far as these Greeks are concerned, you get a package deal. By owning options, your position responds favorably to stock-price movement (the position gets longer as the stock price increases and gets shorter as the stock price decreases). The position responds positively to increases in implied volatility (and negatively to decreases in implied volatility) and will lose value over time. By being short options, your position responds adversely to stock-price movement (the position gets shorter as the stock price increases and gets longer as the stock price decreases). The position also responds negatively to increases in implied volatility (and positively to decreases in implied volatility) and will gain value over time as the time premium of the short option decays.

Hedging Summary

There is literally no limit to the number of positions that you can create through a combination of stock and options. There are a number of positions that have developed over time and that have attained widespread acceptance. These are the subject of the next chapter. Each works best in a specific situation, works tolerably in others, and is inappropriate for still other market expectations. Please examine these closely, paying attention to the conditions under which they are designed to work, what their risks and rewards are, and other strategies that might apply to a particular situation.

Chapter 9

Option Strategies

Introduction

We now turn our attention toward examining discrete, options-based investment strategies of two different types:

- Direct alternatives to traditional buying and selling stock, which offer either greater downside protection, increased profit potential through the use of leverage, or both
- Approaches that usually involve limited risk in order to profit from a wide variety of market expectations, which are either not exploitable via traditional stock trading or which are risky to employ when using stock alone

With these strategies, you will have the capability to generate profits with limited risk from almost any market sentiment. As with traditional investment strategies, there are no guarantees. The starting point will always be your general expectation (usually concerning a particular stock, but sometimes concerning a market sector or a broader measure of the market). This general expectation will point to several strategies that you should consider. You should examine these indicated strategies against your market expectations and their respective risk-to-reward profiles in order to determine the appropriate strategy to employ. Your knowledge of option pricing, particularly implied volatility versus your forecast volatility, will provide insight to aid in your selection. For example, when comparing the risk/reward profiles of two likely alternatives, if they both involve the purchase of options and one of them involves options that are relatively less expensive than those that the other strategy requires, this situation might tip the balance toward selecting the strategy that has the cheaper options.

Market Outlooks

We will examine four market outlooks with trading strategies corresponding to each:

- **Bullish**—The expectation of an increase in price. This category has two subcategories:
  - **Moderately bullish**—Although the outlook is for higher prices, the increase is not likely to be dramatic.
  - **Extremely bullish**—Expecting a dramatic, explosive increase in price (generally anticipated to occur in the short term)

- **Bearish**—The expectation of a decrease in price. This category has two subcategories:
  - **Moderately bearish**—Although the outlook is for lower prices, the decrease is not likely to be dramatic.
  - **Extremely bearish**—Expecting a dramatic sell-off in the stock (generally anticipated to occur in the short term)
- **Neutral (frontspread)**—Expecting little price movement over a given time period. Neutral strategies enable the trader to make money in a market where prices remain the same or move little.
- **Volatile (backspread)**—The anticipation that prices will move dramatically, but the direction of that move is not clear

Our goal in separating our discussion of strategies into the four general categories of bullish, bearish, neutral, and volatile is to provide our readers (after determining your market outlook) with a reference for the potential strategies. This chapter will also discuss risk-reduction strategies for managing an existing stock portfolio.

Spreads

A number of these strategies involve option spreads. You construct a spread by being long an option(s) and being short an option(s) of the same type in the same underlying asset. For example, buying a call and selling another call with a different strike or a different expiration is a spread. Buying a put and selling another put with either a different strike or a different expiration is also a spread. In contrast, buying a call and either buying or selling a put is not a spread. Spreads offer the investor an array of strategies for attempting to benefit from almost any anticipated market condition while reducing risk. For example, you can use a spread to take a bull position or a bear position, for selling high volatility and buying low volatility, or to finance the purchase of other options. The degree of risk reduction varies among the different types of spreads. While some spreads have limited risk, others have risks that are comparable to buying the underlying security outright. There are several different types of spreads:

1. **Calendar spread (in other words, a time or horizontal spread)**—With this type of spread, all options are of the same type and have the same strike price and underlying asset, yet they have different expiration dates. The purchase (sale) of one option has a different expiration date from the sale (purchase) of another. Buying one XYZ March 85 call, for example, and selling one XYZ February 85 call would be a calendar spread.

2. **Diagonal spreads**—This kind of spread is similar to the time spread in that the options are of the same type and underlying asset; however, the expiration date and the strike prices are different. This time spread uses different strike prices. Buying one XYZ March 90 call and selling one XYZ February 85 call is an example of a diagonal spread.

3. **Vertical spread**—A vertical spread consists of options of the same type, on the same underlying asset, and with the same expiration date, but these options have different strike prices. Buying one XYZ May 90 put and selling one XYZ May 85 put is an example of a vertical spread.

4. **Ratio spreads**—A ratio spread is any of these types of spreads in which the number of options purchased differs from the number of options sold. Buying one XYZ July 90 call and selling two XYZ July 95 calls is an example of a ratio spread.

Legging

Several strategies involve three or more options strikes. As a practical matter, you cannot put on these positions simultaneously at reasonable prices. In order to achieve these positions at prices that produce an acceptable risk/reward profile, you must put on the positions in a series of separate trades. This process is called legging. Although the analysis of these specific positions includes a discussion of how to approach legging, we should give you some general comments concerning legging at this point.

Until a position is fully legged into, your ability to complete the position at an acceptable price is subject to the risk of changing prices in the positions that you have not yet executed. The key to legging is knowing which order to execute the trades in order to minimize that risk.

To minimize this risk, we look at the supply and demand factor of each building block in the options strategy. Once we determine the supply and demand for each building block, the trader can leg into the position first from the building block that has the most demand and finish the implementation with the building block that has the most supply. This procedure is called legging the hard side first. The hard side is the trade that is the most difficult to put on. If the stock is rising rapidly in price and the trader wishes to purchase the stock, because the stock is rising, this side is considered the demand side. The demand side refers to what the majority of traders are doing, whether buying or selling. If a stock is rising quickly, we would say that there is demand for the stock—hence, there would be more buyers than sellers. Selling the stock would be easy, because there are many buyers. We would then call this side the supply side. Because buying the stock in a rising market situation is difficult (getting a good price is difficult because of the high demand), we call this side the hard side.Consider the following example of legging the hard side first. Assume that you are legging into a covered call in which the stock price is rising. Realizing that it will be harder to purchase the stock at a good price than it will be to sell the call, you should buy stock as the first part of the leg. Selling the call would be the easier of the two sides to fill, because the rising price of the stock should increase the demand for the call. If the trader decides to sell the call first in a rising market, he or she is taking the chance that he or she might not be filled on the stock at his or her price.

When a trader puts on a leg and cannot complete the rest of the position because the price for remaining legs has become unacceptable, the trader is said to be legged out. He or she now has a position that has gone against him or her, and it will be hard to close it without incurring a loss.

Some of the option positions that we cover in this book can only be legged into. Do not even bother calling your broker with any fancy spread terminology such as a butterfly or iron butterfly. The market makers on the trading floor will just laugh your broker right out of the trading pit. There is no market maker in the world who will hand over free money, especially to a customer.

Bullish Strategies

Bullish strategies are among the most common strategies that individual investors use, probably resulting from the general view of the market that we acquire through the media and elsewhere is that rising stock prices are good, and falling stock prices are bad. In actuality, your position relative to that market movement—not the movement itself—is either good or bad for you. For example, if you position benefits from a declining market and the market does decline, that is good, while if instead it rallied, that would be bad.

Most investors, then, are programmed to buy low and sell high. These are bullish investors who want to gain a profit from a rise in value or stock price. In fact, when investors tend to think of bullish strategies, the only thing that typically pops into their head is to purchase stock. To be sure, this strategy is great when the stock rises in price, but when a hefty sum of the investor's capital is committed to the position, this endeavor can be risky. In other words, while long stock purchase is not necessarily the wrong idea, it can be capital intensive and can create risk parameters that the individual investor might not totally understand. In this chapter, we will show alternatives to purchasing stock, learn how to reduce market directional risk and capital exposure, and discuss the relevance of leverage.

The first bullish strategy we will consider is long stock. Because long stock is the most commonly employed strategy and the one with which most traders are familiar, it will offer a good comparison study against the other bullish strategies described in this chapter.

Figure 9-1   *Bullish long stock.*
            Black line = long 100 shares of stock for $50/share.

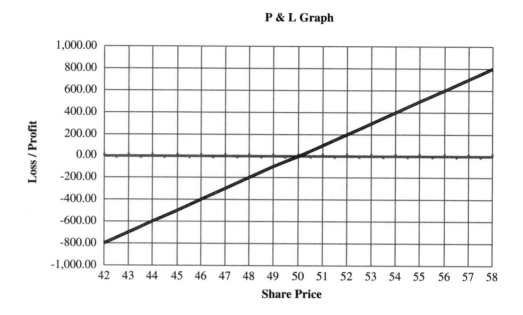

Bullish: Long Stock

Long stock is the most common position among investors. Long stock simply refers to the outright ownership of stock (see Figure 9-1).

Example.   An investor who has no position in XYZ purchases 100 shares of XYZ at $50 per share. The investor is now long 100 shares of XYZ.

- **Reward**—This situation has unlimited up-side profit. Each $1 increase in the market price of the stock results in $100 worth of profit.
- **Break-even**—The stock is unchanged at $50.
- **Risk**—This situation has an unlimited down-side loss until the stock price equals zero. Each $1 decrease in the market price of the stock results in $100 worth of loss.

Bullish Long Stock (Margined)

In a margin account, your broker will loan you half of the cost of purchasing a stock. Thus, for the same capital investment, you can acquire twice as much stock. You will, of course, pay interest on the borrowed funds (see Figure 9-2).

Example.   An investor who has no position in XYZ purchases 200 shares of XYZ at $50 per share, using $5,000 of his own money and borrowing $5,000 from his broker. The investor is now long 200 shares of XYZ.

Figure 9-2   *Bullish long stock (margined).*
Black line = long 200 share of stock for $50/share on margin.

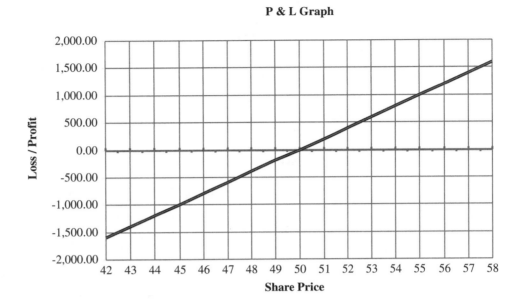

- **Reward**—This situation has unlimited up-side profit. Each $1 increase in the market price of the stock results in $200 worth of profit.*
- **Break-even**—The stock is unchanged.*
- **Risk**—This situation has unlimited down-side loss until the stock price equals zero. Each $1 decrease in the market price of the stock results in $200 worth of loss.*

Let's compare this information with long stock:

- **Reward**—The reward is twice as much gain as long stock.
- **Risk**—There is twice as much loss as long stock.

Bullish Long Calls

You can use calls to take bullish positions. As in the previous case of bullish long stock (margined), this approach results in substantially more gain if the stock does increase dramatically in price if you use leverage. That is, you can acquire the up-side potential of many more shares of stock via options than by actually buying the stock. To illustrate this point, we will compare the profit and loss out option expiration: (1) purchasing three of the near-term 50-level calls for $2 each when the stock is

---

*We over simplify here to make the broader point. The precise result will include the cost of borrowing.

Figure 9-3 *Profits and losses upon expiration.*
Gray line = long stock.
Black line = long (3) 50 level calls for $2 ($2 × 3 × 100 = $600) at expiration.
Thin gray line = long (3) 50 level calls for $2 ($2 × 3 × 100 = $600) with 21 days to expiration.

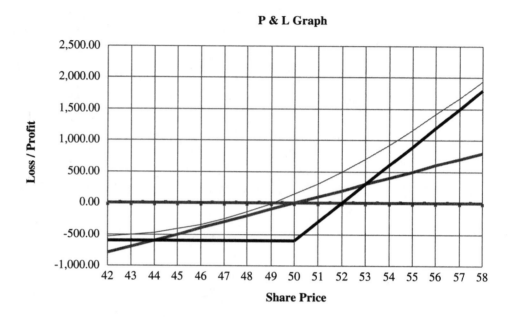

trading at $50 per share, and (2) purchasing 100 shares for $50 per share (see Figure 9-3). Like the long stock positions, the long call will profit to the upside as the underlying stock increases in value. Unlike the long stock positions, the maximum loss is the amount paid for the calls (in this case, $2 or a total of $600).

You can implement this strategy by using ITM, ATM, or OTM calls. Each type has its own risk/reward profile. You must understand the conditions that are necessary for profit for a particular type of call prior to acquiring it to implement a bullish strategy. Let's consider each in turn.

Example. XYZ stock is trading for $50. The July 45 call is trading for $6; the July 50 call is trading for $2; and the July 55 call is trading for $1. For illustrative purposes, assume that in each case, three contracts are purchased.

ITM calls will react much like stock. Most of the cost will be intrinsic value with less time premium. In this example, the July 45 call will have $5 worth of intrinsic value and $1 worth of time premium. The total purchase price for three contracts is $1,800. As measured at July option expiration:

- **Reward**—There is unlimited upside profit. For each $1 that the stock closes above $51, we have $300 worth of profit.
- **Break-even**—The stock closes at $51.

- **Risk**—Loss is limited to $1,800 (the amount paid for the calls). For each $1 that the stock closes below $51, we have $300 worth of loss. A maximum loss results if the stock finishes at or below $45.

Compared to long stock, we can see the following (see Figure 9-4):

- **Reward**—On a per-share basis, gain is reduced by the amount of time premium in the option purchase price ($1 less per share in the current example). On a leveraged basis, gain is a multiple of stock gain (reduced by the aggregate time premium, which is three times the profit minus $300 in the current example).
- **Break-even**—The break-even point is the current stock price increased by the amount of time premium in the contract ($51 in the current example).
- **Risk**—On a per-share basis, loss is increased by the amount of the time premium but is capped at the option purchase price ($1 plus a price reduction from $50 in the current example). On a leveraged basis, loss is a multiple of the stock loss—increased by the aggregate time premium but capped at the total paid for the contracts ($1,800 in the current example).

ATM calls are cheaper than ITM calls but are more expensive than OTM options. ATM calls are less likely to result in a profit than ITM calls,

Figure 9-4 *Three purchased contracts.*
Gray line = long stock.
Black line = long 3 45 level calls for $6 ($6 × 3 × 100 = $1800) at expiration.
Thin gray line = long 3 45 level calls for $6 ($6 × 3 × 100 = $1800) with 21 days to expiration.

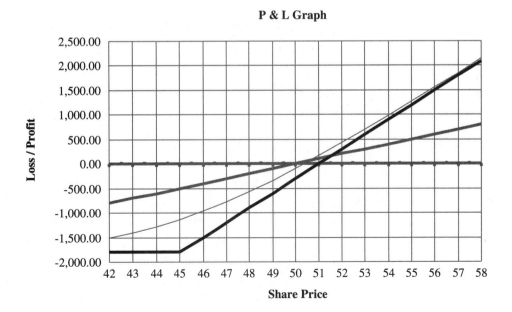

and each contract will produce less profit than one ITM call. ATM calls are more likely to result in a profit than OTM calls, and each contract will produce more profit than one OTM call. ATMs require an increase in stock price or an increase in volatility prior to option expiration in order to be effective. Time decay is an important consideration when purchasing ATM options, because 100 percent of the purchase price is time premium. The total purchase price for three July 50 call contracts is $600. We measured the following at July option expiration:

- **Reward**—This situation has an unlimited upside profit. For each $1 that the stock closes above $52, we have $300 worth of profit.
- **Break-even**—The break-even point is when the stock closes at $52.
- **Risk**—Loss is limited to $600, which is the amount paid for the calls. For each $1 that the stock closes below $52, we have $300 worth of loss. A maximum loss results if the stock closes at or below $50.

Compare this situation to long stock (see Figure 9-5):

- **Reward**—On a per-share basis, gain is reduced by the amount of time premium in the option purchase price ($2 less per share in the current example). On a leveraged basis, gain is a multiple of stock

Figure 9-5   *Comparison to long stock.*
            Gray line = long stock.
            Black line = long 3 50 level calls $2 ($2 × 3 × 100 = $600) at expiration.
            Thin gray line = long 3 50 level calls $2 ($2 × 3 × 100 = $600) with 21 days to expiration.

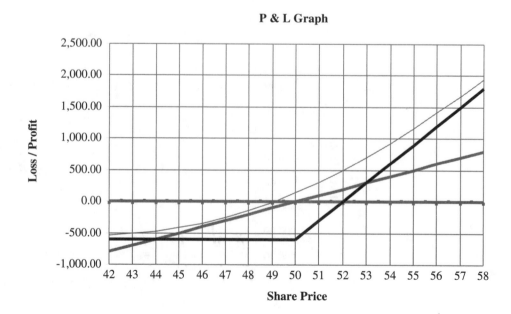

P & L Graph

gain—reduced by the aggregate time premium (three times the profit minus $600 in the current example).
- **Break-even**—The current stock price increased by the amount of time premium in the contract ($52 in the current example)
- **Risk**—On a per-share basis, $1 of loss for each dollar the stock closes below the current price of the stock increased by the amount of time premium ($52 in the current example), but capped at the option purchase price ($200). On a leveraged basis, loss is capped at the total amount paid for the contracts ($600 in the current example).

OTM calls are cheaper than the ATM or ITM options. These are less likely to result in a profit, and each contract will produce less profit than either an ATM call or an ITM call. OTM calls require a quick and large increase in stock price or a dramatic increase in volatility in order to be effective. 100 percent of the purchase price is the time premium. The total purchase price for three July 55 call contracts is $300. We measured the following at July option expiration:

- **Reward**—This situation has unlimited upside profit. For each $1 that the stock closes above $56, we have $300 worth of profit.
- **Break-even**—The stock closes at $56.
- **Risk**—Loss is limited to $300, which is the amount paid for the calls. For each $1 the stock closes below $51, we have $300 worth of loss. A maximum loss results if the stock closes at or below $55.

Compare this information to long stock (see Figure 9-6):

- **Reward**—On a per-share basis, the option gain is the stock gain reduced by the sum of (i) the option purchase price and (ii) the difference between the option exercise price and the price of the stock. We have a $1 option purchase price plus $5 (the option exercise price of $55 minus the $50 stock price equals $6).
- **Break-even**—The current stock price plus the option purchase price, plus the difference between the option exercise price and the price of the stock ($50 + $1 + $5 = $56 in the current example)
- **Risk**—On a per-share basis, risk refers to $1 of loss for each dollar the stock closes below the break-even price. This price, however, is capped at the option purchase price ($100). On a leveraged basis, loss is capped at the total amount paid for the contracts ($300 in the current example).

Whichever option you choose to purchase, if the call option is not ITM at expiration, it will have no intrinsic value and will expire worthless.

There are two ways to analyze a speculative bullish position by using calls. The first is from a leveraged risk perspective, and the second is from a per share (or stock equivalent) strategy.

Figure 9-6   *Comparison with long stock.*
Gray line = long stock.
Black line = long 3 55 level calls $1 ($1 × 3 × 100 = $300) at expiration.
Thin gray line = long 3 55 level calls $1 ($1 × 3 × 100 = $300) with 21 days to expiration.

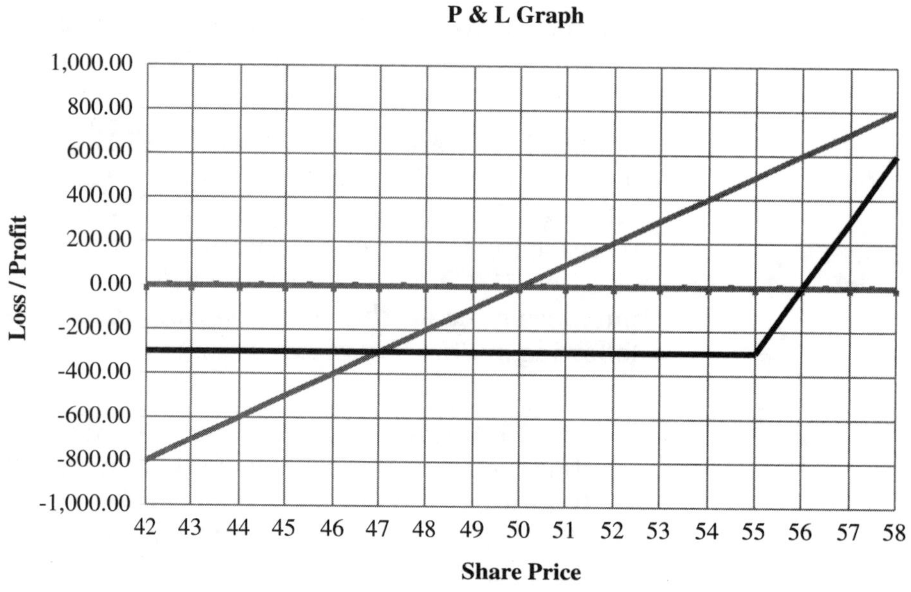

P & L Graph

Leveraged Risk

The leveraged risk perspective compares investment outcomes when the trader is willing to commit a specific dollar amount. We are not endorsing this approach; rather, we intend to highlight the leverage that is possible when using options. In the following example, the trader will invest $6,000 in stock XYZ. Currently, the stock is trading at $60, but the investor is speculating that the price will increase to $65–$70 per share by July expiration. The investor has collected the data and has created a matrix to help with the decision process. Because the investor cannot predict the future, he or she has calculated the returns in the matrix in order to identify their intrinsic value upon expiration at several specified stock prices.

You can easily create this matrix by using a spreadsheet program such as Microsoft Excel.

Example of a Leveraged Position.   XYZ stock is trading for $60. The July 55 call is trading for $6; the July 60 call is trading for $3; and the July 65 call is trading for $1.50. Compare investing the entire amount:

Long stock: 100 shares at $60
Long stock: 200 shares at $60 on margin

Call option: 10 July 55 calls at $6
Call option: 20 July 60 calls at $3
Call option: 40 July 65 calls at $1.50

The profit or loss of each alternative at a variety of expiration values for the stock is summarized in Table 9-1 (profit is in bold).

Figures 9-7 through 9-11 indicate the profit and loss for these positions.

Which bullish approach is best? The answer depends on a combination of your temperament, your tolerance for risk, and your assessment of the probabilities of where the stockmight be at expiration. For example, if you felt strongly that the stock would finish between $60–$70 at expiration, you would focus primarily on the profit and loss results for the various strategies with the stock in those ranges. You would exclude the July

Table 9-1   *Profit and Loss for Each Alternative*

Stock Price	50	55	60	65	70	75	80
100 sh	−$1,000	−$500	$0	$500	$1,000	$1,500	$2,000
200 sh/margin	−$2,000	−$1,000	$0	$1,000	$2,000	$3,000	$4,000
July 55 calls	−$6,000	−$6,000	−$1,000	$4,000	$9,000	$14,000	$19,000
July 60 calls	−$6,000	−$6,000	−$6,000	$4,000	$14,000	$24,000	$34,000
July 65 calls	−$6,000	−$6,000	−$6,000	−$6,000	$14,000	$34,000	$54,000

Figure 9-7   *Black line = long 100 shares of stock for $60/share.*

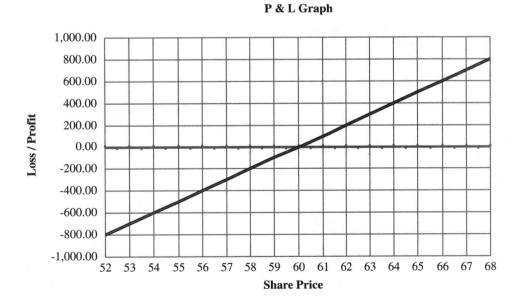

P & L Graph

Figure 9-8   *Black line = long 200 shares of stock for $60/share.*

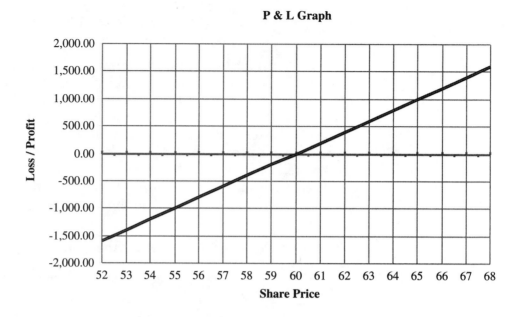

Figure 9-9   *Gray line = long stock.*
Black line = long 10 July 55 calls for $6 ($6 × 3 × 100 = $6000)
at expiration.
Thin gray line = long 10 July 55 calls for $6 ($6 × 3 × 100 =
$6000) with 21 days to expiration.

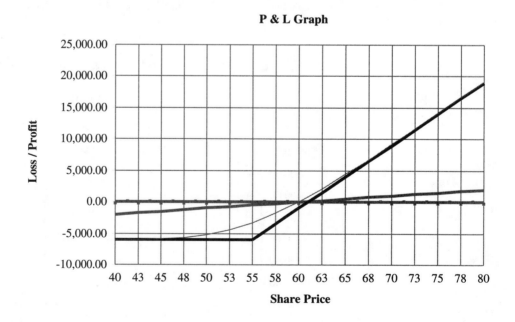

65 calls, because in the anticipated price range, the July 60 calls offer the
same profit potential but offer a lower risk of loss. You would probably
also exclude the stock purchases, because they provide such a limited

Figure 9-10   *Gray line = long stock.*
             Black line = long 20 July 60 calls for $3 (20 × $3 × 100 =
             $6000) at expiration.
             Thin gray line = long 20 July 60 calls for $3 (20 × $3 × 100 =
             $6000) with 21 days to expiration.

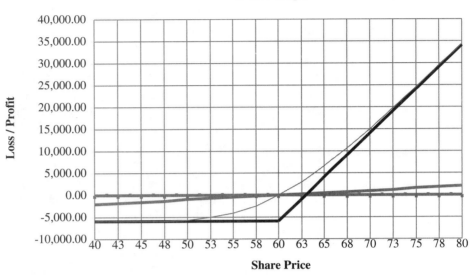

Figure 9-11   *Gray line = long stock.*
             Black line = long 40 July 65 calls for $1.50 (40 × $1.50 × 100 =
             $6000) at expiration.
             Thin gray line = long 40 July 65 calls for $1.50 (40 × $1.50 ×
             100 = $6000) with 21 days to expiration.

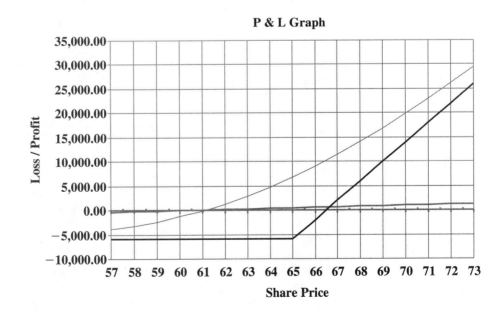

profit compared to the July 55 calls (with only a slight reduction in risk). If you felt that it was more likely that the stock would finish closer to $70 than to $60, you might decide to purchase the July 60 calls. If you do not like losing money on trades, however, you might buy the July 55 calls (which have a maximum loss of $1,000 in the range compared to a loss of the entire $6,000 for the July 60 calls).

The Delta Position

You would use the delta strategy to control an exact number of shares. The trader wishes to control 100 shares of XYZ and will commit the corresponding dollar amount, depending on which he or she decides to purchase. In this case, the trader believes that the stock has a potential of making a terrific move to the up side—let's say up to $80 or more per share. Maybe he or she is speculating on unexpected news or predicting a takeover rumor that will increase the demand for the stock and send it higher. He or she is concerned about the down-side risk. What if the news is unfavorable? The stock could drop precipitously in price. He or she only wants to commit a little capital to the position in order to control only 100 shares of stock.

Example of a Delta Position.   XYZ stock is trading for $60. The July 55 call is trading for $6; the July 60 call is trading for $3; and the July 65 call is trading for $1.50. In this case, we only acquire control of 100 shares.

Long stock: 100 shares at $60 = $6,000
Long stock: 100 shares at $60 on margin = $3,000
Call option: One July 55 call at $6 = $600
Call option: One July 60 call at $3 = $300
Call option: One July 65 call at $1.50 = $150

The profit, loss, and *return on investment* (ROI) of each alternative at a variety of expiration values for the stock are summarized in Table 9-2.

Table 9-2   *Profit, Loss, and ROI of Each Alternative*

Stock Price	$60		$65		$70		$75		$80	
	P&L	ROI (%)	P&L	ROI (%)	P&L	ROI (%)	P&L	ROI (%)	P&L	ROI (%)
100 sh	0	0	$500	8	$1,000	17	$1,500	25	$2,000	33
margin	0	0	$500	17	$1,000	33	$1,500	50	$2,000	67
July 55	−$100	−17	$400	67	$900	150	$1,400	233	$1,900	317
July 60	−$300	−100	$200	67	$700	233	$1,200	400	$1,700	567
July 65	−$150	−100	−$150	−100	$350	233	$850	567	$1,350	900

Figure 9-12 *Black line = long 100 shares of stock for $60/share = $6,000.*

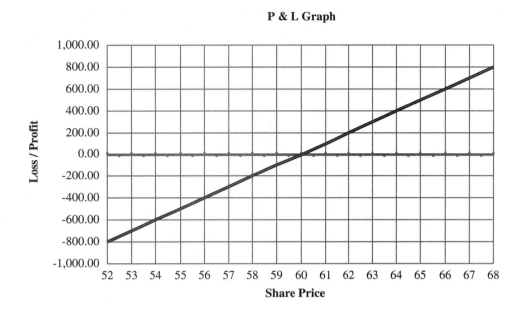

Figure 9-13 *Black line = long 200 shares of stock for $60/share = $6,000.*

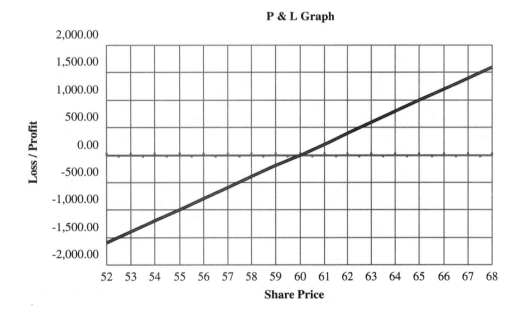

Figures 9-12 through 9-16 indicate the profit and loss for these positions.
The trader decides to purchase the July 65 call. The call only costs
$1.50 ($150), and not only is he or she willing to risk that capital for the
position, but he or she can afford to do so. The trader believes that the
stock could reach $80 or higher. Notice in the $80 column that the rate of
return on the July 65 call is 900 percent and the profit is $1,350.00,

Figure 9-14 *Gray line = long stock.*
            Black line = long 1 July 55 call at $6 = $600 ($1 × 6 × 100 =
            $600) at expiration.
            Thin gray line = long 1 July 55 call at $6 = $600 ($1 × 6 × 100
            = $600) with 21 days to expiration.

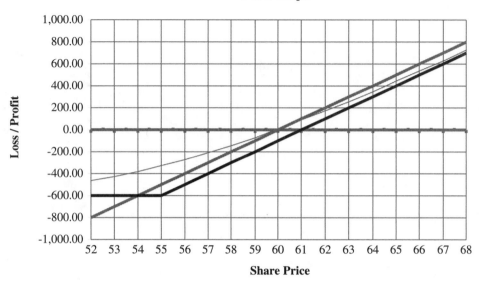

Figure 9-15 *Gray line = long stock.*
            Black line = long 1 July 60 call at $3 = $300 ($1 × 3 × 100 =
            $300) at expiration.
            Thin gray line = lone 1 July 60 call at $3 = $300 ($1 × 3 × 100
            = $300) with 21 days to expiration.

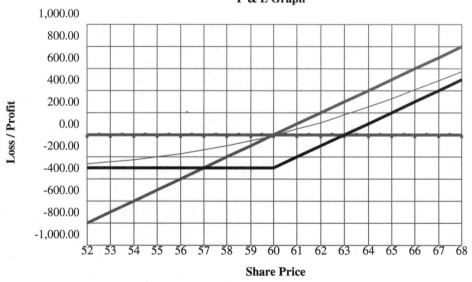

Figure 9-16   *Gray line = long stock.*
Black line = long 1 July 65 call at $1.50 = $150 (1 × $1.50 =
$150) at expiration.
Thin gray line = long 1 July 65 call at $1.50 = $150 (1 × $1.50
= $150) with 21 days to expiration.

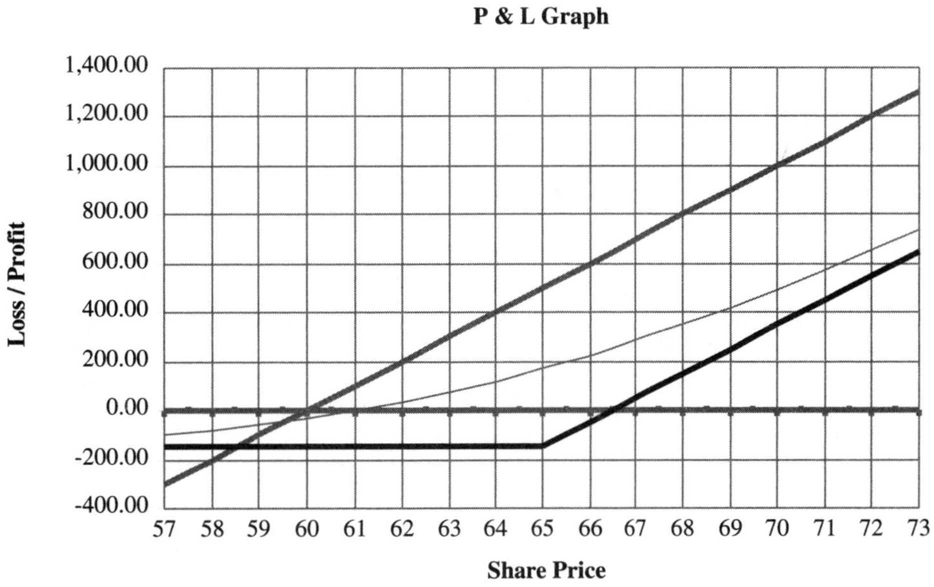

P & L Graph

compared to owning the stock outright and committing $6,000 worth of capital only to see a profit of $2,000 for a 33 percent return. The call has given the trader an incredible amount of leverage for little capital outlay. The trader's maximum risk in this position is $150.

Managing the Position

We have focused on analyzing long calls based on their profit/loss, as measured upon expiration. There is no requirement for the calls to be held until expiration. At any point prior to expiration, the holder of the options has three choices:

• Liquidate the position.
• Let it ride.
• Sell further-out calls.

Let's examine each of these options in the context of a position that has increased in value since it was put on.

With XYZ trading at $50, you purchased two October 50 calls trading for $3 for a total investment of $600. The stock has almost immediately risen to $55, and the October 50 calls are now trading for $6. The October

Figure 9-17   *A position that has increased in value.*
               Black line = bull spread at expiration.
               Thin gray line = bull spread with 21 days to expiration.

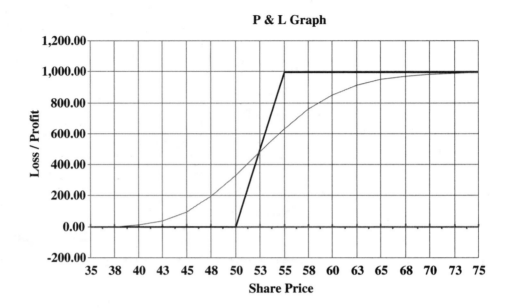

55 calls are trading for $3, and the October 60 calls are trading for $1. Your alternatives are:

1. **Liquidate the position**—Your calls are now worth $6. If you sell them, you will receive $1,200 for a net profit of $600. This option might be attractive if you think that the stock won't go much higher in price.
2. **Let it ride**—As long as you keep the calls, you own the up side. If you think that the stock has more room to run, you can wait and see what happens. When you compare this situation to owning the stock, you only have $1 left of time premium in the option price.
3. **Sell further-out calls**—Two candidates that you should strongly consider are: (a) selling two October 55 calls and (b) selling four October 55 calls and buying two October 60 calls. Let's consider these choices separately.
    a. **Sell two October 55 calls**—This action converts the long call position into a call bull spread (see Figure 9-17). We will cover this concept in detail in the next bullish strategy. By selling the October 55 calls for the same price that you purchased the October 50 calls, you guarantee that you cannot do worse than break even. For each $1 that the stock closes at expiration above $50, you will have $200 worth of profit—topping off at a stock price of $55. After $55, the loss on the October 55 calls will offset further gain on the October 50 calls. Thus, your potential profit would range from $0 to $1,000. If you thought that the stock price was unlikely to fall below $53 (which would result in a $600 profit—the same as you

would achieve by liquidating the position), this option would be a viable alternative to liquidating the calls now.

b. **Sell four October 55 calls and buy two October 60 calls—** This option converts the long call position into a long butterfly, which we will cover in detail in "The Truth about Butterflies" section in this chapter. This butterfly would have been put on for a $400 credit (purchased two October 50 calls for $600, sold four October 55 calls for $1,200, and purchased two October 60 calls for $200). As we measured at expiration, the profit/loss graph of this position is shown in Figure 9-18).

This position would result in a profit ranging from $400 to $1,400 upon expiration, depending on the stock price upon expiration. The minimum figure would result from a stock price either at or below $50 or at or above $60. The maximum profit would occur if the stock closed at $55 upon expiration.

A Moderately Bullish Bull Spread

Remember that a spread is generally a strategy that involves the purchase of one option and the sale of an identical amount of another option of the same kind. A bull spread is a position in which an option at a particular strike price (either a call or a put) is bought, and a higher strike price of the same type of option (with the same expiration date) is sold.

Figure 9-18 *Profit/loss graph.*
Black line = long 2 Oct 50 puts for $600, short 4 Oct 45 puts for $1,200 and long 2 Oct 40 puts for $200 at expiration.
Thin gray line = long butterfly with 21 days to expiration.

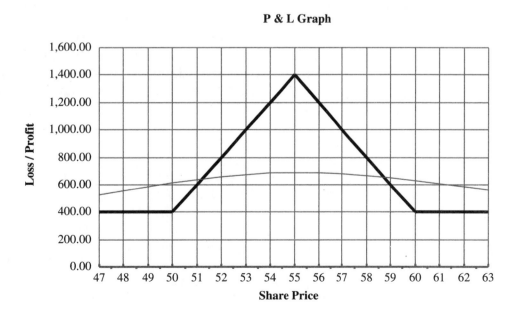

This spread is used to speculate on an uptrend in the market price of the underlying security. The maximum profit is reached when the underlying security rises above the strike that is sold. A bull spread can be constructed with either puts or calls.

Call Bull Spread

The investor establishes a call bull spread when he or she purchases the lower strike call and sells the higher strike call. (The investor pays a debit.)

- **Reward**—This situation has a limited reward. The maximum profit is the difference between strike prices minus the debit paid. The maximum profit results when the underlying finishes, at expiration, above the higher strike.
- **Break-even**—The stock closes upon expiration at a price that is equal to the lower strike price increased by the amount of the debit.
- **Risk**—The risk in this situation is limited. The debit paid is the maximum loss. The maximum loss occurs when the underlying finishes, at expiration, below the lower strike.

Outlook on Stock.   Moderately bullish.

Put Bull Spread

A put bull spread is established when the investor purchases the lower strike put and sells the higher strike put. (The investor collects a credit.)

- **Reward**—The reward in this instance is limited. The maximum profit is the credit received. The maximum profit results when the underlying finishes, at expiration, above the higher strike.
- **Break-even**—The stock closes at expiration at a price that is equal to the higher strike price reduced by the amount of the credit.
- **Risk**—The risk in this situation is limited. The maximum loss is the difference between strike prices minus the credit received. The maximum loss occurs when the underlying finishes, at expiration, below the lower strike.

Outlook on Stock.   Moderately bullish.

Case Study.   Let's consider a trader who expects a stock that is currently trading for $50 to drift upward in price (but not explosively so), with an anticipated target of $54–$56 at near-term expiration. At the same time, the trader does not wish to expose himself to a significant down-side risk. The near-term 45-level calls are trading for $7; the 50-level calls are trading for $4; and the 55-level calls are trading for $2. Based on an expiration value of $55, purchasing the 45-level call would risk $7 in order to make $3, while purchasing the 50-level call would risk $4 in order to make $1.

Therefore, the trader decides to purchase the 50-level call for $4 ($400) and sell the 55-level call for $2 ($200). The 55-level call will help subsidize the cost of the 50-level call. This technique is called a bull spread. Instead of committing $4 ($400) to the position, the trader is only committing $2 ($200), which equates to 400 − 200 = 200. The trader's maximum risk is $200 with a reward of $300. The bull spread maximum price can only be the difference between the two strikes; in this case, $5 (55 level strike − 50 level strike = $5). Because the trader spent $2 for the spread, his maximum profit would be $3.

- **Reward**—The reward potential is $300 (the difference between the strikes $5 minus the debit paid, which is $2).
- **Risk**—The risk potential is $200 (the price paid for the spread).
- **Break-even**—The stock closes at $52 upon expiration.

  - **An example of a July 50–55 put bull spread (see Figure 9-19)**—The trader buys one XYZ July 50 put for $4 ($4 × 100 = $400). Then, he or she sells one XYZ July 55 put for $7 ($7 × 100 = $700). The net credit is $3 ($300).

- **Reward**—The reward potential is $300 (credit received).
- **Risk**—The risk potential is $200 (the difference between the strike's $5 minus the credit received, which is $3).
- **Break-even**—The stock closes at $52 upon expiration.

These examples illustrate both the long call spread and the short put spread. Notice that the profit and loss graph for each of the examples is

Figure 9-19   *Example of a July 50–55 bull spread.*
              Black line = bull spread at expiration.
              Thin gray line = bull spread with 21 days to expiration.

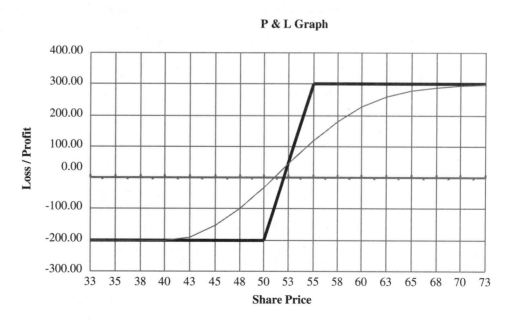

P & L Graph

identical. This situation again shows that calls and puts work similarly and are actually measurements of curvature. If you were to only view the profit and loss graph, you could determine that it is a bull spread, but you could not determine how it was created. In both examples, the 50-level call or put is purchased, and the 55-level call or put is sold. A market maker would look at this position and deduce that the trader is long the 50 strike and short the 55 strike. Notice how he did not mention whether the position consisted of calls or puts, but rather long or short curvature. Take a moment to look at this phenomenon on the profit and loss graph (refer to Figure 9-19).

An alternative position would be to consider the July 45–50 bull spread. As we just saw, the risk/reward profiles of the put and call bull spreads are identical, so we do not need to examine them separately.

Example of a July 45–50 Call Bull Spread. XYZ is trading at $50 per share. The trader buys one XYZ July 45 call for $7 ($7 × 100 = $700). He then sells one XYZ July 50 call for $4 ($4 × 100 = $400). The net debit is $3 ($3 × 100 = $300).

- **Reward**—The reward potential is $200 (the difference between the strike's $5 minus the debit paid, which is $3).
- **Risk**—The risk potential is $300 (the price paid for the spread).
- **Break-even**—The stock closes at $48 at expiration.

Let's compare the risk/reward profile of this call bull spread with the 50–55 call bull spread discussed earlier (see Table 9-3).

The tradeoff is clear. The 45–50 spread is much more likely to result in a profit, and that profit will be lower than the maximum profit from the 50–55 spread. Furthermore, in the event of a large move in the stock price, the potential loss will be higher than for the 50–55 spread. The maximum gain and maximum loss numbers depend upon the actual prices for these options. The particular example used here involved options that had a high implied volatility. The effect of lower volatility would be to reduce the maximum gain and increase the maximum loss for

Table 9-3   *Risk / Reward Profile Compared to the 50–55 Call Bull Spread*

Risk/Reward Profile	45–50 bull spread	50–55 bull spread
Maximum gain	$200	$300
Stock price producing maximum gain	$50 or above	$55 or above
Breakeven stock price	$48	$52
Maximum loss	$300	$200
Stock price producing maximum loss	$45 or below	$50 or below

the 45–50 spread and increase the maximum gain and reduce the maximum loss for the higher strike spread.

We saw that the put and call bull spreads that cover the same strikes are essentially the same spread. We also noted that there can be more than one set of strikes at which to put on the position, such as choosing between the 45–50 and 50–55 spreads that we have used as examples and discussed previously. What factors should you consider when selecting the most appropriate bull spread? Consider the following points:

1. **Selecting the strikes to use**—Compare the maximum gain/maximum loss profiles of each set of strikes. If they are similar, then the lower strike (the 45–50 spread in our example) would be the choice—whereas if the higher strike spread offers a much greater reward with a lower loss, you should select this option (given your bullish sentiment).
2. **Puts or calls**—Based on the current pricing, it might be cheaper to put the call spread on rather than the put spread (or vice-versa). Remember, they are the same position. There might be slight margin requirement differences between the put and call spreads. Check with your broker.

Bullish: Ratio Bull Spread (Long)

The ratio bull spread is designed to create leverage (control of upside potential) without committing as much capital as you would by purchasing the calls outright. This goal is achieved by purchasing calls and financing the long call position by selling a call(s) with a lower strike and higher price than the ones purchased. The ratio bull spread can be put on in any ratio that the trader desires: buy two, sell one; buy three, sell one; buy four, sell one; buy three, sell two; and so on. Whatever the ratio, the trader is simply purchasing more options than he or she is selling in order to create leverage at a reduced price. The long calls should always be OTM, while the short strike can be ITM, ATM, or OTM. We suggest selling the ATM to slightly OTM calls, because they will have the most premium attached. We will focus on the 3:1 ratio bull spread by presenting an illustration.

Example. The trader believes that stock XYZ is going to make a tremendous move above $60 per share, but she does not want to pay for the long contracts. XYZ is trading for $50. The trader buys three XYZ July 55 calls for $1 ($1 × 3) × 100 = $300). She sells one XYZ July 50 call for $3 ($3 × 100 = $300). The net position cost is $0 (see Figure 9-20).

Notice in the profit and loss graph that the trader has no risk if the stock closes below $50 at option expiration. Her position will break even. The maximum risk of the position is that the stock closes on expiration day at the strike where the trader is long (in this case, the $55 strike). If this situation occurs, the short July 50 call will be worth a debit of $5, while the long July 55 calls will expire worthless. The maximum loss is

Figure 9-20 *3:1 ratio bull spread.*
Black line = ratio bull spread at expiration.
Thin gray line = ratio bull spread with 21 days to expiration.

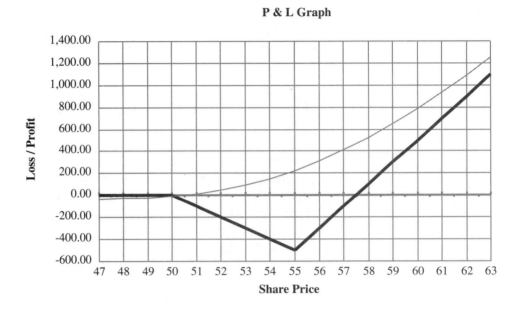

calculated by the difference between the short strike and the long strike adjusted for the credit/debit for which the trader put on the position. In this case, the position was put on for even, and the difference in the strikes is $5 (the 55-level call minus the 50-level call). The maximum risk is therefore $5 ($5 − $0). Remember that this graph shows intrinsic value at expiration, and the loss is not totally incurred until such time.

Let's consider an example of a ratio bull spread (long) consisting of a call bear spread plus a long OTM call.

- **Reward**—The reward here is unlimited. As the stock continues to rise through the long strike, the position incurs intrinsic value. The more calls that the trader owns, the larger his or her rate of return as the stock continues to rise.
- **Risk**—The risk in this situation is limited. The maximum risk of this position is the difference between the long and short strikes minus the credit/debit cost of the position to put on. The maximum loss is realized when the stock closes at the strike that the trader is long the call contracts. The outlook of the stock is bullish to extremely bullish.

Managing the Position

This position does well if the stock price explodes. In the previous example, as measured upon option execution, for each dollar that the stock moves higher than $55, the July 55 calls gain $3 in value while the July 50 call loses $1. This situation results in a net gain of $2 for each dollar move.

Remembering the Greeks, this position is approximately delta neutral to start, with both long gamma and long vega. In other words, prior to expiration, this position will gain in value whenever volatility increases or the stock price increases. The best of both worlds results when the stock price increases, causing option-implied volatility to increase as well. This situation will tend to happen when the stock has been in a trading range and breaks out of the range to the upside. This scenario is excellent for this position if the option sold is at the top of the trading range. If so, and if the stock stays in the trading range, then the short option will expire as worthless—while if the stock breaks out of the range, the call volatility might explode.

Bearish Strategies

Bearish strategies enable the individual investor to generate profit in a declining marketplace. Unfortunately, most investors have a hard time being bearish because they have been taught that a downward turning market is a bad thing. Using their trading insight to see differently is hard for them. The media supports this perspective, as well. CNBC and other television programs that report about the market are always excited when the market rises and are surprised and concerned when it falls. Not surprisingly, then, we often run into individual investors who remain bullish regardless of the situation. They hope for bounces in the market and try to pick bottoms. Attempting to pick a bottom is like trying to catch a falling safe, however.

Individual investors need to realize that the market is its own animal and that it will continue to rise and fall. As investors and traders, we have a choice about whether we would like to take advantage of these trends— regardless of their direction. Again, a declining market is bad only relative to your position. If you are the owner of the stock that is declining in price, you are looking at a loss. There are many other positions to take, however, that do not respond negatively to a down turn in the market.

In the bearish strategy section, we will learn ways to generate profits in declining markets. The most common of these strategies is short stock. Unfortunately, short stock is a capital-intensive position that requires the trader to have margin or equity in his or her account for protection in case the stock were to rise in price. Nevertheless, we will begin this chapter by reviewing the short stock position so that we can look at it in comparison with option strategies in order to show how you can use options to reduce market exposure, reduce capital risk, and create leverage.

Bearish: Short Stock

Remember that an investor is short stock when he or she borrows stock from a brokerage firm in order to sell it with the speculation that the stock will decrease in value. To close out the position and repay the loan, the investor buys the stock on the open market and returns the shares to the broker—ideally, after it has declined in price.

Let's consider an example. An investor who has no position in XYZ borrows 100 shares from his or her broker and sells them for $50 per share. The investor then has $5,000 in his or her account and is obligated to return 100 shares of XYZ to the broker at some time in the future. The investor then waits to purchase back the stock after it has declined in price.

- **Reward**—This situation has unlimited down-side profit until the stock price equals zero. Each $1 decrease in the market price of the stock results in $100 worth of profit.
- **Break-even**—The stock is unchanged at $50.
- **Risk**—This situation has unlimited upside loss. Each $1 increase in the market price of the stock results in $100 worth of loss.

The short stock position has the same risk profile as long stock. In this case, however, the individual investor is looking for a decrease—not an increase—in stock price. The risk/reward profile is 1:1. For every $1 that the stock increases in price, the position loses $100. Conversely, for every $1 that the stock price decreases, the position gains $100 (see Figure 9-21).

Short stock has directional risk, which can become extreme if the stock were to gap up. When stock makes several gaps up, short sellers might fuel this rapid rise. What is commonly referred to as a short squeeze or short covering rally occurs when the short sellers are forced to buy back the stock because the increasing stock price has created losses in their account. A short covering rally or short squeeze, however, actually

Figure 9-21   *Risk/reward profile.*
            Black line = 100 shares short stock for $50/share.

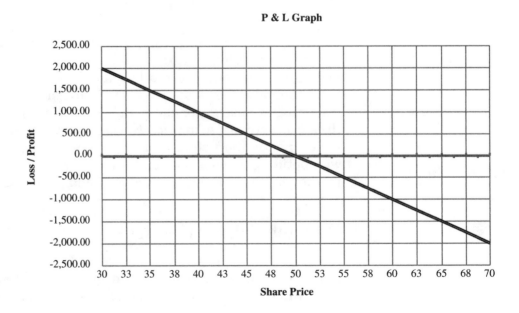

makes the stock rise accelerate due to the extra purchasing from the short stockholders. Not only are there natural buyers, but there are also short stock re-purchasers. This supply-demand imbalance can send a stock's price skyrocketing.

Short squeezes and short covering rallies can be dangerous situations for short stock sellers. Long stockholders face the exact same risk in a crashing market. Once the market is moving against your position, it is hard to get out unscathed.

Bearish: Long Puts

Like selling stock short, puts can be used to create short positions in the marketplace. While most brokerage firms require a huge amount of capital in order to enable a client to sell stock short, there are no margin requirements for purchasing puts. Just as long calls can create a speculative upside position, long puts enable you to create speculative downside positions with limited risk. Using puts rather than short stock will result in substantially more gain if the stock decreases dramatically in price if leverage is used (in other words, acquiring the downside potential of many more shares of stock via options rather than by actually selling the stock). To illustrate this point, we will compare the profit and loss upon option expiration graphs of (1) purchasing three of the near-term 50-level puts for $2 each when the stock is trading at $50 per share to (2) selling 100 shares for $50 per share. Like the short stock positions, the long put will profit to the down side as the underlying stock declines in value. Unlike the long stock positions, the maximum loss is the amount paid for the puts (in this case, $2, or a total of $600). Refer to Figure 9-22.

You can implement this strategy by using ITM, ATM, or OTM puts. Each type has its own risk/reward profile. You *must* understand the conditions that are necessary for profit for a particular type of put prior to acquiring it in order to implement a bearish strategy. Let's consider each point in turn.

For example, XYZ stock is trading for $50. The July 55 put is trading for $6; the July 50 put is trading for $2; and the July 45 put is trading for $1. For illustrative purposes, assume in each case that three contracts are purchased.

ITM puts will react much like stock will. Most of the cost will be intrinsic value with less time premium. In this example, the July 55 put will have $5 worth of intrinsic value and $1 worth of time premium. The total purchase price for three contracts is $1,800. We measured the following upon July option expiration:

- **Reward**—In this case, there is unlimited downside profit. For each $1 that the stock closes below $49, we have $300 worth of profit.
- **Break-even**—The stock closes at $49.
- **Risk**—The loss is limited to $1,800 the amount paid for the puts. For each $1 that the stock closes above $49, we have $300 worth of loss. A maximum loss results if the stock finishes at or above $55.

Figure 9-22   *Profit and loss upon expiration graphs.*
Gray line = short stock.
Black line = long 3 50 level puts for $2 ($2 × 3 × 100 = $600) at
expiration.
Thin gray line = long 3 50 level puts for $2 ($2 × 3 × 100 =
$600) with 21 days to expiration.

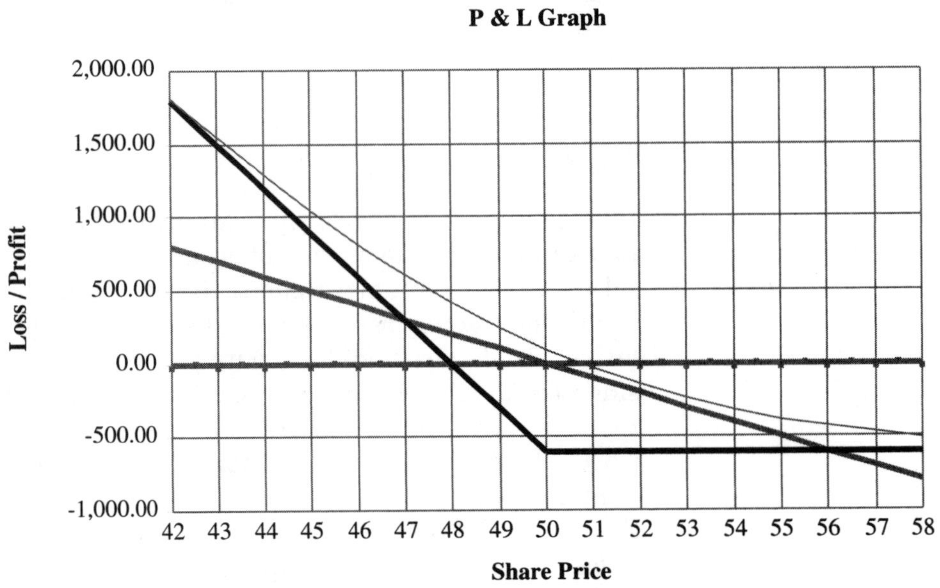

P & L Graph

Compare this situation to short stock (see **Figure 9-23**):

- **Reward**—On a per-share basis, gain is reduced by the amount of time premium in an option's purchase price ($1 less per share in the current example). On a leveraged basis, gain is a multiple of stock gain and is reduced by the aggregate time premium (three times the profit minus $300 in the current example).
- **Break-even**—The current stock price decreased by the amount of time premium in the contract ($49 in the current example)
- **Risk**—On a per-share basis, loss is increased by the amount of time premium but is capped at the option purchase price ($1 plus the price increase from $50 in the current example). On a leveraged basis, loss is a multiple of the stock loss and is increased by the aggregate time premium. Loss is capped, however, at the total price paid for the contracts ($1,800 in the current example).

ATM puts are cheaper than ITM puts but are more expensive than OTM options and are less likely to result in a profit than ITM puts. Each contract will produce less profit than one ITM put. These puts are more likely to result in a profit than OTM puts, and each contract will produce more profit than one OTM put. ATM puts require a decrease in stock price or an increase in volatility prior to option expiration in order to be effective. 100 percent of the purchase price is the time premium. The total

Figure 9-23   *Short stock.*
Gray line = short stock.
Black line = long 3 55 level puts for $6 ($6 × 3 × 100 = $1800)
at expiration.
Thin gray line = long 3 55 level puts for $6 ($6 × 3 × 100 =
$1800) with 21 days to expiration.

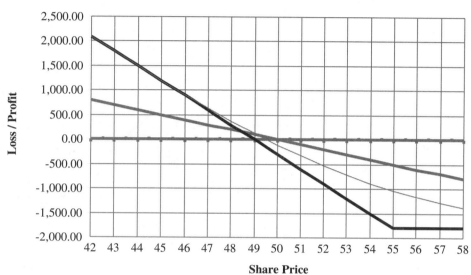

P & L Graph

purchase price for three July 50 put contracts is $600. We measured the following upon July option expiration:

- **Reward**—The reward in this situation is unlimited upside profit. For each $1 that the stock closes below $48, we have $300 worth of profit.
- **Break-even**—The stock closes at $48.
- **Risk**—The loss in this situation is limited to $600, which is the amount paid for the puts. For each $1 that the stock closes above $48, we have $300 worth of loss. A maximum loss results if the stock closes at or above $50.

Compare this situation to short stock (see Figure 9-24):

- **Reward**—On a per-share basis, gain is reduced by the amount of time premium in the option purchase price ($2 less per share in the current example). On a leveraged basis, gain is a multiple of stock gain and is reduced by the aggregate time premium (three times the profit minus $600 in the current example).
- **Break-even**—The current stock price decreased by the amount of time premium in the contract ($48 in the current example)
- **Risk**—On a per-share basis, risk refers to each $1 of loss for each dollar that the stock closes above the current price of the stock

Figure 9-24   *Short-stock comparison.*
Gray line = short stock.
Black line = long 3 50 level puts $2 ($2 × 3 × 100 = $600) at
expiration.
Thin gray line = long 3 50 level puts $2 ($2 × 3 × 100 = $600)
with 21 days to expiration.

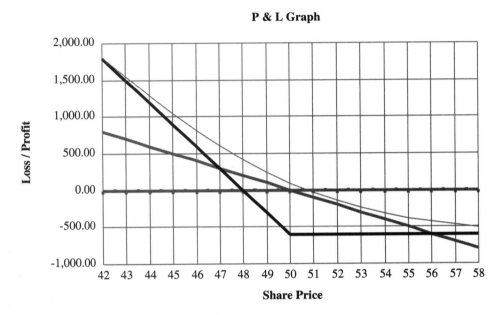

decreased by the amount of time premium ($48 in the current exam-
ple). The price is capped at the option purchase price ($200), how-
ever. On a leveraged basis, loss is capped at the total amount paid for
the contracts ($600 in the current example).

OTM puts are cheaper than the ATM or ITM options. OTM options
are less likely to result in a profit, and each contract will produce less
profit than either one ATM or one ITM put. These puts require a quick
and large increase in stock price or an extreme increase in volatility in
order to be effective. 100 percent of the purchase price is time premium.
The total purchase price for three July 45 put contracts is $300. We mea-
sured the following upon July option expiration:

- **Reward**—This situation has unlimited down-side profit. For each
  $1 that the stock closes below $44, we have $300 worth of profit.
- **Break-even**—The stock closes at $44.
- **Risk**—Loss is limited to $300, which is the amount paid for the puts.
  For each $1 that the stock closes above $44, we have $300 worth of
  loss. A maximum loss results if the stock closes at or above $45.

Compare this information to short stock (see Figure 9-25):

- **Reward**—On a per-share basis, option gain is the stock gain reduced
  by the sum of (1) the option purchase price and (2) the difference
  between the option exercise price and price of the stock ($1 option

Figure 9-25 *Short-stock comparison.*
Gray line = short stock.
Black line = long 3 45 level puts for $1 ($1 × 3 × 100 = $300) at expiration.
Thin gray line = long 3 45 level puts for $1 ($1 × 3 × 100 = $300) with 21 days to expiration.

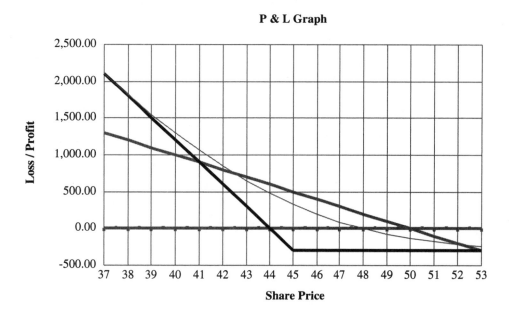

P & L Graph

purchase price plus $5). The $5 comes from the current stock price of $50 minus the option strike price of $1, which equals $6.

- **Break-even**—The option's strike price minus the option purchase price ($45 − $1 = $44 in the current example)
- **Risk**—On a per-share basis, $1 of loss for each dollar that the stock closes above the break-even price (but capped at the option purchase price, which is $100). On a leveraged basis, loss is capped at the total amount paid for the contracts ($300 in the current example).

Whichever option you choose to purchase, if the put option is not ITM upon expiration, it will have no intrinsic value and will expire as worthless.

There are two ways to analyze the speculative bear position by using puts. The first is from a leveraged risk perspective, and the second is from a per-share or stock-equivalent strategy.

Leveraged Risk

The leveraged risk perspective compares investment outcomes when the trader is willing to commit a specific dollar amount. You should not perceive this discussion as the authors' endorsement of such an approach, this information is intended to highlight the leverage that is possible by using options. In the following example, the trader will invest $6,000 in stock XYZ. The stock is currently trading at $60, the investor is speculating that the price will fall to $50–$55 per share by July expiration. The investor has collected the data and has created a matrix to help with the decision-making process. Because the investor cannot predict the future, he or she has calculated the returns in the matrix in order to identify their intrinsic value upon expiration at several specified stock prices. You can easily create this matrix by using Microsoft Excel.

Example of a Leveraged Position.   XYZ stock is trading for $60. The July 65 put is trading for $6; the July 60 put is trading for $3; and the July 55 put is trading for $1.50. Compare investing the entire amount:

Short stock: 100 shares at $60
Put option: 10 July 65 puts at $6
Put option: 20 July 60 puts at $3
Put option: 40 July 55 puts at $1.50

The profit (loss) of each alternative at a variety of expiration values for the stock is summarized in Table 9-4 (profit is in bold).

Figures 9-26 through 9-29 indicate the profit and loss for these positions.

Table 9-4   *Profit and Loss of Each Alternative*

Stock Price	45	50	55	60	65	70	75
100 sh	$1,500	$1,000	$500	$0	−$500	−$1,000	−$1,500
July 65 puts	$14,000	$9,000	$4,000	−$1,000	−$6,000	−$6,000	−$6,000
July 60 puts	$24,000	$14,000	$4,000	−$6,000	−$6,000	−$6,000	−$6,000
July 55 puts	$34,000	$14,000	−$6,000	−$6,000	−$6,000	−$6,000	−$6,000

Figure 9-26   *Black line = short 100 shares of stock for $60/share.*

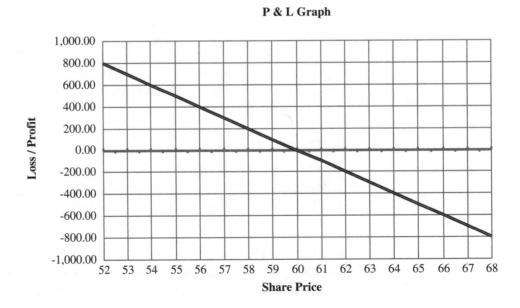

Figure 9-27 *Gray line = short stock.*
Black line = long 10 July 65 puts for $6 (10 × $6 × 100 =
$6,000) at expiration.
Thin gray line = long 10 July 65 puts for $6 (10 × $6 × 100 =
$6,000) with 21 days to expiration.

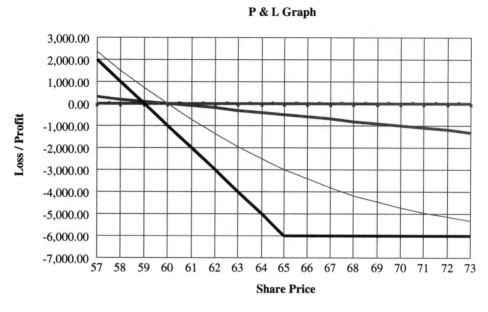

Figure 9-28 *Gray line = short stock.*
Black line = long 20 July 60 puts for $3 (20 × $3 × 100 =
$6,000) at expiration.
Thin gray line = long 20 July 60 puts for $3 (20 × $3 × 100 =
$6,000) with 21 days to expiration.

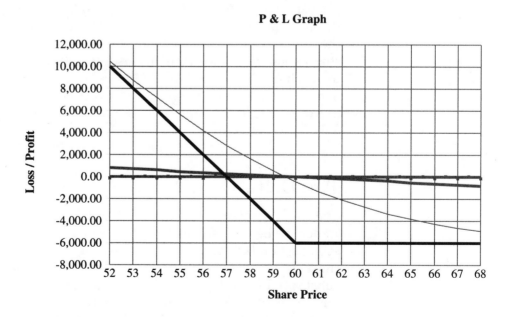

Which bearish approach is best? The answer depends on a combination of your temperament and your assessment of the probabilities of where the stock might be at expiration. For example, if you felt strongly

Figure 9-29   *Gray line = short stock.*
Black line = long 40 July 55 puts for $1.50 (40 × $1.50 × 100 =
$6,000) at expiration.
Thin gray line = long 40 July 55 puts for $1.50 (40 × $1.50 ×
100 = $6,000) with 21 days to expiration.

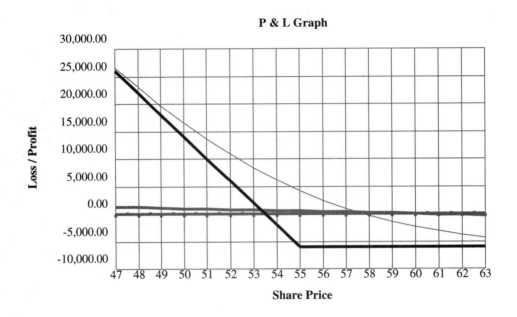

that the stock would finish between $50–$60 at expiration, you would focus primarily on the profit and loss results for the various strategies with the stock in those ranges. You would exclude the July 55 puts, because in the anticipated price range, the July 60 puts offer the same profit potential but a lower risk of loss. You would probably also exclude the stock purchase, because it provides such a limited profit compared to the July 65 puts (with only a slight reduction in risk). If you felt that the stock would most likely finish closer to $50 than to $60, you might decide to purchase the July 60 puts. On the other hand, if you do not like losing money on trades, you might buy the July 65 puts (which have a maximum loss of $1,000 in the range) compared to a loss of the entire $6,000 for the July 60 puts.

The Delta Position

The delta strategy is used to control an exact number of shares. The trader wishes to control 100 shares of XYZ and will commit the corresponding dollar amount, depending on which he or she decides to purchase. In this case, the trader believes that the stock has a potential of a substantial sell-off—let's say, to $40 per share or below. The trader is concerned about upside risk, however. What if the trader's expectation of the move is incorrect, the stock could increase in price, therefore he or she only wants to commit a small amount of capital to the position in order to control only 100 shares of stock.

Example of the Delta Position. XYZ stock is trading for $60 per share. The July 65 put is trading for $6; the July 60 put is trading for $3; and the July 55 put is trading for $1.50. In this case, we only acquire control of 100 shares:

Short stock:	100 shares at $60 = $6,000
Put option:	one July 65 put at $6 = $600
Put option:	one July 60 put at $3 = $300
Put option:	one July 55 put at $1.50 = $150

The profit (loss) and *return on investment* (ROI) of each alternative at a variety of expiration values for the stock are summarized in Table 9-5.

The following graphs (Figures 9-30 through 9-33) indicate the profit and loss for these positions.

Table 9-5   *Profit and Loss and ROI*

Stock Price	$40		$45		$50		$55		$60	
	P&L	ROI (%)	P&L	ROI (%)	P&L	ROI (%)	P&L	ROI (%)	P&L	ROI (%)
100 sh	$2,000	33	$1,500	25	$1,000	17	$500	8	0	0
July 55	$1,400	233	$900	150	$400	67	−$100	−17	−$600	−100
July 60	$1,200	400	$700	233	$200	67	−$300	−100	−$300	−100
July 65	$850	567	$350	233	−$150	−100	−$150	−100	−$150	−100

Figure 9-30   *Short stock.*
Black line = short 100 shares of stock for $60 / share.

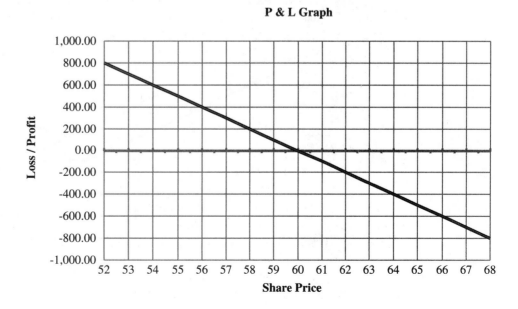

P & L Graph

Figure 9-31   *Short stock / ITM put.*
Gray line = short stock.
Black line = long 1 July 65 puts for $6 (1 × $6 × 100 = $600) at expiration.
Thin gray line = long 1 July 65 puts for $6 (1 × $6 × 100 = $600) with 21 days at expiration.

P & L Graph

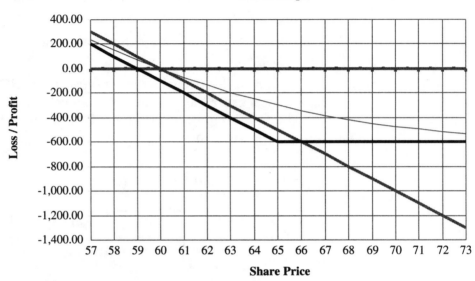

Figure 9-32   *Short stock / ATM put.*
Gray line = short stock.
Black line = long 1 July 60 puts for $3 (20 × $3 × 100 = $300) at expiration.
Thin gray line = long 1 July 60 puts for $3 (20 × $3 × 100 = $300) with 21 days to expiration.

P & L Graph

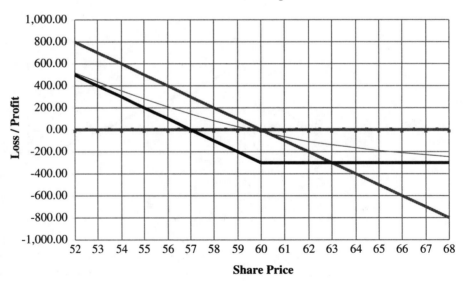

Figure 9-33   *Short stock / OTM put.*
Gray line = short stock.
Black line = long 1 July 55 puts for $1.50 (1 × $1.50 × 100 =
$150) at expiration.
Thin gray line = long 1 July 55 puts for $1.50 (1 × $1.50 × 100
= $150) with 21 days to expiration.

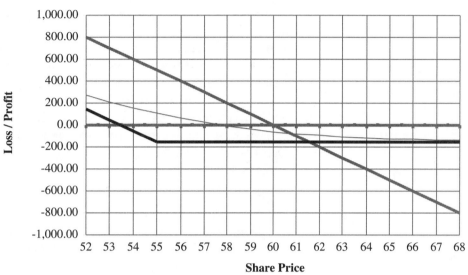

The trader decides to purchase the July 55 put. This put only costs $1.50 ($150), and not only is the trader willing to risk that capital to the position, but he or she can afford to do so. The trader believes that the stock could reach $40 or lower. Notice in the $40 column that the rate of return of the July 55 put is 567 percent and that the dollar return is $850, as compared to selling the stock outright and committing $6,000 of capital (only to see a return of $2,000, or 33 percent). The put has given the trader an incredible amount of leverage for little capital outlay. The trader's maximum risk in this position is $150.

Managing the Position

We have focused on analyzing long puts based on their profit/loss (as measured upon expiration). There is no requirement for the puts to be held until expiration. At any point prior to expiration, the holder of the options has three options:

• Liquidate the position.
• Let it ride.
• Sell further-out puts.

Let's examine each of these options in the context of a position that has increased in value since it was put on:

With XYZ trading at $50, you purchased two October 50 puts that were trading at $3 (for a total investment of $600). The stock has almost immediately fallen to $45, and the October 50 puts are now trading at $6. The October 45 puts are trading at $3, and the October 40 puts are trading for $1. Your alternatives are

1. **Liquidate the position**—Your puts are now worth $6. If you sell them, you will receive $1,200 (a net profit of $600). This option might be attractive if you think that the stock does not have much more downside.

2. **Let it ride**—As long as you keep the puts, you own the downside. If you think that the stock has more room to fall, you can wait and see what happens. As compared to shorting the stock, you only have $1 left of time premium in the option price.

3. **Sell further-out puts**—Two candidates that you should strongly consider are (1) selling two October 45 puts and (2) selling four October 45 puts and buying two October 40 puts. Let's consider these choices separately.

   a. **Selling two October 55 puts**—This action converts the long put position into a put bear spread. We will cover this concept in detail in the next section on bearish strategy. By selling the October 45 puts for the same price that you purchased the October 50 puts, you guarantee that you cannot do worse than break even. For each $1 that the stock closes at expiration below $50, you will have $200 worth of profit—topping out at a stock price of $45. Below $45, the October 45 puts will offset the October 50 puts. Thus, your potential profit would range from $0 to $1,000. If you thought that the stock price was unlikely to fall below $47 (which would result in a $600 profit—the same as you would achieve by liquidating the position), this alternative would be viable (instead of liquidating the puts now).

   b. **Selling four October 45 puts and buying two October 40 puts**—This action converts the long put position into a long butterfly, which we cover in detail in "The Truth about Butterflies" section of this chapter. This butterfly would have been put on for a $400 credit (purchased two October 50 puts for $600, sold four October 45 puts for $1,200, and purchased two October 40 puts for $200). As measured at expiration, the profit/loss graph of this position is shown in Figure 9-34.

This position would result in a profit ranging from $400 to $1,400 upon expiration—depending on the stock price at expiration. The minimum figure would result from a stock price either at or below $40 or at or above $50. The maximum profit would occur if the stock closed at $45 at expiration.

Moderately Bearish: Bear Spread

A bear spread is a position in which an option at a particular strike price (either a call or a put) is sold, and a higher strike price of the same type

Figure 9-34 *Long butterfly profit and loss graph.*
Black line = long 2 Oct 50 puts for $600, short 4 Oct 45 puts for
$1,200, and long 2 Oct 40 puts for $200 at expiration.
Thin gray line = long butterfly with 21 days to expiration.

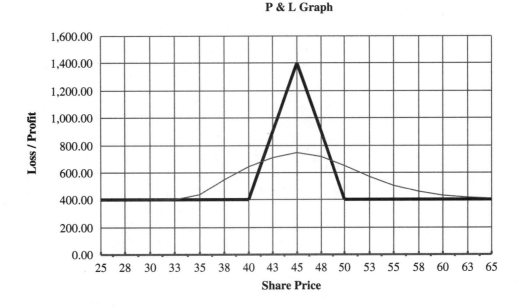

of option (with the same expiration date) is bought. This spread is used to speculate on a down trend in the market price of the underlying security. The maximum profit is reached when the underlying security falls below the strike that is sold. A bear spread can be constructed with either puts or calls.

Put Bear Spread

The investor establishes a put bear spread when he or she purchases the higher strike put and sells the lower strike put. (The investor pays a debit.)

- **Reward**—The reward in this situation is limited. The maximum profit is the difference between strike prices minus the debit amount that is paid. The maximum profit occurs when the underlying finishes, at expiration, below the lower strike price.
- **Break-even**—Stock closes upon expiration at a price that is equal to the higher strike price decreased by the amount of the debit.
- **Risk**—The risk is limited in this situation. The debit paid is the maximum loss. The outlook on this stock is moderately bearish. The maximum loss occurs when the underlying finishes above the higher strike.

Call Bear Spread

A call bear spread is established when the investor purchases the higher strike call and sells the lower strike call. (The investor collects a credit.)

- **Reward**—The reward in this case is limited. The maximum profit is the credit received. The maximum profit occurs when the underlying finishes, at expiration, below the lower strike.
- **Break-even**—The stock closes upon expiration at a price that is equal to the lower strike price increased by the amount of the credit. The maximum loss occurs when the underlying finishes, at expiration, above the higher strike.
- **Risk**—The risk is limited. The maximum loss is the difference between strike prices minus the credit received.

Outlook on Stock.   Moderately bearish. Let's consider a trader who expects a stock that is currently trading for $50 to drift lower in price (but not explosively) with an anticipated target of $44–$46 upon near-term expiration. At the same time, the trader does not wish to expose himself or herself to significant up-side risk. The near-term 55-level puts are trading for $7; the 50-level puts are trading for $4; and the 45-level puts are trading for $2. Based on an expiration value of $45, purchasing the 45-level put would risk $7 in order to make $3, while purchasing the 50-level put would risk $4 in order to make $1.

Therefore, the trader decides to purchase the 50-level put for $4 ($400) and sell the 45-level put for $2 ($200). The 45-level put will help subsidize the cost of the 50-level put. This situation represents a bear put spread. Instead of committing $4 ($400) to the position, the trader is only committing $2 ($200), or $400 − $200 = $200. The trader's maximum risk is $200 with a reward of $300. The bear spread maximum price can only be the difference of the two strikes; in this case, $5 (50-level put −45-level put = $5). Because the trader spent $2 for the spread, his or her maximum profit would be $3.

Example of a Put Bear Spread.   XYZ is trading at $50 per share. The trader buys one XYZ July 50 put for $4 ($4 × 100 = $400), then sells one XYZ July 45 put for $2 ($2 × 100 = $200). The net debit is $200.

- **Reward**—The reward potential is $300 (the difference between the strikes, which is $5, minus the amount of debit paid, which is $2).
- **Risk**—The risk potential is $200 (the price paid for the spread).
- **Break-even**—The stock closes at $48 upon expiration.

Example of a Call Bear Spread.   The trader sells one XYZ July 45 call for $7 ($7 × 100 = $700), then buys one XYZ July 50 call for $4 ($4 × 100 = $400). The net credit is $300 (see Figure 9-35).

- **Reward**—The reward potential is $300 (amount of credit received).
- **Risk**—The risk potential is $200 (the difference between the strikes, which is $5, minus the credit amount received, which is $3).
- **Break-even**—The stock closes at $48 upon expiration.

These examples illustrate both the put bear spread and the call bear spread. Notice that the profit and loss graph for each of the examples is

Figure 9-35 *Call bear spread example.*
Black line = bear spread at expiration.
Thin gray line = bear spread with 21 days to expiration.

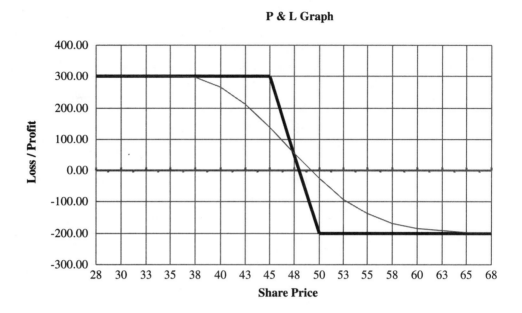

P & L Graph

Table 9-6 *Risk / Reward Profile Comparison*

Risk/Reward Profile	50–55 bear spread	45–50 bear spread
Maximum gain	$200	$300
Stock price producing maximum gain	$50 or below	$45 or below
Breakeven stock price	$52	$48
Maximum loss	$300	$200
Stock price producing maximum loss	$55 or above	$50 or above

identical. This situation again shows that puts work similarly and are actually a measurement of curvature. If you were to only view the profit and loss graph, you could determine that it is a bear spread, but you could not determine how it was created. In both examples, the 50-level option is bought and the 45-level option is sold. A market maker would look at this position and deduce that the trader is long the 50 strike and short the 45 strike. Notice how the market maker did not mention whether the position consisted of puts; rather, he or she indicated long or short curvature. Take a moment and look at the profit and loss graph to examine this phenomenon.

Let's compare the risk/reward profile of the July 50–55 put bear spread with the 45–50 put bear spread discussed previously (see Table 9-6 and Figure 9-36).

Figure 9-36   *Profit and loss graph comparison.*
              Black line =$^{45}/_{50}$ bear spread at expiration.
              Gray line =$^{50}/_{55}$ bear spread at expiration.

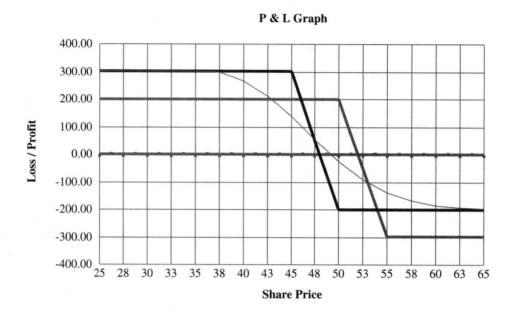

The tradeoff is clear. The 50–55 spread is much more likely to result in a profit, and that profit will be lower than the maximum profit from the 45–50 spread. In the event of a large upward move in the stock price, the potential loss will be higher for the 50–55 spread than for the 45–50 spread.

> **NOTE**
>
> The maximum gain and maximum loss numbers will depend on the actual prices of these options. The particular example that we used here involved options that had a high implied volatility. The effect of lower volatility would be to reduce the maximum gain and increase the maximum loss for the 50–55 spread and increase the maximum gain and reduce the maximum loss for the lower strike spread.

We have seen that the put and call bull spreads covering the same strikes are essentially the same spread. We also noted that there might be more than one set of strikes at which to put on the position, such as choosing between the 45–50 and 50–55 spreads that we have used as examples and discussed previously. What factors should we consider when selecting the most appropriate bull spread? Consider the following points:

1. **Selecting the strikes to use**—Compare the maximum gain/ maximum loss profiles of each set of strikes. If they are similar, then the higher strike (the 50–55 spread in our example) would be the choice. On the other hand, if the lower strike spread offers a much

greater reward with a lower loss, you could select this option (given your bearish sentiment).

2. **Puts or calls**—Based on current pricing, it might be cheaper to purchase the call spread than the put spread (or vice-versa). Remember, however, that they are the same position. There might be slight margin requirement differences between the put and call spreads. Check with your broker.

Bearish: Ratio Bear Spread (Long)

The ratio bear spread is designed to create leverage (control of downside potential) without committing as much capital as you would by purchasing the puts outright. You use this technique by purchasing puts and financing the long put position by selling a put or puts with a higher strike and price than the ones purchased. The ratio bear spread can be put on in any ratio that the trader desires: buy two, sell one; buy three, sell one; buy four, sell one; buy three, sell two; and so on. Whatever the ratio, the trader is simply purchasing more options than he or she is selling in order to create leverage at a reduced price. The long puts should always be OTM, while the short strike can be ITM, ATM, or OTM. We suggest selling the ATM to slightly OTM puts, because they will have the most premium attached. We will focus on the 3:1 ratio bear spread here. An illustration is best for this purpose.

Example.   The trader believes that stock XYZ is poised for a significant sell-off to $40 per share or lower, but he does not want to pay for the long contracts (see Figure 9-37). XYZ is trading for $50. The trader buys three XYZ July 45 puts for $1 ($1 × 3) × 100 = $300) and sells one XYZ July 50 put for $3 ($3 × 100 = $300). The net position cost is $0.

Figure 9-37   *Black line = ratio bear spread at expiration.*
Thin gray line = ratio bear spread with 21 days to expiration.

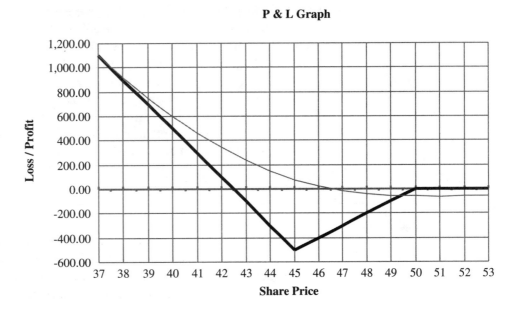

P & L Graph

Notice in the profit and loss graph that the trader has no risk if the stock closes above $50 upon option expiration. His or her position will break even. The maximum risk in the position is that the stock closes on expiration day at the strike that the trader is long (in this case, the $45 strike). If this situation occurs, the short July 50 put will be worth a debit of $5 while the long July 45 puts will expire as worthless. The maximum loss is calculated by the difference between the short strike and the long strike (adjusted for the credit/debit for which the trader put on the position). In this case, the position was put on for even, and the difference in the strikes is $5 (the 55-level put minus the 50-level put). The maximum risk is therefore $5. Remember that this graph shows the intrinsic value upon expiration, and the loss is not totally incurred until such time. The ratio bear spread is long (the put bear spread plus a long OTM put).

* **Reward**—The reward is unlimited. As the stock continues to fall through the long strike, the position incurs intrinsic value. The more puts that the trader owns, the larger his or her rate of return as the stock continues to fall.
* **Risk**—The risk is limited. The maximum risk of this position is the difference between the long and short strikes minus the credit/debit amount that the position cost in order to be put on. The maximum loss is realized when the stock closes at the strike that the trader is long the put contracts. The outlook of this stock is bearish to extremely bearish.

Managing the Position

This position does well if the stock price explodes. In the previous example, as measured at option execution, for each dollar the stock moves above $55, the July 55 puts gain $3 in value while the July 50 put loses $1 (for a net gain of $2 for each dollar move).

This position is approximately delta neutral at the beginning, with both long gamma and long vega. In other words, prior to expiration, this position will gain in value whenever volatility increases or the stock price decreases. The best result would be when the stock price decreases, causing option-implied volatility to increase. This situation tends to happen when the stock has been in a trading range and breaks out of it to the downside. This scenario is excellent for this position if the option sold is at the bottom of the trading range. If so, and if the stock stays in the trading range, then the short option will expire as worthless. On the contrary, if the stock breaks out of the range, the put volatility might explode.

Neutral Strategies

The term *neutral* as used in this chapter refers to a definite expectation that a stock or a market is directionless and is unlikely to make a substantial move in either direction during the time period that is under consideration. Neutral most definitely *does not* mean that the trader has no opinion about the immediate prospects for the stock or market as a whole. Neutral strategies are specifically designed to profit in a flat, nonvolatile market. All of these strategies involve selling options in an attempt to generate income from time decay.

Some of these strategies have limited risk; others have significant risk in one direction; and still others assume significant risk regardless of whether the stock goes up or down:

- **Limited risk**—Results from purchasing the same number of options of the same type as are sold. The potential profit comes from selling options that have more time premium and purchasing options that have less time premium. The decay of the excess premium is the anticipated source of income.
- **One-direction risk**—Results from selling more options of the same type than are purchased. In the case of such a strategy involving calls, the risk is that the stock will increase significantly in value. The imbalance in calls will result in increasing losses as the stock continues to rise in price. Where puts are used, the reverse is true. The risk is that the stock will decline substantially in price.
- **Unlimited risk**—Results when positions involving one-direction call risk are combined with one-direction put risk. In other words, more calls and more puts are sold than purchased.

Covered Call Writing/Buy Write

Covered call writing is a strategy in which an investor owns the underlying security and writes (sells) a call option against this position. A buy write is when the investor purchases the underlying security and writes (sells) a call option simultaneously. In both cases, OTM calls are most commonly sold (see Figure 9-38).

This position consists of 100 shares of stock (in this case, purchased for $88 per share and short one 90-level call for $3).

The covered call/buy write strategy is the most utilized neutral market strategy. When implemented with OTM calls, not only does it enable the investor to capture premium in a flat marketplace, but it also enables the investor to be slightly bullish at the same time. Whichever type of call is used (ITM, ATM, or OTM), the premium received from the option sale acts as an offset to a down turn in the price of the stock. This premium can be subtracted from the initial stock purchase to give the individual investor a downside break-even point. OTM calls would obviously provide less downside protection than the more expensive ITM or ATM calls.

We strongly recommend for you to sell ATM or OTM options. Remember, ITM options consist mostly of intrinsic value, so if the stock price remains unchanged or moves higher, the only gain will be the decay of the time premium (which is a small portion of the option's purchase price).

You should understand this strategy as a variation on long stock. This strategy differs from being long stock only in that the call seller has

Figure 9-38 *Covered call writing / buy write.*
Black line = Long 100 shares of stock for $88/share and short one 90 level call for $3.
Thin gray line = Long 100 shares of stock for $88/share and short one 90 level call for $3 with 21 days to expiration.

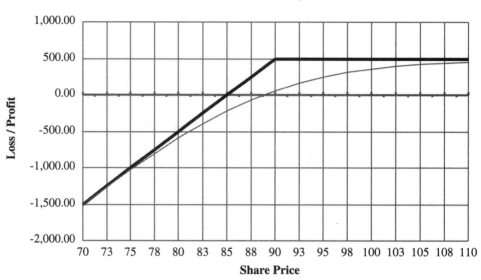

rented his or her right to gain from the price of the stock exceeding the strike price of the call for a period of time (until expiration of the call) for money. There are three potential outcomes of this position:

- If the call option expires as unexercised, the option expires and the investor is simply back to being long the stock. The investor is, however, enriched by the premium that he or she received from the sale of the option.
- If the call option finishes ITM and is not repurchased by the seller, it will be exercised and the stock will be purchased or called from the writer (seller) of the option at the option's strike price.

> **NOTE**
>
> Even in this worst-case scenario, you are still profiting from the rise in the price of the stock—just not as much as you would have if you had not sold the covered call.

- You are not bound to hold the position until the option expires. Repurchasing the option that was sold will close the option position and leave you with the long stock position with which you started. Although you might have lost money on the option, your stock would have appreciated even more. The intrinsic value of the option is offset by the stock gain.

We highlight these alternatives in the following examples.

Example Number 1. One hundred shares of XYZ stock are purchased for $75 per share, and one July 80 call is sold for $3. If upon July expiration the stock is trading at $78, the July 80 call expires as worthless. The buy write would result in a $6-per-share profit (a $3-per-share increase in the price of the stock from $75 to $78 plus the $3 per share received from selling the option). In contrast, if the stock had been purchased without selling the call, the investor would have an unrealized profit of $3 per share.

Example Number 2. One hundred shares of XYZ stock are purchased for $75 per share, and one July 80 call is sold for $3. If upon July expiration the stock is trading at $88 and the July 80 call is not repurchased, the call would be exercised and the stock would be sold for $80 per share. In this event, the buy write would result in an $8-per-share profit (a $5-per-share profit from selling the shares for $80 each when the option is exercised plus the $3 per share received from selling the option). By contrast, if the stock had been purchased without selling the call, the investor would have an unrealized profit of $13.

Example Number 3. This example is the same as the previous example, except that after several weeks (but still prior to July expiration), the stock is trading at $81 and the July 80 call is trading for $4. If the call were repurchased, while you would have lost $1 per share on the option, your stock would have gone up $6 per share for a net profit of $5 per share. Then, you would be back to owning the stock long. (If you are surprised that the option would increase by only $1 in price when the stock had increased by $6, remember that while calls increase in price as the price of the stock increases, the time premium is decaying—and several weeks have elapsed since the option was sold.) Be careful when considering repurchasing calls that have significant amounts of time premium in them. In this example, the $4 price of the July 80 call includes $3 of time premium and $1 of intrinsic value. This amount provides a $3 cushion on the upside and a $4 cushion on the downside between now and the expiration date. Repurchasing the call early makes sense when you expect a significant increase in the stock's price prior to the option's expiration.

Example Number 4. This example is the same as the previous examples, except that upon July expiration on Friday, the stock is trading at $82 and the August 85 call is trading for $4. If you do not want to have your stock called away and you want to sell another covered call, you can accomplish both tasks at once by buying back the July 80 call and simultaneously selling the August 85 call. This action is known as a roll.

Covered call writers come primarily in two stripes. First, there are those who are looking for a reasonably predictable return on their investment and who want to sell long-term options. Second, there are those who periodically sell shorter-term options in order to supplement their returns but are primarily interested in a long-term investment in a stock.

Long-Term Strategy

The first category might include someone who is managing his or her own retirement plan with a target return of at least 20 percent for each equity investment. The option of choice would likely be a LEAP. When reviewing the current prices of the LEAP options, you should separate an option's intrinsic value from its time premium. The option's time premium, not its sale price, is taken into account when calculating the potential profit of the covered call or buy write.

Let's assume that the retirement account is long 100 shares of stock XYZ and that the stock is currently trading at $99 per share. Let's further assume that the nearest-term LEAP 100-level call with about 12 months until its expiration is currently $29^{7}/_{8}$ ($29.875) bid. These calls are OTM and have no intrinsic value, which means that the price of the call is all time premium. Assume that this option was sold against the XYZ stock that was owned (see Figure 9-39):

- If the option expired as worthless, the $29.875 received per share from selling the option would represent a 30.2 percent return on the $99 current value of the stock, and the stock would still be owned.
- If the option finished ITM, the investor could either allow the stock to be called away or repurchase the call prior to its expiration so that the stock would remain in the account. If the stock were called away, the total gain would be $30.875 per share (the option premium of $29.875 plus the difference between the stock's value of $99 and the strike price of the call of $100). In either event, the return on the investment would be 31.2 percent. The choice would be up to the investor. Because this

Figure 9-39   *Black line = covered call at expiration.*
Thin gray line = covered call with 21 days at expiration.

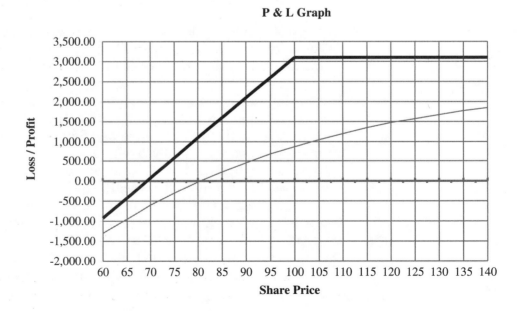

P & L Graph

example took place in a tax-deferred retirement account, tax issues would not impact the choice. If this situation occurred in a taxable account, you would need to consider the tax consequences of the alternatives. If you are faced with this choice in a taxable account, you should consult with your tax advisor prior to making a decision.

- A LEAP-covered call or buy write is a long-term investment. In other words, once the position is established, the trader generally does not actively manage it until the stock is close to expiration. One exception would be a situation in which the trader becomes concerned about a major sell-off of the stock. At this juncture, the trader might consider purchasing puts in order to protect his or her long stock position from such an event.
- Any price decline between the initiation of the position and expiration would obviously reduce the investment return. If the stock fell below $69.125, the investment would result in a loss—because the price decline would exceed the premium received from the sale of the call option.

Short-Term Strategy

Most covered calls/buy writes use OTM calls. The type of stock chosen for this strategy is one that the owner believes is unlikely to go down (at least, in the short term) and that is currently unlikely to experience explosive upward price movement. Nonetheless, the stock is a candidate for continued growth (otherwise, why hold the stock at all?). Under these circumstances, ATM calls are too likely to finish ITM. This situation would give the investor two unpalatable choices: either having the stock called away or repurchasing the calls. The ideal scenario for this type of strategy is to sell the nearest OTM on a monthly basis and to have the stock drift slowly higher. As a result, the options will never finish ITM. This situation would be a home run.

Consider the following hypothetical situation. Stock ABC is trading at $50. Your target for the stock is $60 one year from now. The implied volatility of the ABC options is 35. If the stock slowly increased to $60 and you always sold the nearest OTM call at a 35 volatility, you would collect approximately $14 in option premium (which would expire as worthless over the course of the year). This result would increase the investor's return from 20 percent if it was just based on the appreciation in the stock to $48 (including the $14 in premium captured).

This approach requires an active role for the trader, because he or she will be selling short-term calls frequently and might need to respond if the stock starts to make a large move.

Bull Spread Covered Write/Buy Write

We covered bull spreads in the section called "Bullish Strategies." In that section, we examined the purchase of 50-level calls and the selling of 55-level calls with the stock trading at $50 when we were bullish on the stock. A slight variation also works well as a neutral strategy. In this variation, with the stock trading at $50, the 45-level call would be purchased and the 50-level call would be sold. Because the 50-level call will have more time premium than the 45-level call, it will profit from time decay. Remembering our synthetics, this time decay will be the equivalent (with the stock trading at $50) of purchasing the stock and selling the 50-level call, thus putting on the buy write and then purchasing the 45-level put.

- Because the net premium received here is less than the traditional buy write's net premium because the put is purchased, this situation will produce less income than the buy write.
- This situation is offset by the fact that the position will be protected from loss should the price of the stock plummet below $45. In that event, the 45-level call might retain some value—thus further reducing the loss if that contract is sold.

Horizontal Calendar Spread

A horizontal calendar spread, frequently also referred to as a horizontal time spread, is a strategy in which an option is sold and an option of the same type and exercise price (but with a further-out expiration date) is purchased. When the outlook for the stock is neutral, the ATM call or put options are used. With a mildly bullish outlook, use the nearest strike OTM call options. A mildly bearish outlook would call for the nearest strike OTM puts. Consider the following example.

In late February, XYZ stock is trading for $90—and its options are trading with a 35 volatility. Samples of options prices are shown in Table 9-7).

Notice that the horizontal calendar spread is put on for a debit. You pay more for the farther-out option than you receive for the near-term option. If the stock does not move significantly in price by expiration of the near-term option, time will erode the price of the near-term option at a faster rate than the farther-term option—especially if the ATM options are used. This situation will widen the spread in price between the two options, producing a profit. Assuming that at March expiration, the options are still trading with 35 volatility, let's compare how several time spreads will perform when the stock closes at March expiration at $85, $90, and $95 (see Table 9-8).

You should note that if the stock remains at $90, the spreads that involve the ATM March 90 strike will perform the best. The decay of the

Table 9-7 *Samples of Options Prices*

Calls	Options	Puts	Calls	Options	Puts	Calls	Options	Puts
6.82	MAR85	1.48	8.32	APR85	2.64	9.58	MAY85	3.57
3.80	MAR90	3.45	5.47	APR90	4.78	6.80	MAY90	5.77
1.87	MAR95	6.53	3.40	APR95	7.73	4.69	MAY95	8.67

Table 9-8   *Performance of Time Spreads*

Spread	Initial Debit	March Expiration Value		
		85	**90**	**95**
MAR85P – APR85P	1.16	3.26	1.48	.58
MAR85P – MAY85P	2.09	4.52	2.64	1.45
MAR90P – APR90P	1.33	1.36	3.45	1.65
MAR90P – MAY90P	2.32	2.47	4.78	2.89
MAR90C – APR90C	1.67	1.68	3.80	2.01
MAR90C – MAY90C	3.00	3.11	5.47	3.61
MAR95C – APR95C	1.53	0.67	1.87	4.01
MAR95C – MAY95C	2.82	1.76	3.40	5.78

ATM calls is much faster than the decay of either the ITM March 85 or OTM March 95 options. If the stock drifts towards another strike, however, the spreads that perform the best are those spreads at that strike.

At expiration of the near-term option, the position could be closed out or the long option could be retained. Holding the long position could produce a substantial profit if the stock made a dramatic move in the appropriate direction (up for a call and down for a put). You risk a loss when you hold the long position (either from time decay or the stock moving in the wrong direction).

The maximum risk of this position is the full amount of the debit amount paid in order to initiate the position. A loss of this magnitude will result only if the stock moves so significantly prior to the near-term expiration that both options lose their entire premium.

You should note that these spreads are volatility sensitive. Recall from our discussion of the Greeks that the more time until expiration, the more impact that a change in volatility wields. Thus, these spreads are long vega. If volatility increases, then the longer-term options will increase more in price than the near-term options—increasing the spread and thus increasing the profit. The reverse is true if volatility declines. Compare the impact on the spreads if volatility increased to 50 or decreased to 20 just after the spreads were established (see Table 9-9).

The March 85–April 85 put spread that you just paid $1.16 for would be worth $1.85 at a 50 volatility and only $.48 at a 20 volatility. All spreads have increased in value at a 50 volatility and have lost value when volatility goes to 20. This situation indicates that these spreads would merit serious consideration when volatility is low—when the chances of a volatility increase are greater than the chances of a further decline in volatility.

Table 9-9   *Impact on the Spreads*

Spread	Initial Debit	Spread Value	
		Vol = 20	Vol = 50
MAR85P – APR85P	1.16	.48	1.85
MAR85P – MAY85P	2.09	.91	3.27
MAR90P – APR90P	1.33	.70	1.95
MAR90P – MAY90P	2.32	1.21	3.40
MAR90C – APR90C	1.67	1.03	2.27
MAR90C – MAY90C	3.00	1.86	4.05
MAR95C – APR95C	1.53	.76	2.30
MAR95C – MAY95C	2.82	1.49	4.11

Diagonal Calendar Spread

In this variation on a horizontal calendar spread, the option purchased is of the same type but not the same exercise price as the near-term option sold. In the case of a call calendar spread, the option that has the next-highest exercise price to the option sold is used. In the case of a put calendar spread, however, the option that has the next-lowest exercise price is used.

The March 90–April 85 put spread, the March 90–May 85 put spread, the March 90–April 95 call spread, and the March 90–May 95 call spread are all be examples of a vertical calendar spread.

Several important differences from the horizontal time spread result because a lower-priced option is purchased in a vertical calendar spread:

- Its initial cost is less and can even result in a credit.
- It will perform better when the stock moves in the wrong direction (down in the case of a call spread and up in the case of a put spread).
- When the stock moves strongly in the direction of the type of contract (up in the case of a call spread and down in the case of a put spread), it will perform worse because the long contract will not increase in price as quickly as the lower exercise price option used in the horizontal version. In fact, the maximum loss is the initial debit plus the difference in strike prices between the contracts sold and purchased. This situation will occur when both options become so deep ITM that there is little premium remaining in their prices. At that point, their market values will differ only by the difference in strike prices.

- If the stock does not move, this position will outperform the horizontal time spread both on an absolute basis and on the rate of return. This situation happens because there is less decay in the value of the long option used in the vertical time spread than in the horizontal time spread.

Using the pricing example from the previous discussion of horizontal calendar spreads, we can see that a comparison of the initial credit (debit) of the vertical spread to the value of the position upon March expiration at a variety of stock prices is shown in Table 9-10.

To determine the result, combine the initial credit (debit) with the value of the position upon March expiration. For example, upon March expiration with the stock closing at $85, the March 90–April 85 put spread would have resulted in a $.74 loss (the $.81 credit received initially reduced by the negative value of the position at expiration). This position does extremely well when the stock closes near the near-term strike at expiration. This position produces a profit when the stock moves against the near-term position (above the near-term put strike or below the near-term call strike) and does not fare well when the stock moves favorably for the near-term position (below the near-term put strike or above the near-term call strike).

This position is also long vega, meaning that it increases in value when volatility increases and declines in value when volatility decreases.

Straddle (Short)

A short straddle involves selling the same number of contracts of both a put and a call with the same exercise price and expiration. For example, if an investor sold a July 60 call and a July 60 put, he or she would have sold the July 60 straddle one time. Most often, the ATM straddle is utilized.

By selling the call unhedged, the investor is assuming unlimited upside risk. By selling the put unhedged, the investor is assuming unlimited (at least, until the stock goes to $0) downside risk. This combination of

Table 9-10 *Comparison of Initial Credit and Value of Position*

Spread	Initial Credit (Debit)	March Expiration Value		
		85	90	95
MAR90P – APR85P	.81	(1.55)	1.48	.54
MAR90P – MAY85P	(.12)	(.22)	2.64	1.42
MAR90C – APR95C	.40	.64	1.87	(1.20)
MAR90C – MAY95C	(.89)	1.72	3.40	.47

risk makes the short straddle position extremely risky and difficult to manage.

> **NOTE**
>
> Do not take the presence of this discussion as an endorsement of this strategy. We present this information solely to introduce the concept of the short straddle, which will be useful in the presentation of other strategies that incorporate straddles.

When considering a short straddle, the trader should calculate the break-even points of the short straddle and then compare them to his predicted stock move.

Formula: Short Straddle.   Consider the following situation in which the strike price minus the call price plus the put price equals the low break-even point and the strike price plus the call price plus the put price equals the high break-even point.

- **Reward**—The reward here is limited. If the underlying security remains between the break-even points, then the position will result in a profit. The maximum profit will result if the stock price closes at the short option strike price upon expiration.
- **Risk**—The risk is unlimited. If the underlying security rises above or falls below the break-even points, then you incur a loss. Let's consider an example.

Example of a Short Straddle.   ABC stock is trading at $71. The trader sells one ABC May 70 call for $4 and sells one ABC May 70 put for $3. The break-even points(refer to Figure 9-40) are:

- High break-even point = $77 (70 strike + $4 call premium + $3 put premium)
- Low break-even point = $63 (70 strike − $4 call premium + $3 put premium)

The theory behind the short straddle is straightforward. As long as the stock stays close to the strike that is sold, time decay works to create profit. If the stock closes at the strike that is sold upon expiration, both the call and the put expire as worthless—and the entire premium received from selling the straddle is retained. The risk is that the stock will move in one direction or another. The straddle seller is betting that the movement of the stock will be less than the combined premium obtained from selling the options. The put premium is subsidizing the call risk, and the call premium is hedging the put risk.

The formula for deciding whether the short straddle is the right position for the trader's market outlook is:

Figure 9-40 *Black line = short straddle at expiration.*
Thin gray line = short straddle with 21 days to expiration.

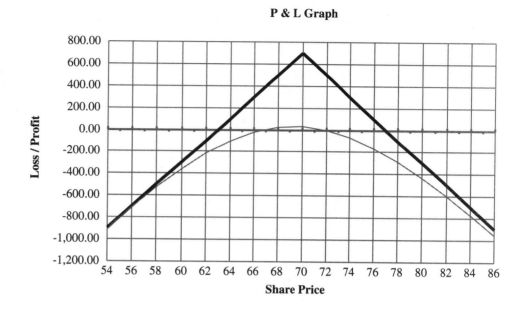

predicted stock move < option premium = short straddle

Remembering our synthetic relationships, we recall the following information:

short synthetic call = short stock + short put
short synthetic put = long stock + short call

In other words, we have two alternate ways to construct the short straddle: one, by using a synthetic put, and two, by using a synthetic call:

short synthetic straddle (synthetic put)
Sell two May 70 calls at $4
Buy 100 shares of stock at $71

The purchase of 100 shares of stock combined with the sale of one May 70 call creates a synthetic short put for $3 (Call price 4 + strike price 70 = 74 − stock price 71 = 3)

Short synthetic straddle (synthetic call)
Sell two May 70 puts at $3
Sell 100 shares of stock at $71

Figure 9-41   *Profit and loss graph.*
Black line = short synthetic straddle at expiration.
Thin gray line = short synthetic straddle with 21 days to expiration.

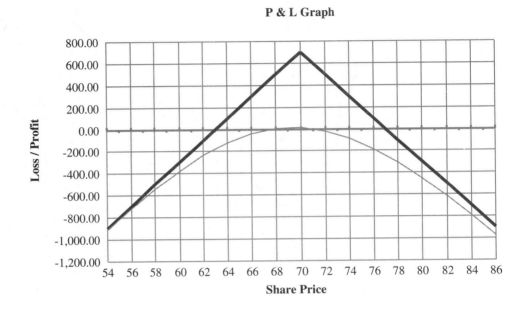

The sale of 100 shares of stock combined with the sale of one May 70 put creates a synthetic short call for $4 (Put price 3 + stock price 71 = 74 − strike price 70 = 4)

Both of these synthetically constructed short straddles have the identical risk profiles of the short straddle. By examining the profit and loss graph (see Figure 9-41), we find that it would be impossible for someone to know which way the strategy was implemented.

Managing the Position

Once you have established the position, the issue then becomes how to manage the position. Let's consider the decisions that you might have to make (see the following example and Figure 9-42).

Example.   XYZ is trading at $50. A straddle takes place when you

- Sell one XYZ July 50 call for $2.5 ($2.5 × 100 = $250).
- Sell one XYZ July 50 put for $2.75 ($2.75 × 100 = $275).
- The net credit equals $5.25 ($525).

In the example, the trader speculates that the stock will trade close to $50 by expiration. The trader has sold the straddle for $5.25, and if the stock closes upon expiration at $50, the trader will collect the entire premium. The

Figure 9-42   *Straddle example.*
              Black line = short straddle at expiration.
              Thin gray line = short straddle with 21 days to expiration.

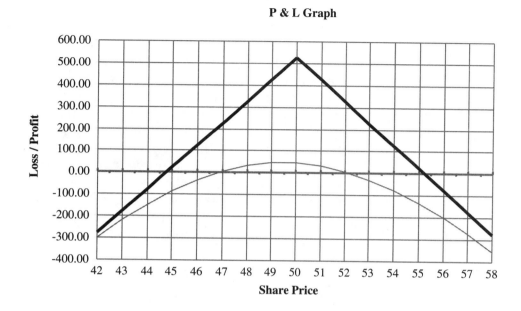

P & L Graph

trader must also calculate his or her break-even points, with the low break-even point being $44.75 ($50 − $5.25) and the high break-even point being $55.25 ($50 + $5.25). As long as the stock closes between the two break-even points and the position has not been adjusted, the trader will make a profit.

Let's assume that the stock price increases to $54. If the investor does nothing and the stock continues to run, the position will produce a loss—possibly a large loss. If the investor knew that the stock would continue to increase, the response would be simple: buy 100 shares of stock. The gain from the stock would offset the loss from the short call. In fact, if 100 shares were purchased for $54 and the stock continued to increase or stayed the same, the adjusted position (short straddle plus long stock) would result in a gain of $1.25. Take the time to check out this situation. What if the stock retreats back to $50 after the shares are purchased, however? The investor still has the potential of making $525 from the straddle, but the stock purchase has lost $400. What if the stock continues to decline? Then, you should sell the stock. But if the stock is sold, the new break-even points are $48.75 and $51.25. The position still has a substantial risk, and the reward is significantly reduced.

This example highlights the difficulty of managing a short straddle. You are constantly guessing. If the stock price is going to move away from the strike, then you should make an adjustment—but this adjustment will cost you money if the stock moves back in the other direction.

If we have not given you enough reasons to avoid selling straddles, keep in mind that brokerage firms will require a large amount of capital in order to margin this position. The risk factor is unlimited and undefined.

Strangle (Short)

A short strangle involves selling the same number of contracts of both a put and a call with different exercise prices but with the same expiration date. For example, if an investor sold a July 65 call and a July 55 put, that would be selling a strangle. Most often, the nearest OTM puts and calls are utilized. If the following discussion seems familiar, it is only because the strangle has substantially the same risk/reward profile as the straddle. The major differences are in degree, not kind. The strangle collects less premium than the straddle, so it potentially has less reward—but it makes a larger move in the price of the stock in order to create a loss (as compared to the straddle). Nonetheless, both positions are designed to make a profit when the stock is relatively docile, and both can incur substantial losses if the stock moves strongly in either direction.

By selling the call unhedged, the investor is assuming unlimited upside risk. By selling the put unhedged, the investor is assuming unlimited downside risk (at least, until the stock goes to $0). This combination of risk makes the short strangle position extremely risky and difficult to manage.

> **NOTE**
>
> Do not take the presence of this discussion as an endorsement of this strategy. We present this information here solely to introduce the concept of the short strangle, which is important for you to know for the presentation of other strategies that incorporate strangles.

As in the case of the short straddle, when considering a short strangle, the trader should calculate the break-even points of the short strangle and then compare them to his or her predicted stock move.

Here is the formula for the short straddle:

Put strike price − (call price + put price) = low break − even point

Call strike price + (call price + put price) = high break − even point

- **Reward**—The reward in this case is limited. If the underlying security remains between the break-even points, the position will result in a profit. The maximum profit will result if the stock price closes upon expiration between the put strike price and the call strike price.
- **Risk**—The risk in this case is unlimited. If the underlying security rises above or falls below the break-even points, then a loss is incurred.

Let's consider an example of a short strangle. ABC stock is trading at $71. The trader sells one ABC May 75 call for $2 and sells one ABC May 65 put for $1.50. See Figure 9-43.

Figure 9-43   *Short strangle example.*
Black line = short strangle at expiration.
Thin gray line = short strangle with 21 days to expiration.

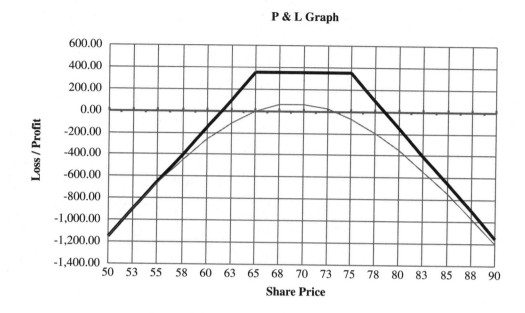

As with the short straddle, the theory behind the short strangle is straight forward. As long as the stock stays above the strike of the put and below the strike of the call, decay works to create profit. If the stock closes within this range upon expiration, both the call and the put expire as worthless—and the entire premium received from selling the strangle is retained. The risk is that the stock will move strongly in one direction or another. The straddle seller is betting that the movement of the stock outside the target range will be less than the combined premium obtained from selling the options. The put premium is subsidizing the call risk, and the call premium is hedging the put risk.

Remembering our synthetic relationships, we recall the following information:

Short synthetic call = short stock + short put

Short synthetic put = long stock + short call

In other words, we have two alternate ways to construct the short strangle: one by using a synthetic put, and the other by using a synthetic call:

Short synthetic strangle (synthetic put)
Sell one May 75 call for $2
Sell one May 65 call for $7.50
Buy 100 shares of stock at $71

The purchase of 100 shares of stock combined with the sale of one May 65 call creates a synthetic short put for $1.50 (the call price of $7.50 plus the strike price of $65 = $72.5 − the stock price of $71 = $1.50):

Short synthetic strangle (synthetic call)

Sell one May 65 put for $1.50

Sell one May 75 put for $6

Sell 100 shares of stock at $71

The sale of 100 shares of stock combined with the sale of one May 75 put creates a synthetic short call for $2:

Put price of $6 + stock price of $71 = $77 − strike price of $75 = $2

Both of these synthetically constructed short strangles have the identical risk profiles of the short strangle. By examining the profit and loss graph, we see that it would be impossible for someone to know which way the strategy was implemented (see Figure 9-44).

Managing the Position

Once you have established the position, the issue then becomes how to manage the position. Let's consider the decisions that you might have to make. See the following example and Figure 9-45.

Figure 9-44   *Profit and loss graph.*
Black line = synthetic short straddle at expiration.
Thin gray line = synthetic short straddle with 21 days to expiration.

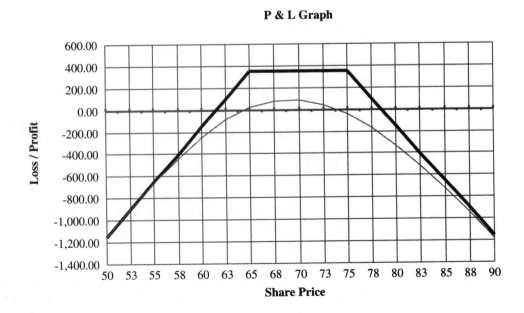

Figure 9-45   *Strangle example.*
                  Black line = short straddle at expiration.
                  Thin gray line = short straddle with 21 days to expiration.

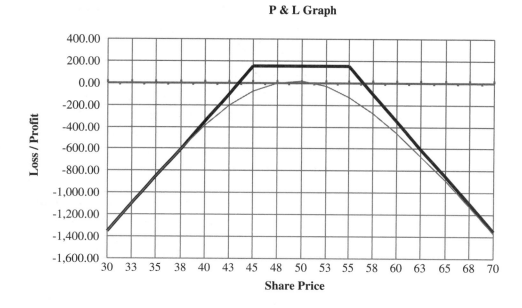

Example.   XYZ is trading at $50. The trader sells one XYZ July 55 call for $.75 ($.75 × 100 = $75). The trader sells one XYZ July 45 put for $.75 ($.75 × 100 = $75). The net credit is $1.50, or $150.

In the example, the trader speculates that the stock will trade close to $50 upon expiration. The trader has sold the strangle for $1.50. If the stock closes at expiration within the range of $45–$55, the trader will collect the entire premium. The trader must also calculate his or her break-even points, with the low break-even point being $43.50 ($45 − $1.50) and the high break-even point being $56.50 ($55 + $1.50). As long as the stock closes between the two break-even points and the position has not been adjusted, the trader will make a profit.

Let's assume that the stock price increases to $54. If the investor does nothing and the stock continues to run, the position will produce a loss—possibly a large loss. If the investor knew that the stock would continue to increase, the response would be simple: buy 100 shares of stock. The gain from the stock would offset the loss from the short call. In fact, if 100 shares were purchased for $54 and the stock continued to increase or stayed the same, the adjusted position (short strangle plus long stock) would result in a gain of $2.50. Take time to check out this situation. But what if the stock retreats back to $50 after the shares are purchased? The investor still has the potential of making $150 from the straddle, but the stock purchase has lost $400. What if the stock continues to decline? Then, you should sell the stock. But if the stock were sold, the best that the position could achieve would be a loss of $250. The position still has substantial risk, and the potential reward becomes a likely loss.

This example highlights the difficulty of managing a short strangle. You are constantly guessing. If the stock price moves away from the strike, you should make an adjustment—but this adjustment will cost you money if the stock moves back in the other direction.

Compare this situation to a short straddle. The advantage of a short strangle over the short straddle is a wider range of stock movement without the risk of exercise. The disadvantage over the short straddle is less premium to collect with the same risk parameters once the stock has broken through a break-even point.

You can form strangles at any difference between strikes. In the earlier example, the strike difference was $10, but the trader could just as easily sell the $^{40}/_{60}$ strangle (giving the individual investor a $20 window instead of a $10 window). Remember that the farther OTM that the strike is, the less premium received. The $^{40}/_{60}$ strangle might only trade .75. Each trader must determine his or her own risk-versus-reward profile and analyze the position before execution. If the trader were to sell the $^{40}/_{60}$ strangle for $^3/_4$, he or she has given himself or herself a $20 neutral berth in which he or she has no exercise risk. As soon as the stock moves through one of the strikes, however, the trader's risk becomes unlimited and uncertain. The investor must make the determination whether .75 of profit is worth the risk if the stock breaks through the strike.

Ratio Bull Spread (Short)

The short ratio bull spread is a call bull spread with another call of the same strike and expiration sold in order to further subsidize the cost of the call purchased. For example, with the stock at $50, purchasing one May 50 call and selling two May 55 calls would be a short ratio bull spread.

Of course, the ratio bull spread limits the profitability versus the short straddle, but it also reduces directional risk to the position. Some of the profit received from the sale of the calls pays for the long call of the lower strike.

If we break down this position into two separate components, we see that it is simply a bull call spread with an extra short call.

We can also break down this position into several synthetic positions. We can sell puts and sell stock, turning the puts into synthetic calls.

Example of a Ratio Bull Spread (Short).   This is a call bull spread plus a short OTM or ATM call.

- **Reward**—The reward in this instance is limited (the difference between the long and short strikes plus or minus the credit or debit of the net position).
- **Risk**—The risk in this situation is unlimited. As the stock continues past the short strike, the position continues to lose on a 1:1 ratio. The outlook on this stock is neutral (slightly bearish).

Here is another example (see Figure 9-46). XYZ stock is trading at $52.50. The trader buys one XYZ July 50 call for $3 ($3 × 100 = $300) and sells two XYZ July 55 calls for $1.75 ($1.75 × 2 × 100 = $350). The net credit in this situation equals $.50 ($50).

Figure 9-46   *Ratio bull spread (short) example.*
Black line = short ratio bull spread at expiration.
Thin gray line = short ratio bull spread with 21 days to expiration.

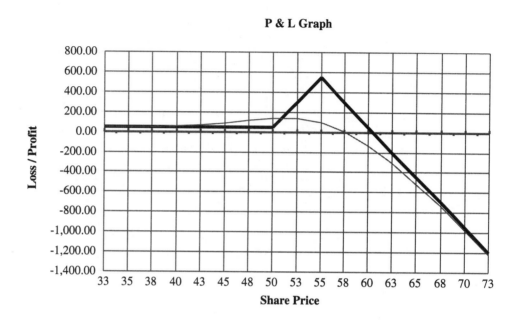

In this example, the trader believes that the stock will remain between $50 and $60. The greatest profit potential is the stock closing at $55 upon expiration. At that point, the position will be worth $5 (the July 50 call will be worth $5 and the July 55 calls will be worthless). Below $55, the July 50 call will be worth less than $5, and the July 55 calls will continue to be worthless. For each $1 increase above $55, although the July 50 call value will increase by $1, this value will be more than offset by the $2 increase in the value of the short calls. At $60, the position will break even. The July 50 call will be worth $10, and each short July 55 call will have a value of $5. Below $50, both the July 50 and July 55 calls will expire as worthless—leaving the position valued at the net debit or credit for which it was put on. Above $60, the position will show a loss.

As this example indicates, this position contains significant risk if the stock were to rise in price higher than $60. The trader must have an understanding of the risk profile and have strategies to reduce that risk if the stock were to rise. The trader might consider purchasing stock or purchasing 60-level calls if he or she is concerned that the stock might rise higher than $60. Note that purchasing a July 60 call would convert this position to a long butterfly, which we will discuss shortly.

Because the position contains a short call position, the individual investor must put up capital margin in his or her trading account.

Ratio Bear Spread (Short)

The short ratio bear spread is similar to the short ratio bull spread, only in this case, the individual investor is concerned about a dramatic rise in stock price. The trader believes that the stock will stay within a trading range throughout the life of the option position but is concerned about positive news or a positive event affecting the stock. Such positive events might be earning surprises, takeover rumors, bullish market sentiments, and so on. The formula is similar to the short ratio bull spread with one slight modification:

> Predicted stock move and option premiums = short ratio bear spread (but concerned about positive event)

The position offers a similar risk profile to the short straddle position but offers protection for upside directional risk. As the stock falls below the break-even price, the position will continue to lose money at a 1:1 ratio.

Example of a Ratio Bear Spread (Short).   This is a put bull spread plus a short OTM put.

- **Reward**—The reward in this case is limited.
- **Risk**—The risk in this situation is unlimited. The outlook on this stock is neutral (slightly bullish).

Let's look at an example (see Figure 9-47). XYZ stock is trading at \$52.5. The trader buys one XYZ July 55 put for \$3 (\$3 $\times$ 100 = \$300) and sells two XYZ July 50 puts for \$1.75 (\$1.75 $\times$ 2 $\times$ 100 = \$350). The net credit in this case is \$.50 (\$50).

Both the short ratio bull and bear spreads benefit from the stock price slowly approaching the short strike price. By increasing the ratio (the

Figure 9-47   *Ratio put spread.*
Black line = short ration bear spread at expiration.
Thin gray line = short ratio bear spread with 21 days to expiration.

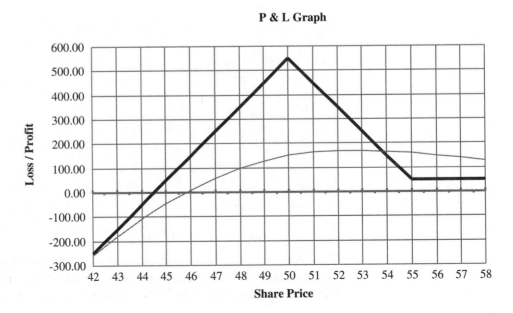

number of options sold), the investor increases his or her profit potential at the serious consequence of increasing his or her risk potential. We recommend not exceeding the 1:2 ratio (buying one and selling two).

Closing neutral strategies enables the trader to generate profit in a flat marketplace. Some of these strategies have a significant amount of delta risk (market directional risk). In each of these strategies, the goal is to collect the premium. The trader is effectively an insurance company predicting that no volatile event will occur in order for him or her to collect the premium without having to pay a claim. Let's now briefly review the risks of each of the neutral strategies.

The covered call/buy write risk is unlimited (decline in stock price until the stock reaches zero). The horizontal spread risk is limited, however (the amount paid for the spread). The vertical spread risk is also limited (the difference between the strikes plus the debit/credit of the spread). The short straddle risk is unlimited (stock rises or falls beyond the break-even points). Furthermore, the short strangle risk is unlimited (stock rises or falls beyond the break-even points), and the short ratio bull spread risk is unlimited (stock rises above the break-even point). Finally, the short ratio bear spread risk is unlimited (stock falls below the break-even point).

Volatile Strategies ("Backspread")

Options enable the trader to take positions in the marketplace that ordinarily would not be available to him or her (due to the intensive capital requirements). We have already learned how option trading enables the investor to take advantage of bullish, bearish, and neutral market sentiments in ways that are not available to those who trade in stock alone. The opportunities do not end here, however. The option investor can add to his or her arsenal an array of strategies for volatile markets, as well. Each of the strategies covered in this chapter enable the investor to take advantage of anticipated swings in the marketplace and/or increases in option-implied volatility due to anticipations of such swings.

Option strategies that are designed to profit from volatile market situations are known in the trade as backspreads. A trader whose general trading mode of operation involves implementation of these strategies is referred to as a backspreader. A backspreader is able to take a bullish and bearish stance simultaneously. Suppose that the investor's outlook on the marketplace is volatile and that he or she believes that the stock will either rise or fall in price. This speculation usually coincides with an event of uncertainty in the future, such as earnings announcements, a ruling in a court case, an upcoming Federal Reserve meeting, or other events that are likely to affect volatility. The investor concludes that the event will create uncertainty in the marketplace and would like to profit from the uncertainty. You should note, however, that with uncertainty in the marketplace, the implied volatility of an option rises—and correspondingly, the option's price rises. This situation happens for two reasons: one, because of the demand of the options as the event approaches, and two, from the event itself. Market makers, therefore, will raise the implied volatility because of the upcoming event.

Traders Guide.   There is a simple formula for determining whether a situation merits a volatile backspread strategy:

- If the predicted stock move is greater than the option's premium (known as a volatile strategy)
- If the trader deduces that the stock move will be greater than the premium on the option, then a volatile strategy is worth implementing. Remember, though, that the stock move must happen before the expiration of the option strategy in order for the strategy to be viable.

You can determine the stock move from two main sources, based on your type of trading personality. A swing or technical-analysis trader will use his or her historical data, charts, and technical analyses to predict a trading range of the stock. A position trader or market maker uses standard deviations and historical options volatility to determine this information. In either case, the results are similar—and the trader must come to his or her own conclusion about the predicted range of the stock move.

The long straddle and the long strangle are the primary strategies that traders use to profit from a volatile market. We will examine these strategies in detail in this section.

Straddle (Long)

We examined the short straddle under "Neutral Strategies" in this chapter. The long straddle is the inverse position. In a long straddle, you buy both a put and a call with the same exercise price and expiration. For example, buying 10 March 50 calls and 10 March 50 puts is referred to as buying the March 50 straddle 10 times. The most common of the volatile strategies, the straddle position enables the investor to profit from a significant price movement in the stock, regardless of its direction. If the stock declines in price, the long put appreciates in value. If the stock increases in price, the long call appreciates. If the stock move is substantial, the value of the straddle will grow. By combining both a long call and a long put position of the same strike, the individual trader is taking both bullish and bearish positions simultaneously.

When considering a long straddle, the trader should calculate the position's break-even points and then compare them to his or her predicted stock move. If the predicted stock move is $10 and the straddle is trading for $5, the trader would purchase the straddle in order to gain $5 dollars on the predicted move. If the anticipated stock move is $5, however, and the straddle is trading at $10, this option would not be a candidate for a long straddle position.

Here is the formula for the long straddle position:

Strike price − (call price + put price) = low break-even point

Strike price + (call price + put price) = high break-even point

- **Reward**—The reward in this situation is unlimited. The underlying security has to rise above or fall below the break-even points in order to realize a profit.
- **Risk**—The price risk is limited. The maximum loss is the total purchase price of the straddle. A loss is incurred if the underlying security stays between the break-even points and the position is not adjusted.

This stock's Greek exposure is gamma, vega, and theta. The outlook on this stock is volatile. The trader speculates that the stock price will make a significant move either up or down by expiration.

Example of a Long Straddle.   XYZ is trading at $50. The trader buys one XYZ July 50 call for $1.50 ($1.50 × 100 = $150) and buys one XYZ July 50 put for $1.50 ($1.50 × 100 = $150). The net debit in this case is $3 ($300). See Figure 9-48.

The break-even points are

- **High break-even point**—$53 (50 strike + $1.50 call premium + $1.50 put premium)
- **Low break-even point**—$47 (50 strike − $1.50 call premium − $1.50 put premium)

Figure 9-48   *Long straddle.*
Black line = long 1 July 50 call for $1.5 ($1.5 × 100 = $150).
Long 1 July 50 put for $1.5 ($1.5 × 100 = $150) at expiration.
Thin gray line = Long 1 July 50 call for $1.5 ($1.5 × 100 = $150).
Long 1 July 50 put for $1.5 ($1.5 × 100 = $150) with 21 days to expiration.

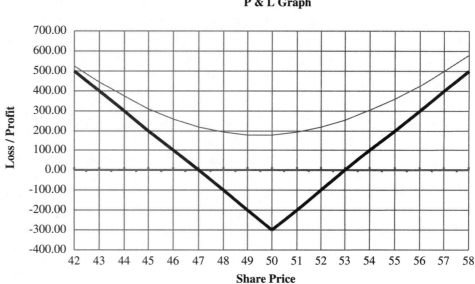

P & L Graph

There are numerous ways to establish a straddle synthetically. The following list shows some examples:

- Buying 20 March 50 calls and selling 1,000 shares of stock. The selling of 1,000 shares of stock combined with 10 March calls creates 10 synthetic puts. Thus, the trader has 10 March 50 calls and 10 synthetic March 50 puts.
- Buying 20 March 50 puts and buying 1,000 shares of stock. The purchase of 1,000 shares of stock combined with 10 March 50 puts creates 10 synthetic calls. Thus, the trader has 10 March 50 puts and 10 synthetic March 50 calls.

Both of these synthetically constructed long straddles have the identical risk/reward profile of the long straddle. By examining the profit and loss graph, we find that it would be impossible for someone to know which way the strategy was implemented. Although this situation indicates that (in theory) it does not matter how the position is constructed, where margins are important, margin requirements will be much higher for the synthetic straddles because they involve stock positions (which carry with them high margin requirements).

Market Risks: Analyzing the Greeks

Let's assume that the ATM straddle is purchased. Because the position involves both a put and a call of the same strike and expiration, we know the following information:

- **Delta**—With both options being ATM, their deltas will initially offset each other so that the position should start off having close to zero deltas. The straddle will not initially have a directional bias.
- **Gamma**—Both the put and the call have positive gamma. If the call goes ITM, its delta will increase—and the put's negative delta will move closer to zero (with the net result being that the position will become increasingly long delta as the stock moves higher). Conversely, as the price of the stock declines below the strike, the negative deltas of the put will be getting larger while the positive deltas of the call are decreasing. This situation will result in increasing short deltas as the stock goes lower. The value of the straddle will respond favorably to price movement away from the strike. Conversely, movement back towards the strike price will generally reduce the straddle's value.
- **Theta**—Both contracts are subject to time decay. Time is the enemy of the straddle.
- **Vega**—Both contracts are long vega. If volatility increases, so will their respective prices. If volatility declines, their prices will decline as well. Price is sensitive to changes in implied volatility. The more time until expiration, the greater the effect.

Managing a Long Straddle

Some strategies are not high maintenance. They are put on based on a set of expectations, and the anticipated events either happen or do not happen. The position either works or does not work. A common mistake that many inexperienced investors (and occasionally, professional traders) make is to treat a straddle as one of these strategies. Straddles do not fall into that category. Although anticipated price movement might be the reason for putting on a straddle, a sudden increase in implied volatility might produce an instant profit without stock movement. The stock might start to move, perhaps erratically, prior to any newsworthy event. For these reasons, you should closely monitor and adjust the position. Let's examine a hypothetical straddle.

Example.   XYZ is trading at $50. Implied volatility is 35, and there are 60 days until July expiration. The July 50 call is purchased for $3, and the July 50 put is purchased for $2.63. Thus, the straddle is purchased for a debit of $5.63. Note that if the implied volatility immediately contracted to 25, the value of the straddle would be reduced to $4.05—while if the implied volatility suddenly expanded to 45, the straddle would be worth $7.22. In this latter case, the position could be liquidated for a quick profit of $1.59. Getting back to our hypothetical example, assume that after one week the stock is trading for $45 and the volatility remains at 35. The straddle would be worth $6.42 ($5.57 for the put and $.85 for the call), and the position would have a delta of −50 (−75 delta for the put and +25 delta for the call). We have three choices:

1. **Liquidate the position**—We could lock in a profit of $.69 ($69) by selling the puts and calls.
2. **Adjust the position**—The adjustment would depend on our current expectation of the stock. We have three adjustments that would recover at least $250 of our initial investment in the straddle of $563:

    a. **Sell the put**—If we are bullish, we can sell the put and recover virtually all of our initial investment. If the price of the stock does rise (subject to time decay), the call will rise in value. The maximum loss is $6 (the initial straddle purchase price of $563 offset by the sale of the put for $557). The upside potential only remains. As measured upon expiration, we are long 100 shares above $50 and have no position below $50.

    b. **Contract neutral**—If we are bullish, we could buy 100 shares of stock at $45. Purchasing the shares would achieve two things: first, it would convert the put into a synthetic call, and second, it would lock in a minimum value for the position of $500 at expiration. (If the stock closed at expiration at $45, the put would be worth $5; the call would be worthless; and the stock would be unchanged.) For each $1 below $45 that the stock closed at expiration, the loss from the stock would be completely negated by the increase in the value of the put over $5 and the call would remain worthless. The value of the position would remain at $500. For each $1 above 45 and up to $50 that the stock closed at expiration, the put contract would lose $100 in value (which would be offset by the increase in the value of the stock, leaving the value of the position also at $500). Above $50, after the put became worthless, it would stop offsetting the gain in the stock. Both the stock and the call would add value to the position. For example, if the stock closed at $52, the call would be worth $2; the stock would show a $700 profit; and the put would be worthless (for a position value of $9). The maximum loss is $63 (initial straddle purchase price of $563 offset by the minimum value of the adjusted position at expiration of $500). The upside potential only remains. As measured at expiration, the position is long 100 shares below $50 and long 200 shares above $50.

c. **Delta neutral**—If we were unsure, then the approach taken by most professional options traders would be to buy 50 shares of stock and become delta neutral. Because we still own contracts, we are therefore still long gamma—and movement in either direction will benefit our position. The effect of purchasing the 50 shares is to guarantee a position value upon expiration of no worse than $250. This worst-case result would occur if the stock closed upon expiration at exactly $50. Both the put and the call would expire as worthless, but our 50 shares would have gained $5 in price for a total gain of $250. Notice that if after purchasing the 50 shares the price declined from $45 to $40 upon expiration, the position would be worth $750 ($1,000 value for the put and a $250 loss on the stock). If, on the other hand, the stock reversed and closed upon expiration at $55, the position would have a value of $1,000 ($500 from the call and $500 worth of profit from the 50 shares that appreciated in value from $45 to $55). The maximum loss is $313 (initial straddle purchase price of $563 offset by the minimum value of the adjusted position at expiration of $250). This position has both upside and downside potential. As measured at expiration, this position is short 50 shares below $50 and long 150 shares above $50.

3. **Do nothing**—We could do nothing and hope that the stock continues to lose value. The maximum loss is the entire investment of $563. Both upside and downside potentials remain. As measured at expiration, this position is short 100 shares below $50 and long 100 shares above $50.

Let's compare the results of a delta-neutral adjustment and a do-nothing investor in the case of a stock that oscillates up and down around the $50 mark, finally closing upon expiration at $50. If we never adjust, both the put and the call will expire as worthless—and our entire investment will be lost. Contrast that situation with delta adjustments each time the stock reaches either $45 or $55. Assume for simplicity that the net delta of the straddle (not counting any stock adjustments) was −50 with the stock at $45 and +50 whenever the stock reached $55. Let's further assume that the stock went to $45, then up to $55, then back down to $45, then back up to $55, and then closed at expiration at $50. The first time that the stock reached $45, 50 shares would be purchased to become delta neutral. At $55, the position would be long 100 deltas (50 deltas from the straddle and 50 from the stock purchased at $45). The 50 shares previously purchased for $45 would be sold for a profit of $500, and an additional 50 shares would be sold short in order to become delta neutral. When the stock next reached $45, the position would be short 100 deltas—so 100 shares would be purchased in order to return the position to delta neutral. This situation would result in another profit of $500 derived from repurchasing the 50 shares sold short at $55. When the stock returned to $55, the position would be long 100 deltas again—resulting in the sale of the 50 shares purchased at $45 (for a profit of $500) and the short sale of 50 more shares in order to return the position to delta neutral. When the stock closed at expiration at $50, both the puts and the calls would expire as worthless—but the 50 shares sold short at $55 could be repurchased for another $250 gain. The result of this scenario would be that the delta-neutral adjuster, although the calls and puts both expired as worthless, made $1,750 through his or her stock adjustment for a net profit of $1,087. In contrast, the non-adjuster lost his or her entire investment of $563.

A straddle will accumulate short deltas as the stock decreases in price, enabling the investor to purchase the underlying stock, and will accumulate long deltas as the underlying increases in value, enabling the trader to sell the stock.

Strangle Long. In the long strangle, a put at a lower strike price and a call at a higher strike price—both with the same expiration date—are purchased. Generally, they are two strikes apart (the nearest strikes to the ATM strike). For example, purchasing one July 45 put and one July 55 call would constitute a strangle. In this example (the July 45–55 strangle), the strangle position is similar to the straddle except that the capital outlay is significantly smaller than for the straddle (because OTM options carry significantly lower premiums than the ATM options that are typically used to construct straddles). The tradeoff is the increased likelihood that the position will lose money and the fact that a smaller profit will result when a large stock move does occur.

> **NOTE**
>
> If the low break-even and high break-even points of the straddle and strangle are close to each other, the strangle will produce virtually the same profit with less capital at risk.

Here are the formulas:

Put strike price − (call price + put price) = low break-even point

Call strike price + (call price + put price) = high break-even point

- **Reward**—The reward in this situation is unlimited. The underlying security has to rise above or fall below the break-even points in order to realize a profit.

Figure 9-49 *Long strangle example.*
Black line = long 1 July 55 call for $.75 ($.75 × 100 = $75).
Long 1 July 45 put for $.75 ($.75 × 100 = $75).
Thin gray line = long 1 July 55 call for $.75 ($.75 × 100 = $75).
Long 1 July 45 put for $.75 ($.75 × 100 = $75) with 21 days until expiration.

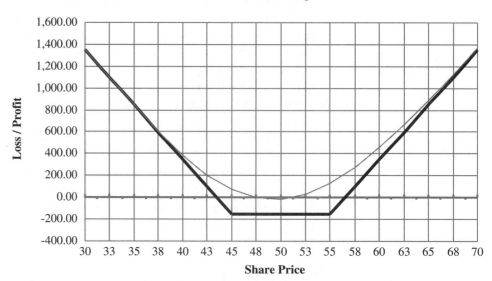

- **Risk**—The price risk here is limited. The maximum loss is the total purchase price of the strangle that will result if the stock is trading between the break-even points upon expiration.

The Greek sensitivity in this situation is gamma, vega, and theta. The outlook on this stock is volatile.

The trader is speculating that the stock price will make an extreme move either up or down by expiration.

Example of a Long Strangle (see Figure 9-49).   XYZ stock is trading at $50. The trader buys one XYZ July 55 call for $.75 ($.75 × 100 = $75) and buys one XYZ July 45 put for $.75 ($.75 × 100 = $75). The net debit is $1.50, or $150.

The break-even points are

Low break-even point = $43.50 (50 strike − $1.50 call premium − $1.50 put premium)

High break-even point = $56.50 (50 strike + $1.50 call premium + $1.50 put premium)

Market Risks: Analyzing the Greeks

Strangles have a similar Greek sensitivity to straddles. The following discussion is therefore the same as the previous discussion about straddles. Let's assume that the stock is trading at $50 and that the 45–55 strangle is purchased. Because the position involves both a put and a call that have the same expiration date, we know the following information:

- **Delta**—Because both options are OTM and are equally away from the current stock price, their deltas will initially offset each other so that the position should start off having close to zero deltas. The strangle will not initially have a directional bias.
- **Gamma**—Both the put and the call have positive gammas. Hence, as the underlying stock increases in price, the delta of the call will increase and the put's negative delta will move closer to zero. The net result is that the position will become increasingly long delta as the stock moves higher. Conversely, as the price of the stock declines, the negative deltas of the put will increase while the positive deltas of the call will decrease, resulting in increasing short deltas as the stock goes lower. The value of the strangle will respond favorably to price movement away from the ATM strike. Conversely, movement back towards the ATM strike price will generally reduce the strangle's value.
- **Theta**—Both contracts are subject to time decay. Time is the enemy of the strangle.
- **Vega**—Both contracts are long vega. If volatility increases, so will the contracts' respective prices. If volatility declines, their prices will decline as well. Price is sensitive to changes in implied volatility. The more time until expiration, the greater the effect.

Managing a Long Strangle

The long strangle is commonly a low-maintenance position because it is generally put on based on the expectation of an extreme move in the underlying stock. In comparison to the long straddle position, the probability of the long strangle position making money is decreased. Although similar to the long strangle in that a sudden increase in implied volatility might produce a profit without stock movement, the impact of the value of the option will not be as large because the options are OTM. Therefore, as the stock might start to move (perhaps erratically) prior to a newsworthy event, the position will generally still require a large move in the underlying stock in order to show a substantial profit.

The trader is looking for movement in the stock (just like the straddle) and can lock in his or her profit in the same three ways that we described in the straddle position:

1. **Contract neutral**—Selling/buying stock against the calls/puts on a 1:1 ratio; converting all calls to synthetic puts or all of the puts to synthetic calls
2. **Delta neutral**—Selling/buying stock against the calls/puts on a delta-neutral ratio; converting some of the calls to synthetic puts or puts to synthetic calls (thus giving the trader more profit potential if the stock were to continue in the same direction)
3. **Selling out the call or put**—Capturing intrinsic value and some premium and keeping the call/put for a free play in the other direction. The trader also has the ability to sell the straddle short, thus legging into the iron butterfly position (discussed later in this chapter).

Volatile Strategy Summary

Options are versatile tools that enable the trader to take a position in the marketplace regardless of directional move. These volatile strategies are used in the marketplace when the trader believes that the stock will make a significant move but is uncertain about direction.

The formula for all of these strategies is

$$\text{Stock move} > \text{option premium} = \text{volatile strategy}$$

The straddle and the strangle are used when the trader is speculating on an extreme move in the market, regardless of direction, and that implied volatility is low. These positions can be traded as is and are rather simple to maintain. The risk to these positions is the net debit that the trader has paid for the position.

Each of these positions can be designed in several ways by using synthetics, spreads, or building blocks. These are the basic foundations of volatile strategies, and the trader can design his or her own strategies to suit his or her particular market outlook.

Some common questions are

- *Should I always buy straddles?*

   The answer is no. Analyze the stock. If the trader's speculation is that the stock will not move, then he or she should not purchase the straddle. Use the formula to help you decide whether the straddle is worth buying.
- *Should I buy strangles instead of straddles?*

   The answer is, "It depends." The strangle requires less capital commitment, but you have a greater likelihood of losing all of your capital if the stock does not move beyond one of the OTM options. The straddle costs more, but you have a greater chance of recouping some of the cost because there is a good chance that either the straddle call or the put will finish ITM. If you want to sell straddles, you should purchase a strangle first. The strangle offers insurance for the short straddle position (see the butterfly section).
- *When do you purchase a straddle or a strangle?*

   You must consider several factors:

   1. Is there an upcoming event that you believe will have an effect on the stock price (for example, earnings, news, and so on)?
   2. When will this event occur? What expiration month corresponds to the anticipated event (January, February, March, and so on)?
   3. Is the price of the straddle or strangle worth purchasing? Do you anticipate that the stock move will be greater than then the price of the position?

Buy straddle = predicted stock move > premium of the straddle

Buy strangle = predicted stock move > (premium of the strangle
   + difference between the strikes)

The Truth about Butterflies

The butterfly and its close relatives, the iron butterfly and the condor, are distinctive strategies that are worthy of their own discussions. Although we will discuss each of them—both in their long and short versions— some general observations about these strategies will help put the discussions into context:

- All of them are combinations of other spreads that we have already analyzed—Butterflies and condors are bull spreads and bear spreads combined, while the iron butterfly is the combination of a straddle and a strangle.
- All of them involve selling exactly as many options of the same type as are purchased.
- All of them are limited risk, limited reward positions.
- In order to be established at favorable prices, all of them need to be legged into—in theory, you could place an order to buy or sell one of these positions. In practice, however, no floor trader will offer to fill such an order at any appreciable discount from posted prices.
- In addition to being discrete strategies on their own, they each are also potential risk-management adjustments to other strategies. For example, if you started with the 45–50 call bull spread and the stock rallied up, one of your options would be to sell the 50–55 call bear spread—thus converting your bull spread into a long butterfly.

We will discuss six different strategies in this section: long butterfly, short iron butterfly, long condor, short butterfly, long iron butterfly, and short condor. The first three positions are designed to profit from a flat, directionless (neutral) market; the latter three will profit from a substantial price movement regardless of direction. We will first examine the neutral market spreads and then turn our attention to the volatile market strategies.

Neutral Strategies

Butterfly (Long).   A long butterfly consists of buying one contract each at the lowest and highest of the three consecutive strikes while simultaneously selling two contracts of the middle strike.

The formula for a long butterfly is to buy one, sell two, and buy one (which equals the debit paid).

- **Reward**—The reward here is limited. The difference between the consecutive strike prices minus the debit paid equals the maximum profit (which occurs if the options expire with the underlying security trading at the short strike).
- **Risk**—The risk is limited (the total debit paid for the butterfly lost if the options expire with the underlying security trading either above or below long strikes).

The outlook on this stock is neutral. The trader speculates that the stock price will be near the middle strike upon expiration.

Example of a Long Call Butterfly. XYZ is trading at $50. The trader buys one XYZ July 45 call for $5.75 ($5.75 × 100 = $575). The trader then sells two XYZ July 50 calls for $2.75 ($2.75 × 2 × 100 = $550). The trader finally buys one XYZ July 55 call for $.75 ($.75 × 100 = $75). The net debit is $1 ($100).

- **Reward**—The reward is $4 (the difference between consecutive strikes, which is $5, minus the debit paid, which is $1).
- **Risk**—The risk is $1, and the break-even prices are

  - Low break-even: $46
  - High break-even: $54
  - Profit range: $46–$54

Example of a Long Put Butterfly (see Figure 9-50). XYZ is trading at $50. The trader buys one XYZ July 55 put for $5.75 ($5.75 × 100 = $575) and sells two XYZ July 50 puts for $2.75 ($2.75 × 2 × 100 = $550). The trader then buys one XYZ July 45 put for $.75 ($.75 × 100 = $75). The net debit is $1 ($100).

- **Reward**—The reward is $4 (the difference between consecutive strikes, which is $5, minus the debit paid, which is $1).
- **Risk**—The price risk is $1. The break-even prices are

Figure 9-50   *Long put butterfly.*
Black line = long butterfly at expiration.
Thin gray line = long butterfly with 21 days at expiration.

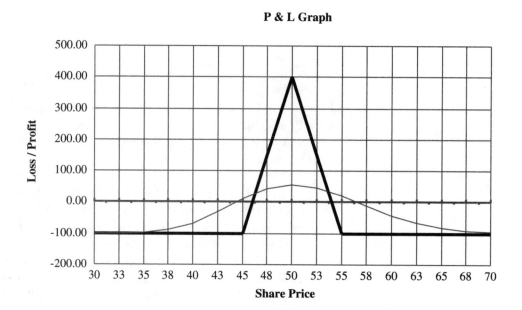

- Low break-even price: $46
- High break-even price: $54
- Profit range: $46–$54.

The attraction of the long butterfly is clear in this graph. If your expectation that the stock price will remain around $50 is accurate, this position will not only be profitable but will also generate a tremendous return on your investment. If you are wrong, then your maximum loss is the amount that you paid in order to establish the position. In this example, the position is profitable if the stock closes at expiration between $46 and $54 with a maximum profit of $4 if the stock closes at $50 (versus a maximum loss of $1 if the stock closes at $45 or lower or $55 or higher).

If investing $1 to possibly return $5 offers an attractive payoff, consider how much better the investment would be if the cost of the position were $.25. The reward would be a maximum of $4.75 with a $.25 risk. In other words, for the same risk (putting the position on four times for $.25 each, rather than one time for $1), you have more than four times the reward.

Establishing the Position. Is it possible to establish a long butterfly for such a small debit or even for a credit? The answer is most certainly yes, but you can only perform this action by constructing the position in pieces and by correctly anticipating the next move of the stock. Let's offer you two ways to achieve this goal by using our example as the factual backdrop:

1. Note that whether you are referring to a long call or to a long put butterfly, the position is actually two spreads combined: a bull spread at the lower strike and a bear spread at the higher strike. Thus, the position can be put on in these two pieces. If you thought that the stock was more likely to increase in price than decrease in the near term, you would leg into the butterfly by starting with the bull spread leg (either the 45–50 bull call spread or the 45–50 bull put spread). If you thought that a decline was imminent, you would start with the bear spread leg (either the 50–55 bear put spread or the 50–55 bear call spread). Obviously, if your initial leg of the butterfly involved puts, you would use the appropriate puts to complete a put butterfly. Furthermore, if a call spread were used as the initial leg, then you would use the appropriate calls to complete the call butterfly. It is possible to use synthetics to create a butterfly.

   a. If you were correct and the stock did increase in price, the remaining leg should be available at a more favorable price. For example, if you had started with the 40/50 bull call spread leg the 50-level call that you will be selling (having more deltas than the 55-level call that you will be buying) should have increased more in price than the 55-level call. Therefore, the remaining call bear spread will generate a larger credit than prior to the stock run-up. Also, if you had put on the 50/55 bear put spread first, the decline in price would have reduced the price of the 45–50 put bull spread.

    b. If you were incorrect and the stock moved in the wrong direction, you would need to decide whether to continue with your initial strategy and complete the butterfly, liquidate the position at a loss, do nothing, or adjust your leg in some other way. For example, if you had put on the 45–50 bull spread and saw the stock decline, you might consider selling another 50-level call and converting the position to a ratio call spread (short).

2. More aggressively, if you thought that the stock was going to rise first, you would start with the purchase of the 45-level call. After the stock rose, you would then quickly sell two 50-level calls and buy one 55-level call. If you thought that the stock was going to decline in price first, you would start with the purchase of the 55-level put. Then, after the stock sold off, you would quickly sell two 50-level puts and buy one 45-level put. Either of these techniques might result in putting the position on for even or possibly for a credit, meaning no risk of loss.

Successful legging into a butterfly requires you to create a profitable first leg. Note that each first leg discussed earlier represents a previously discussed strategy: a bull spread, a bear spread, and the purchase of a naked call. This information highlights an important aspect of butterflies and their close relatives—that they are methods by which other strategies can be adjusted, as well as initial strategies in their own right. For example, if you establish a bull spread or a naked call purchase that has become profitable, as an alternative to liquidating the position in order to make your profit, you can consider converting it into a butterfly.

We now turn our attention to the sibling of the butterfly: the iron butterfly.

Iron Butterfly (Short).   A short iron butterfly involves selling a straddle and buying the related strangle. The formula is

Selling the ATM straddle and buying the OTM strangle = receiving a credit

- **Reward**—The reward is limited. The entire credit is retained if the stock price is at the straddle option strike upon expiration. Profit is reduced dollar for dollar for each dollar that the stock price closes upon expiration from the straddle option price.
- **Risk**—The risk is limited. The price difference between the straddle strike and a strangle strike minus the credit received equals the maximum loss if the stock price rises above or falls below either strangle strike.

The outlook on this stock is neutral. The trader speculates that the stock price will remain between the two long OTM strangle strikes.

Figure 9-51   *Short iron butterfly.*
              Black line = short butterfly at expiration.
              Thin gray line = short butterfly with 21 days to expiration.

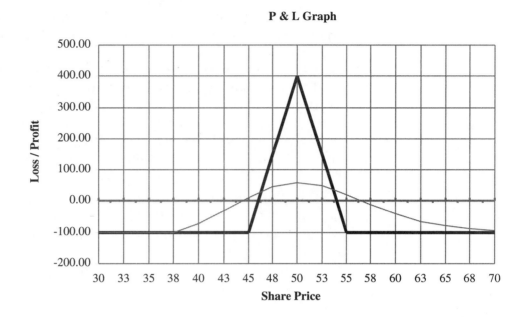

P & L Graph

Example of a Short Iron Butterfly (see Figure 9-51). XYZ stock is trading at $50. The trader buys one XYZ July 45 put for $.75 ($.75 × 100 = $75) and sells one XYZ July 50 put for $2.75 ($2.75 × 100 = $275). The trader then sells one XYZ July 50 call for $2.75 ($2.75 × 100 = $275) and buys one XYZ July 55 call for $.75 ($.75 × 100 = $75). The net credit is $4 ($400).

The break-even prices are

Low break-even price: $46

High break-even price: $54

Profit range: $46–$54

If this graph looks remarkably similar to the **graph of the long but-terfly, you are correct. The short iron butterfly is not only a sibling to the butterfly, but it is also an identical twin. This result is clear if you remem-ber several points that we made previously:

- A put bull spread and a call bull spread using the same strikes have the same risk/reward profile.
- A put bear spread and a call bear spread using the same strikes have the same risk/reward profile.
- A long butterfly is a bull spread at the lower strike and a bear spread at the higher strike.

Instead of viewing the iron butterfly (short) as purchasing the strangle and selling the straddle, let's combine the options in a different way: puts with puts and calls with calls. We then have a combination of the 45–50 put bull spread and the 50–55 call bear spread—a bull spread at the lower strike and a bear spread at the higher strike (in other words, a long butterfly). Thus, the only real difference between the two strategies is which options are used. The butterfly uses either all calls or all puts while the short iron butterfly uses a combination of calls and puts.

If a $4 credit offers an attractive payoff, consider how much better the investment would be if the credit were $4.75. The reward would be a maximum of $4.75 with a $.25 risk. In other words, for the same risk (putting the position on four times for a $.25 risk each time, rather than one time for a $1 risk), you have more than four times the reward.

Establishing the Position. Is it possible to establish a short iron butterfly for such a large credit? The answer is most certainly yes, but you can only perform this action by constructing the position in pieces and correctly anticipating the next move of the stock. Similar alternatives to options that we discussed for legging into a long butterfly are available for legging into a short iron butterfly:

1. If you thought that the stock was more likely to increase in price than decrease in the near term, you would first put on the bull 45–50 put spread. Then, after the stock had risen, you would complete the position by acquiring the bear 50–55 call spread. If you thought a decline was imminent, you would first put on the bear 50–55 call spread and follow it with the bull 45–50 put spread after the decline had occurred.

   a. If you were correct, then the remaining leg should be available at a more favorable price. If you had put on the bull spread, the 50-level calls that have more delta than the 55-level calls should have increased more in price than the 55-level calls. Hence, the remaining bear spread will generate a larger credit than prior to the stock run-up. If you had put on the bear spread first, the decline in price would have increased the credit of the 45–50 bull put spread.

   b. If you were incorrect and the stock moved in the wrong direction, you would need to decide whether to continue with your initial strategy and complete the butterfly, liquidate the position at a loss, do nothing, or adjust your leg in some other way. For example, if you put on the 45–50 bull put spread and saw the stock decline, you might consider selling another 50-level put and converting the position to a ratio put spread (short).

2. More aggressively, if you thought that the stock was going to rise first, you would start with the purchase of the 55-level call. After the stock rose, you would then quickly buy one 45-level put, sell one 50-level call, and sell one 50-level put. This technique will not produce the same results as purchasing the 45-level call as the first leg of the long call butterfly, however, because the 45 call (being ITM) has a much greater delta than the OTM 55 call. Therefore, for a comparable increase in the underlying asset, the 45 call would increase in

price more than the 55 call and would thus reduce the net cost of the butterfly. There would have to be a dramatic increase in the stock price before the increase in the price of the 55 call would reduce the net cost of the iron butterfly to even.

3. The trader may also speculate on the implied volatility being low and purchase the strangle. As the implied volatility rises, the option's premium increases. The trader then sells the straddle at the higher volatility, thus selling the straddle at higher premiums. The net result is a long iron butterfly.

We now turn our attention to the cousin of the butterfly and the iron butterfly: the condor.

Condor (Long). A long condor consists of buying one contract each of the outside strikes of four consecutive strikes while simultaneously selling one contract each of the inside strikes. One of these inside strikes should be the ATM strike. The options must all be of the same type and expiration date. You can use this strategy with all calls or all puts, because it will accomplish the same results.

Buy one + sell one + sell one + buy one = debit paid

- **Reward**—The reward in this situation is limited. The interval between the consecutive strike prices minus the debit paid equals the maximum profit, which you can achieve if the underlying security is within the two short strikes upon expiration.
- **Risk**—The risk is limited. The debit is paid for the condor if the options expire with the underlying security above the highest strike or below the lowest strike.

The outlook on this stock is neutral. The trader is speculating that the stock price will remain between the two long strikes.

Example of a Long Call Condor. XYZ is trading at $50. The trader buys one XYZ July 45 call for $5.75 ($5.75 × 100 = $575) and sells one XYZ July 50 call for $2.75 ($2.75 × 100 = $275). The trader then sells one XYZ July 55 call for $1.25 ($1.25 × 100 = $125) and buys one XYZ July 60 call for $.50 ($.50 × 100 = $50). The net debit is $2.25 ($2.25 × 100 = $225).

The break-even prices are

Low break-even price: $47.25

High break-even price: $57.75

Profit range: $47.25–$57.75

Example of a Long Put Condor (see Figure 9-52). XYZ is trading at $50. The trader buys one XYZ July 60 put for $10.50 ($10.50 × 100 = $1,050) and sells one XYZ July 55 put for $6.25 ($6.25 × 100 = $625). The

Figure 9-52   *Long put condor.*
               Black line = long condor at expiration.
               Thin gray line = long condor with 21 days to expiration.

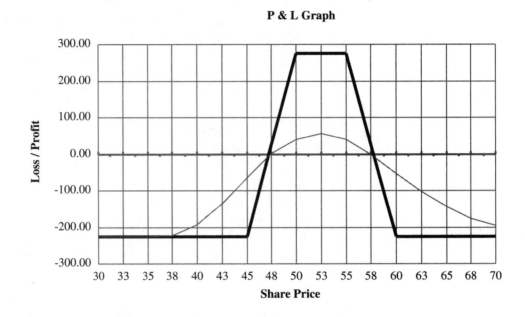

P & L Graph

trader then sells one XYZ July 50 put for $2.75 ($2.75 × 100 = $275) and buys one XYZ July 45 put for $.75 ($.75 × 100 = $75). The net debit is $2.25 ($2.25 × 100 = $225).

The break-even prices are

Low break-even price: $47.25

High break-even price: $57.75

Profit range: $47.25–$57.75

Comparing the risk/reward profile of the long condor to the long butterfly or short iron butterfly, we find the following:

• The condor is more costly to put on, so the **maximum profit is less.** The maximum profit is the difference between the strikes ($5 in our examples) reduced by the cost of the position. The condor is more costly. For example, in the case of the call spread, it differs from the butterfly in that although it contains the identical bull spread (a debit spread), its bear spread (a credit spread) involves higher OTM strikes than the butterfly (the 55-60 bear call spread versus the 50–55 bear call spread in the examples we have been using). This situation will always produce a smaller credit.

• The condor will result in a profit over a wider range of stock prices. The maximum profit results from the stock closing upon expiration at any point between the two interior strikes.

Establishing the Position.   In our experience, a long condor is not a position that you would set out to establish. Rather, this position is generally legged into or initiated as two separate positions. Furthermore, any time that this position could be established at attractive prices, the butterfly or iron butterfly would be available for a small debit or even a credit. The disparity in risk versus reward between these positions would always make the butterfly more attractive. There are circumstances in which a condor might make an attractive adjustment to an existing options position, and that is the context in which we will next examine this position.

We will use the prices in our long call condor example. Assume that we had purchased one July 50 call for $2.75 with the stock trading at $50. Let's further assume that almost immediately the stock climbed to $55 and that the July 50 call was trading at $5.75, the July 55 call was trading at $2.75, the July 60 call was trading at $1.25, and the July 65 call was trading at $.50. Let's further assume that we believe the stock has more room to run. Let's compare adjusting the position by turning it into the 45–50–55 call butterfly versus the 45–50–55–60 condor. The butterfly would be established for a $1.50 credit (bought one July 50 call for $2.75, sold two July 55 calls for $2.75 each, and bought one July 60 call for $1.25). Conversely, the condor would be established for a $.75 credit (bought one July 50 call for $2.75, sold one July 55 call for $2.75, sold one July 60 call for $1.25, and bought one July 65 call for $.50). See Figure 9-53.

If we anticipated that the stock was most likely to remain in the $55–$60 range, the condor would provide a much higher payoff for most stock finishes in that range.

We now turn our attention to the inverse of each of these positions and will discuss their attributes and uses.

Figure 9-53   *Butterfly versus the condor.*
Gray line = long condor at expiration.
Black line = long butterfly at expiration.
Thin gray line = long butterfly with 21 days to expiration.

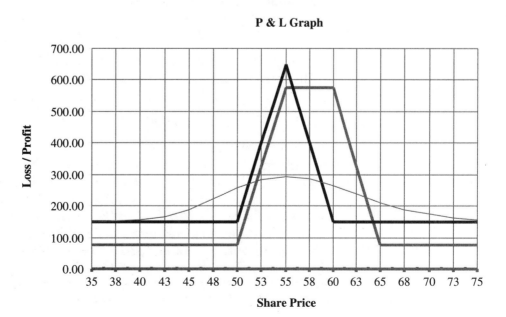

Volatile Strategies

Butterfly (Short).   A short butterfly consists of selling one contract of the lowest and highest of three consecutive strikes while simultaneously buying two contracts of the middle strike. This position is the reverse position of the long butterfly. Not surprisingly, the market expectation for a short butterfly is the opposite expectation for the long butterfly. Where the long butterfly anticipates a flat, passive market, the short butterfly looks for a volatile market—one that will move the stock price strongly away from its present value.

Here is the formula for the short butterfly:

Sell one + buy two + sell one = credit received

- **Reward**—The reward in this situation is limited. The total credit equals the maximum profit if the stock rises above or falls below the two short strikes.
- **Risk**—The risk is limited. The price risk is the difference between consecutive strike prices minus the credit received, which equals the maximum loss if stock closes upon expiration at the long strike.

The outlook on this stock is volatile. The trader is speculating that the stock price will rise above or fall below the short option strikes.

Example of the Short Call Butterfly.   XYZ is trading at $50. The trader sells one XYZ July 45 call for $5.50 ($5.50 × 100 = $550) and buys two XYZ July 50 calls for $2.10 ($2.10 × 2 × 100 = $420). Then, the trader sells one XYZ July 55 call for $.50 ($.50 × 100 = $50). The net credit is $1.80 ($180).

- **Reward**—The reward is $180.
- **Risk**—The price risk is $320 (the difference between consecutive strikes, which is $5, minus the credit received, which is $1.80).

Here are the break-even prices:

Low break-even price: $46.80

High break-even price: $53.20

Profit range: Below $46.80 or above $53.20

Example of a Short Put Butterfly.   XYZ is trading at $50. The trader sells one XYZ July 55 put for $5.50 ($5.50 × 100 = $550) and buys two XYZ July 50 puts for $2.10 ($2.10 × 2 × 100 = $420). The trader then sells one XYZ July 45 put for $.50 ($.50 × 100 = $50). The net credit is $1.80 ($180). See Figure 9-54.

Figure 9-54   *Short put butterfly.*
              Black line = short 45–50–55 butterfly at expiration.
              Thin gray line = short butterfly with 21 days to expiration.

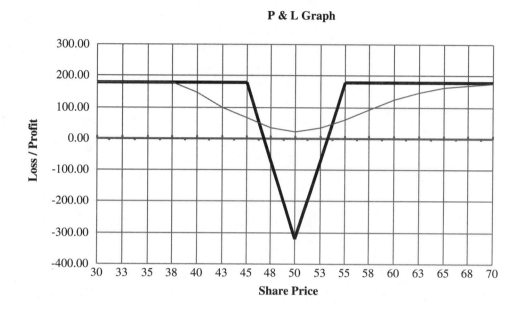

P & L Graph

- **Reward**—The reward is $180.
- **Risk**—The price risk is $320 (the difference between consecutive strikes, which is $5, minus the credit received, which is $1.80).

The break-even prices are

Low break-even: $46.80
High break-even: $53.20
Profit range: Below $46.80 or above $53.20

In comparison to the risk/reward profile of the long butterfly, one might wonder why anyone would ever consider establishing a short butterfly. Its potential reward is much less than that of a long butterfly, and its potential loss is much greater. You should consider a long butterfly in several circumstances:

- When the credit available from establishing the short butterfly is high (low implied volatility) and your expectation is for a big move in the stock (direction uncertain)
- As an adjustment for either a long ratio bull spread (refer to the bullish strategy section of this chapter) or a long ratio bear spread (refer to the bearish strategy section of this chapter)

We will now consider each of these situations.

Anticipating a Volatile Move. A short butterfly captures the entire credit received when establishing the position if the stock closes either below the lowest strike or above the highest strike in the position. Furthermore, because the maximum loss is the difference between consecutive strikes in the position minus the credit, the larger the credit, the smaller the maximum loss. Therefore, if a large credit can be obtained from establishing the position, and the expectation of a volatile move in the stock is high, this strategy is less risky than a straddle. Its return might be substantially less, however, should the stock price change dramatically.

Ratio Spread Adjustment. Use of the short butterfly as an adjustment to either a long ratio bull spread or to a long ratio bear spread is best examined by looking at an example.

Assume that the 1:2 long ratio bull spread was established by selling one XYZ July 45 call for $5.50 and purchasing two XYZ July 50 calls for $2.10 each, for a net credit of $1.30 when the stock is trading at $50. Assume further that the stock shoots up to $55 and that the July 45 calls are at $10.25, the July 50 calls are at $5.50, and the July 55 calls are at $2.10. By selling one July 55 call, you turn the ratio bull spread into a short butterfly—established with a $3.40 credit (selling one XYZ July 45 call for $5.50, buying two XYZ July 50 calls for $2.10 each, and selling one July 55 call for $2.10). Compare this situation to not adjusting the position (see Figure 9-55).

With the stock at $57.40 upon expiration, the butterfly and the ratio bull spread produce a profit of $3.40 ($340). Below $57.40, the butterfly outperforms the ratio bull spread while the ratio bull spread is superior

Figure 9-55   *Comparison to not adjusting the position.*
             Black line = 1:2 ratio bull spread at expiration.
             Gray line = short 45–50–55 butterfly.

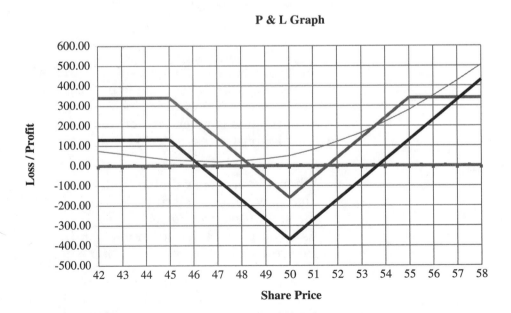

if the stock finishes above \$57.40. You would decide whether or not to convert the position into a butterfly based upon your assessment of the stock.

The situation would be similar in the case of the long ratio bear spread (selling one July 55 put and buying two July 50 puts), except that the adjustment to a short butterfly would involve the sale of one July 45 put.

Managing the Position. You can obtain better prices for the position by legging into it. Let's offer you two ways to achieve this goal by using our example as the factual backdrop:

1. You can separate the position into two parts: a bear spread at the lower strike and a bull spread at the higher strike. If you thought that the stock was more likely to increase in price than decrease in the near term, you would leg into the butterfly by starting with the bull spread leg (either the 50–55 bull call spread or the 50–55 bull put spread). If you thought that a decline was imminent, you would start with the bear spread leg (either the 45–50 bear put spread or the 45–50 bear call spread). Obviously, if your initial leg of the butterfly involved puts, you could use the correct put spread to complete a put butterfly (and vice-versa) if a call spread were used as the initial leg.

   a. If you were correct and the stock did increase in price, the remaining leg should be available at a more favorable price. For example, if you had started with the bull call spread leg (buying the 50-level call and selling the 55-level call), the 45-level call that you will be selling has more deltas than the 50-level call that you will be buying and should have increased more in price than the 50-level call. Therefore, the remaining call bear spread will generate a larger credit than prior to the stock run-up, and if you had put on the bear put spread first (buying the 50-level put and selling the 45-level put), the decline in price will have increased the price of the 50–55 put bull spread that you will be selling.

   b. If you were incorrect and the stock moved in the wrong direction, you would need to decide whether to continue with your initial strategy and complete the butterfly, liquidate the position at a loss, do nothing, or adjust your leg in some other way. For example, if you had put on the 50–55 bull call spread and saw the stock decline, you might consider selling another 55-level call and converting the position to a ratio call spread (short).

2. More aggressively, if you thought that the stock was going to rise first, you would start with the purchase of two 50-level calls. After the stock rose, you would then quickly sell one 45-level call and one 55-level call. If you thought that the stock was going to decline in price first, you would start with the purchase of the 50-level puts. After the stock sold off, you would then quickly sell one 45-level put and one 55-level put. Either of these techniques might result in putting the position on for even or possibly for a credit, meaning no risk of loss.

Iron Butterfly (Long).   The long iron butterfly is the reverse position of the short iron butterfly. In the long iron butterfly, the ATM straddle is bought and the OTM strangle is sold.

Here is the formula for the long iron butterfly:

Buy an ATM straddle and sell the OTM strangle = debit paid

- **Reward**—The reward in this case is limited. The reward is the difference between the straddle strike and either of the strangle strikes minus the debit paid, which equals the maximum profit. This situation results if the stock price closes upon expiration above the strangle call strike or below the strangle put strike.
- **Risk**—The risk is limited. The maximum loss equals the debit paid, which results if the stock price upon expiration is at the straddle strike.

The outlook on this stock is volatile. The trader is speculating that the stock price will rise above the strangle call strike or fall below the strangle put strike upon option expiration.

Example of a Long Iron Butterfly (see Figure 9-56).   XYZ is trading at $50. The trader sells one XYZ July 45 put for $.50 ($.50 × 100 = $50) and buys one XYZ July 50 put for $2.10 ($2.10 × 100 = $210). The trader then buys one XYZ July 50 call for $2.10 ($2.10 × 100 = $210) and sells one XYZ July 55 call for $.75 ($.50 × 100 = $50). The net debit is $3.20 ($320).

Figure 9-56 *Long iron butterfly.*
Black line = long iron butterfly at expiration.
Thin gray line = long iron butterfly with 21 days to expiration.

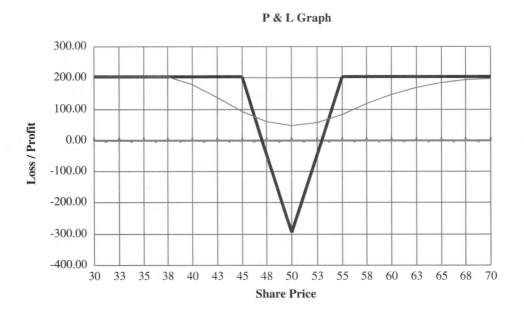

- **Reward**—The reward is $180.
- **Risk**—The risk is $320 (the difference between consecutive strikes, which is $5, minus the credit received, which is $1.80).

The break-even prices are

Low break-even price: $46.80
High break-even price: $53.20
Profit range: Below $46.80 or above $53.20

Consistent with our discovery that a short iron butterfly is equivalent to a long butterfly, the long iron butterfly is the equal to the short butterfly. The only real difference between the two strategies is which options are used. The short butterfly uses either all calls or all puts, while the long iron butterfly uses a combination of calls and puts.

Establishing the Position.   Similar alternatives to those that we discussed for legging into a short butterfly are available for legging into a long iron butterfly:

1. If you thought the stock was more likely to increase in price than decrease in the near term, you would first put on the 50–55 bull call spread. Then, after the stock had risen, you would complete the position by acquiring the 45–50 bear put spread. If you thought a decline was more imminent, you would first put on the 45–50 bear put spread followed by the 50–55 bull call spread after the decline had occurred.

    a. If you were correct, the remaining leg should be available at a more favorable price. If you had put on the bull spread, the 50-level puts (which you intend to purchase and which have more deltas than the 45-level puts that you intend to sell) should have decreased more in price than the 45-level puts. Therefore, the remaining bear spread will require a smaller debit than prior to the stock run-up. If you had put on the bear spread first, the decline in price will have decreased the cost of the 50–55 bull call spread.

    b. If you were incorrect and the stock moved in the wrong direction, you would need to decide whether to continue with your initial strategy and complete the long iron butterfly, liquidate the position at a loss, do nothing, or adjust your leg in some other way. For example, if you had put on the 45–50 bear put spread and saw the stock increase, you might consider selling another 40-level put and converting the position to a ratio put spread (short).

2. More aggressively, if you thought that the stock was going to rise first, you would start with the purchase of the 55-level call. After the

stock rose, you would then quickly buy one 45-level put, sell one 50-level call, and sell one 50-level put. This technique will not produce the same results as purchasing the 45-level call as the first leg of the long call butterfly, because the 45 call, being ITM, has a much greater delta than the OTM 55 call. Therefore, for a comparable increase in the underlying stock, the 45 call would increase in price more than the 55 call and thus reduce the net cost of the butterfly even more. There would have to be a dramatic increase in the stock price before the increase in the price of the 55 call would reduce the net cost of the iron butterfly to even.

Condor (Short).   A short condor consists of selling one contract each of the outside strikes of four consecutive strikes while simultaneously buying one contract each of the two inside strikes. One of the inside strikes is usually the ATM strike. The options must all be of the same type and expiration date (either all calls or all puts). The short condor is similar to the short butterfly or short iron butterfly, except that the trader is reducing his or her capital exposure by purchasing one ATM and one OTM strike instead of two ATMs.

A short condor consists of selling one contract each of the outside strikes while simultaneously buying one contract each of the inside strikes. One of these inside strikes should be the ATM strike.

Here is the formula for the short condor:

Sell one + buy one + buy one + sell one = credit received

- **Reward**—The reward here is limited. The credit received equals the maximum profit if the underlying security closes above the highest strike or falls below the lowest strike upon expiration.
- **Risk**—The risk is limited. The interval between consecutive strike prices minus the credit received equals the maximum loss. A maximum loss will occur if the underlying security is within the two long strikes upon expiration.

The outlook on this stock is volatile. The trader is speculating that the stock price will rise above the highest option price or fall below the lowest option strike upon expiration.

Example of a Short Call Condor.   XYZ is trading at $50. The trader sells one XYZ July 45 call for $6 ($6 × 100 = $600) and buys one XYZ July 50 call for $2.25 ($2.25 × 100 = $225). The trader then buys one XYZ July 55 call for $1 ($1 × 100 = $100) and sells one XYZ July 60 call for $.50 ($.50 × 100 = $50). The net credit is $3.25 ($3.25 × 100 = $325).

- **Reward**—The reward is $325.
- **Risk**—The risk is $175 (the difference between consecutive strikes, which is $5, minus the credit received, which is $3.25).

The break-even prices are

Low break-even price: $48.25
High break-even price: $56.75
Profit range: Below $48.25 or above $56.75

Example of a Short Put Condor (see Figure 9-57). XYZ is trading at $50. The trader sells one XYZ July 60 put for $10.50 ($10.50 × 100 = $1,050) and buys one XYZ July 55 put for $6 ($6 × 100 = $600). The trader then buys one XYZ July 50 put for $2.25 ($2.25 × 100 = $225) and sells one XYZ July 45 put for $1 ($1 × 100 = $100). The net credit is $3.25 ($3.25 × 100 = $325).

- **Reward**—The reward is $325.
- **Risk**—The risk is $175 (the difference between consecutive strikes, which is $5, minus the credit received, which is $3.25).

The break-even prices are

Low break-even price: $48.25
High break-even price: $56.75
Profit range: Below $48.25 or above $56.75

Figure 9-57 *Short put condor.*
Black line = short condor at expiration.
Thin gray line = short condor with 21 days to expiration.

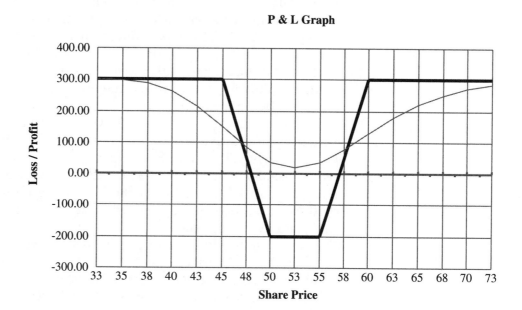

P & L Graph

Comparing the risk/reward profile of the short condor to the short butterfly or long iron butterfly, we find the following:

- The condor results in a higher credit, so the maximum profit is greater and the maximum risk is less. The maximum profit is the difference between the strikes ($5 in our examples) reduced by the cost of the position. The condor produces a higher credit, because (for example) in the case of the call spread, it differs from the butterfly in that although it contains the identical bear spread (a credit spread), its bull spread (a debit spread) involves higher OTM strikes than the butterfly. (We are referring to the 55-60 bull call spread versus the 50–55 bull call spread in the examples that we have been using.) This will always produce a smaller debit.
- The condor has a risk of loss over a wider range of stock prices. The maximum loss for a condor results from the stock closing upon expiration at any point between the two interior strikes, rather than precisely at the long strike in the case of a butterfly or iron butterfly.

In contrast to the long condor, a short condor—depending upon the pricing of the component option—might be a position that you would initiate from the onset. In addition, whenever a short butterfly is considered a position adjustment (such as we have analyzed in the short butterfly section earlier), a condor should also be considered. After first comparing the short condor to the short butterfly as a position adjustment for long ratio bull and bear spreads, we will examine the alternative ways to establish the short condor.

Ratio Spread Adjustment.   For convenience, we will restate the example that we used in the short butterfly section.

Assume that the 1:2 long ratio bull spread was established by selling one XYZ July 45 call for $5.50 and purchasing two XYZ July 50 calls for $2.10 each (for a net credit of $1.30 when the stock is trading at $50). Assume further that the stock moves up quickly to $55 and that the July 45 calls are at $10.25, the July 50 calls are at $5.50, the July 55 calls are at $2.10, and the July 60 calls are at $.50. As we have previously seen, by selling one July 55 call, you turn the bull spread into a short butterfly— established with a $3.40 credit (selling one XYZ July 45 call for $5.50, buying two XYZ July 50 calls for $2.10 each, and selling one July 55 call for $2.10). Alternatively, by selling one of the July 50 calls for $5.50, purchasing one July 55 call for $2.10, and selling one July 60 call for $.50, we create a condor that has a $5.20 credit. You can accomplish this task by selling one XYZ July 45 call for $5.50, buying two XYZ July 50 calls at $2.10 each, selling one July 50 call for $5.50, buying one July 55 call at $2.10, and by selling one July 60 call for $.50. Compare the short condor adjustment to the short butterfly adjustment (see Figure 9-58).

By putting on the condor for a $5.20 credit, we are guaranteed a profit. If we maintained our volatile expectation for the stock, expecting it to finish significantly away from $50, the short condor adjustment would clearly outperform the short butterfly adjustment.

Figure 9-58 *Comparison between the short condor and short butterfly adjustments.*
Gray line = short 45–50–55-60 condor at expiration.
Black line = short 45–50–55 butterfly at expiration.

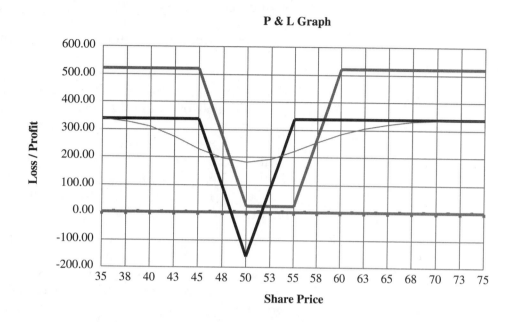

We would decide whether to adjust our position and how to adjust it based on our assessment of the stock at that time.

This situation would be similar in the case of the long ratio bear spread (selling one July 55 put and buying two July 50 puts), except that the adjustment into a short condor would involve the sale of one July 50 put, the purchase of one July 45 put, and the sale of one July 40 put.

Establishing the Position.   You can obtain better prices for the position by legging into it. Let's offer two ways to achieve this goal by using our example as the factual backdrop:

1. Although you can separate the position into two parts—a bear spread at the lower two strikes and a bull spread at the higher two strikes—for legging purposes, we will reconstruct it into a bear spread involving the lowest and second-highest strikes (45–55) and a bull spread involving the second-lowest and the highest strike (50–60). If you thought that the stock was more likely to increase in price than decrease in the near term, you would leg into the butterfly by starting with the bull spread leg (either the 50–60 bull call spread or the 50–60 bull put spread). If you thought that a decline was imminent, you would start with the bear spread leg (either the 45–55 bear put spread or the 45–55 bear call spread). Obviously, if your initial leg of the short condor involved puts, you would use the correct put spread to complete a put short condor (and vice-versa) if a call spread were used as the initial leg.

a. If you were correct and the stock did increase in price, the remaining leg should be available at a more favorable price. For example, if you started with the bull call spread leg (buying the 50-level call and selling the 60-level call), the 45-level call (which you will be selling) has more deltas than the 55-level call that you will be buying. This call should have increased more in price than the 55-level call. Therefore, the remaining call bear spread will generate a larger credit than prior to the stock run-up, and if you had put on the bear put spread first (buying the 55-level put and selling the 45-level put), then the decline in price would have increased the price of the 50–60 put bull spread that you will be selling.

b. If you were incorrect and the stock moved in the wrong direction, you would need to decide whether to continue with your initial strategy and complete the butterfly, liquidate the position at a loss, do nothing, or adjust your leg in some other way. For example, if you had put on the 50–60 bull call spread and saw the stock decline, you might consider selling either another 55-level or 60-level call.

2. More aggressively, if you thought that the stock was going to rise first, you would start with the purchase of one 50-level call. After the stock rose, you would then quickly sell one 45-level call, sell one 60-level call, and purchase one 55-level call. If you thought that the stock was going to decline in price first, you would start with the purchase of a 55-level put. Then, after the stock sold off, you would quickly sell one 45-level put, buy one 50-level put, and sell one 60-level put.

Summary

The butterfly, iron butterfly, and condor are valuable strategies when used in the appropriate context. We have seen the following:

- They are limited-risk, limited-reward positions.
- They can be implemented as standalone strategies or as methods of adjusting other positions.
- They rarely trade as is and require legging into.

Risk-Reduction Strategies

You can use options not only as speculative strategies but also as ways of locking in profit, insuring investments, and reducing the risk of loss of current investments.

Two common scenarios in which sophisticated investors have learned to utilize the risk-reduction properties of options are:

- **When an investment has proved successful and the investor has a large, unrealized profit**—Although the investor is still bullish on the stock and/or does not wish to pay the taxes that would be due on the gain were he to sell the stock, the investor is nervous about the stock in the short term. This concern might involve an upcoming earnings report, the outcome of litigation, or some other news event. How does the investor ride out this rough patch?
- **When an investor is considering initiating a new investment**— The stock has just experienced a significant sell-off, perhaps due to a general market decline. The investor believes that this situation is most likely a short-term situation and that the stock should recover most of its recent loss. There is the possibility, however, that this loss is not the bottom (which might be much lower). Jump in now or wait —that is the dilemma.

In the rest of this chapter, we will discuss how you can use put options in both of these situations (as well as in others) to not only protect capital and/or unrealized profits but to take advantage of risky profit opportunities. Additionally, we will explore a strategy known as a risk collar/ fence, where we will analyze the cost of purchasing the protective puts by selling OTM calls.

Protecting Unrealized Profit

An individual investor who owns a stock that has appreciated since its purchase has an unrealized or paper profit. If the investor wants to maintain this position because he or she believes that the stock might continue to rise in price, he or she is then exposing himself or herself to directional market risk. If the stock goes up, that is good. If it goes down, that is bad. Not only is his or her unrealized profit at risk, but his or her initial capital is also in jeopardy.

If the investor is concerned about short-term down-side risk but is not interested in selling the stock, he or she has three choices:

1. Do nothing and hope for the best.
2. Place a stop order.
3. Purchase a put in order to protect his or her position. The put establishes a minimum amount that the investment will be worth. Essentially, the investor is purchasing insurance to protect his or her capital and unrealized profit. The put strike price will determine how much of the profit and capital that the investor wants to protect. The expiration month of the put will determine the period in which the insurance will be in effect. The price of this insurance varies based on these two factors.

When comparing stop orders to puts, we find the following advantages:

- Puts cost money, but stop orders are free.
- Puts expire, but stop orders stay until you cancel them.

The disadvantages of stop orders, however, are

- Stop orders do not protect against stocks gapping down in price, whereas options work wonderfully in that situation. There are two types of stop orders: limit and market. Consider this example. A stock is trading for $100, and you place a stop order at $95. If the stock suddenly gaps below $95, your result will depend upon whether your order is limit or market. If your order is market, then your stock will be sold at whatever price to which the stock gaps down. If your order is limit, then if the stock gaps down below your limit, nothing will happen. If the limit is below the post-gap price, however, the stock will be sold. Unless you expressly specify that your stop order is limit, it becomes a market order when the stock trades at or below the stop price.
- If your stock drifts down towards your stop order price, it will automatically trigger a sale once the stop price is reached. With a put, you have the luxury of waiting to see what the stock does with the knowledge that you can exercise your option at any time prior to its expiration.

Let's now examine the use of puts in more detail. Here is the simple formula for calculating the protected profit of the position:

Put strike price − initial stock purchase − put price = protected profit

In this example, the individual investor had purchased 100 shares of stock for $85—an $8,500 investment. The investor was right, and the stock increased in value. The stock is currently trading at $105—a $2,000 profit. The investor believes that the stock might continue to rise in price but is currently concerned about downside risk. Maybe there is currently a bearish sentiment in the market, an earnings report, or a news item. The investor is looking to protect not only his initial capital, but also his unrealized profit. The investor does not want to sell the stock for several reasons: first, he might believe that the stock will rise even further in the future. Second, he might not have held the stock for one year and is concerned with short-term capital-gains tax consequences.

The investor decides to purchase the May 105 puts and pays $4 ($400) for the right to sell stock at 105 by May expiration. By purchasing the put, the investor has protected his initial investment of $8,500 and some of his profit. By using the following formula, we can calculate exactly how much profit the investor has protected:

Put strike price of $105 − initial stock purchase of $85 − put price of $4 = protected profit of $16

Figure 9-59   *Protecting profit.*
Black line = long 100 shares for $85, long 1 105 level put for $4
at expiration.
Thin gray line = long 100 shares for $85, long 1 105 level put for
$4 with 21 days to expiration.

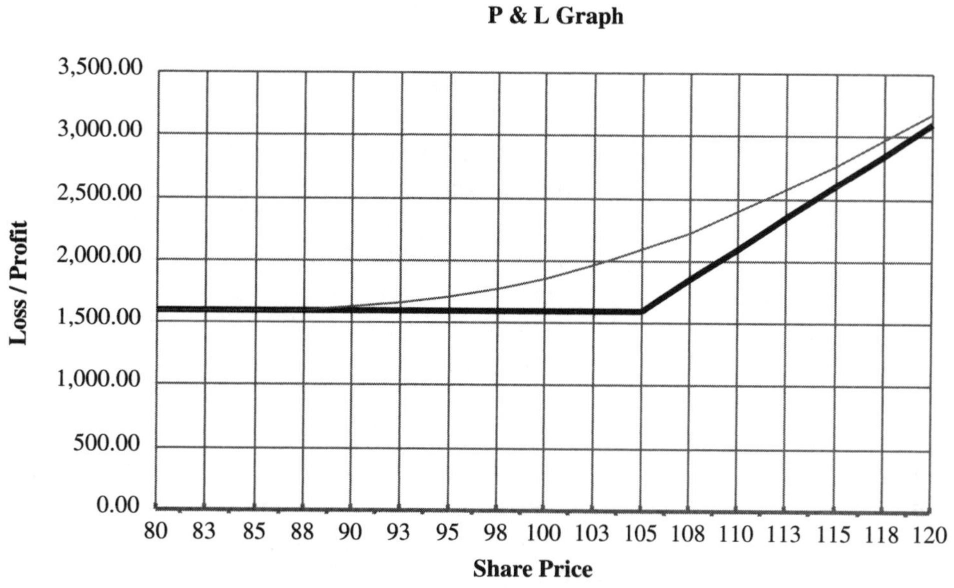

P & L Graph

The investor has protected $1,600 of his profit for the life of the option (see Figure 9-59).

Not only has the investor protected his profit, but he has also managed to keep his long stock position. The put has only protected the profit and has not halted the up-side potential of the position. If the stock continues to rise in price, the investor's position will continue to gain value. Again, we see how we can use options to insure investments (and, in this case, to protect profits).

Consider the following alternatives:

- **XYZ moves up to $130 at expiration**—The stock gain of $25 per share less the put price of $4 equals the net gain of $21 per share of additional profit. Purchase of the put has reduced the investor's profit from $45 per share to $41 per share.
- **XYZ falls to $70 at expiration**—The May 105 put is exercised, selling the stock for $105 per share. The investment has been terminated, and the investor has made $16 per share—thus protecting all but $4 per share of his unrealized gain. Alternatively, the put could be sold at expiration for $35, thereby retaining the stock (which also maintains $16 per share of profit—$31 of gain on the put minus the $15 of unrealized loss on the stock). By comparison, if the put had not been purchased, the investor would still own the stock with an unrealized loss of $15 per share instead of the unrealized profit of $16 per share.

Married Puts

Often, an individual investor considers purchasing stock—believing that the stock will increase in value over time—but is concerned about a short-term and possibly negative situation. In this situation, the individual investor wants to protect his or her position. A possible solution is the married put (see Figure 9-60).

A married put results when stock and puts are purchased at the same time. The married put position gives the purchaser a downside stop until the put option expires. For this strategy, the ATM or OTM puts are purchased, depending on how much downside stop loss the trader is willing to incur. This strategy is used when purchasing a stock in a volatile situation, such as upcoming earnings, news events, and so on—where you believe that the potential reward is substantial but the downside risk is significant. Here is the formula:

$$\text{Stock price} - \text{strike price} + \text{put price} = \text{maximum loss}$$

Notice that the married put has the same profit and loss graph as a long call. Remember that long puts plus long stock equals a long synthetic call. Why not purchase the call instead, then? This question is a good one. One answer might be that the price of the synthetic call might be cheaper than the price at which you can purchase it directly. Another situation that might call for the use of the married put involves the uptick rule. In order to prevent opportunists from exacerbating a market panic by selling stock short while the market is collapsing, the *Securities*

Figure 9-60   *A married put.*
                   Black line = long 100 shares of stock for $47/share and long 1 45 level put at expiration.
                   Thin gray line = long 100 shares of stock for $47/share and long 1 45 level put with 21 days to expiration.

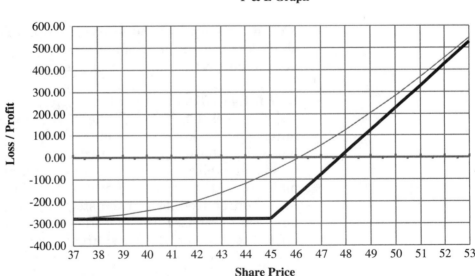

and Exchange Commission (SEC) instituted a rule that only gives short sellers the right to sell when a stock trades up from its last trade (an uptick in price). Someone who is selling stock that they own is not a short seller. In a market panic, the holder of a married put could sell his or her stock without being limited by this rule. If you owned the call instead, any attempt to sell short would be subject to this rule. For this reason, many professional traders trade married puts and conversions in order to assure a supply of long stock for those occasions when it is useful to sell stock in a market meltdown.

Risk Collar/Fence

Usually, when the investor wants to protect his or her long stock position by purchasing puts, he or she is concerned about a volatile event in the marketplace. This event could be any number of concerns, and unfortunately, the investor might have the same idea as many other people in the marketplace. This situation adds to the rise in the implied volatility of the options. With an increase of implied volatility comes the increase in options premiums. This situation causes the OTM put that the investor was interested in purchasing for protection to rise in price. In some cases, the premium rises to a point where it might not be advantageous to the individual investor to purchase. When this situation happens, the individual investor must find a way to finance his or her insurance policy (the put).

The risk collar/fence strategy might be the alternative that the investor needs. This strategy enables the investor to purchase the put and finance it with the sale of a call.

In the case of long stock, the investor is looking to purchase an OTM put and finance the OTM put by selling the OTM call.

Long Underlying Security (Risk Collar/Fence)

Buy an OTM put and sell an OTM call. (The OTM call sale finances the OTM put purchase, which is the down-side protection for the underlying security.) Figure 9-61 illustrates the profit and loss associated with a risk collar.

The position is similar to the bull spread. The purchase of the put and the stock has created a synthetic call, therefore giving the investor the same characteristics as the bull spread.

The risk collar has enabled the investor to lock in limited risk and reduce the put premium by selling the call. The short call with the long stock has created a similar risk-versus-reward profile as for a covered call. The individual investor has limited his or her upside potential with the sale of the call.

Short Underlying Security (Risk Collar)

Buy an OTM call and sell an OTM put. (The OTM put sale finances the OTM call purchase, which is the upside protection for the underlying short security.) See Figure 9-62.

Figure 9-61   *Long underlying security (risk collar / fence).*
Black line = long 100 shares of stock for $50, long 1 45 level put
and short 1 55 level call at expiration.
Thin gray line = long 100 shares of stock for $50, long 1 45 level
put and short 1 55 level call with 21 days to expiration.

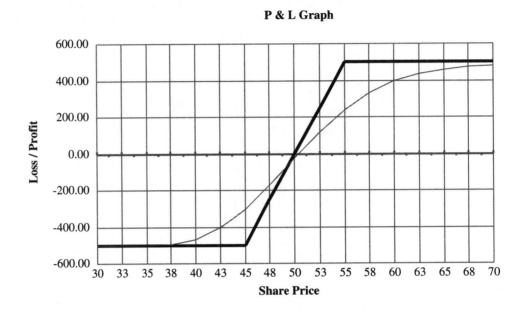

Figure 9-62   *Short underlying security (risk collar).*
Black line = short 100 shares of stock for $50, short 1 45 level
put and long 1 55 level call at expiration.
Thin gray line = short 100 shares of stock for $50, short 1 45
level put and long 1 55 level call with 21 days to expiration.

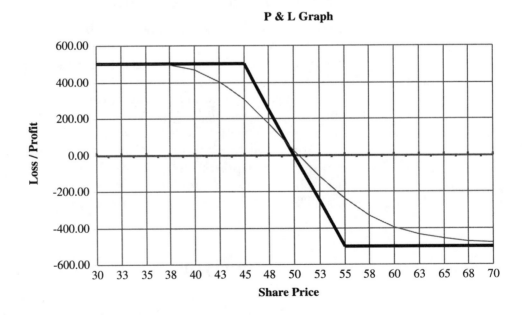

The risk collar/fence can also be used to protect short stock. In this case, the individual investor is purchasing OTM calls to protect the short stock position from a rise in stock price. The OTM put is sold in order to finance the OTM call purchased. This situation creates a similar risk-versus-reward profile as for a bear spread. The short stock and long call have created a synthetic long put position.

You should note that all of these positions have synthetic equivalents.

Quiz

1. An investor who has a pessimistic market outlook is _____.
2. Buying one ABC July 80 call and selling two ABC July 85 calls is referred to as a _____.
3. You are long 10 March 60 calls and short 10 April 60 calls; therefore, you have on a _____.
4. With XYZ trading at $50, you purchased two October 50 puts trading for $3 for a total investment of $600. The stock almost immediately has fallen to $45, and the October 50 puts are now trading for $6. The October 45 puts are trading for $3, and the October 40 puts are trading for $1. What are your alternatives?

   a. _____.

   b. _____.

   c. _____.

5. Predicted stock move < option premium = _____.
6. Consider the following position:

   Sell two May 70 calls at $4 each.

   Buy 100 shares of stock at $71.

   The purchase of 100 shares of stock combined with the sale of one May 70 call equals _____.
7. The short straddle risk equals _____.
8. The short ratio bear spread risk equals _____.
9. If the predicted stock move is greater than the option's premium, this situation equals _____.

10. Identify the following graph:

Black line = Long 1 July 55 call.
Long 1 July 45.
Thin gray line = 21 days to expiration.

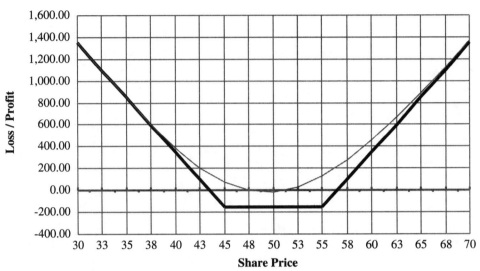

11. Identify the following graph:

Black line =
Thin gray line =

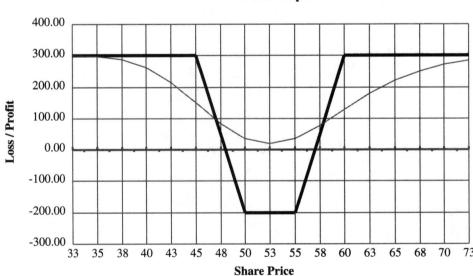

12. Identify the following graph:

Black line =
Thin gray line =

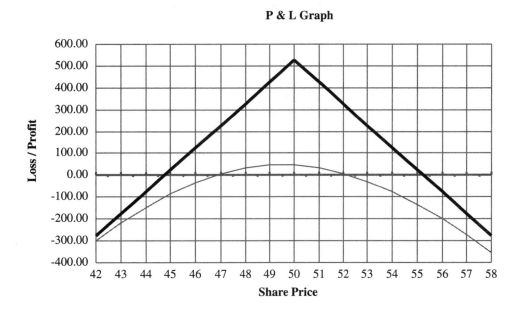

Chapter 10

Market Making

Introduction

Professional floor traders (known in the industry as *market makers*), often think that for the beginning investor, option trading must seem similar to putting together a puzzle without the aid of a picture. You can find the picture if you know where to look. Looking through the eyes of a professional market maker is one of the best ways to learn about trading options under real market conditions. This experience will help you understand how real-world changes in option pricing variables affect an option's value and the risks associated with that option. Furthermore, because market makers are essentially responsible for what the option market looks like, you need to be familiar with their role and the strategies that they use in order to regulate a liquid market and ensure their own profit.

We will provide an overview of the practices of market makers and explore their mindset as the architects of the option business. First, we will consider the logistics of a market maker's responsibilities. How do market makers respond to supply and demand to ensure a liquid market? How do they assess the value of an option based on market conditions and demands? In the second part of this chapter, we will consider the profit-oriented objectives of a market maker. How is market making like any other business? How does a market maker profit? What does it mean to hedge a position, and how does a market maker use hedging to minimize risk?

Who Are Market Makers?

The image of an open outcry pit is not unfamiliar to the American imagination, but many people might not know who the players in that pit are. Market makers, brokers, and the exchange staff occupy a trading pit on an option exchange floor. Hundreds of trading pits are on the floors of the world's 50 or so option exchanges, and combined, they represent the marketplace for option trading. The exchange itself provides the location, regulatory body, computer technology, and staff that are necessary to support and monitor trading activity. Market makers are said to actually make the option market, whereas brokers represent the public orders.

In general, market makers might make markets in up to 30 or more issues and compete with one another for customer buy and sell orders in those issues. Market makers trade using either their own capital or trade for a firm that supplies them with capital. The market maker's activity, which takes place both on the floor of the exchange and increasingly through computer execution, represents the central processing unit of the option industry. If we consider the exchange itself as the backbone of the industry, the action in the trading pit represents the industry's brain and heart. As both a catalyst for trading and a profiteer in his or her own right, the market maker's role in the industry is well worth closer examination.

Individual Trader versus Market Maker

The evaluation of an option's worth by individual traders and market makers, respectively, is the foundation of option trading. Trader and market maker alike buy and sell the products that they foresee as profitable. From this perspective, no difference exists between a market maker and the individual option trader. More formally, however, the difference between you and the market maker is responsible for creating the option industry as we know it.

Essentially, market makers are professional, large-volume option traders whose own trading serves the public by creating liquidity and depth in the marketplace. On a daily basis, market makers account for up to half of all option trading volume, and much of this activity is responsible for creating and ensuring a two-sided market made up of the best bids and offers for public customers. A market maker's trading activity takes place under the conditions of a contractual relationship with an exchange. As members of the exchange, market makers must pay dues and lease or own a seat on the floor in order to trade. More importantly, a market maker's relationship with the exchange requires him or her to trade all of the issues that are assigned to his or her primary pit on the option floor. In return, the market maker is able to occupy a privileged position in the option market—market makers are the merchants in the option industry; they are in a position to create the market (bid and ask) and then buy on their bid and sell on their offer.

The main difference between a market maker and off-floor traders is that the market maker's position is primarily dictated by customer order flow. The market maker does not have the luxury of picking and choosing his or her position. Just like the book makers in Las Vegas who set the odds and then accommodate individual betters who select which side of the bet that they want, a market maker's job is to supply a market in the options, a bid and an offer, and then let the public decide whether to buy or sell at those prices, thereby taking the other side of the bet.

As the official option merchants, market makers are in a position to buy options wholesale and sell them at retail. That said, the two main differences between market makers and other merchants is that market makers commonly sell before they buy, and the value of their inventory fluctuates as the price of stock fluctuates. As with all merchants, though, a familiarity with the product pays off. The market maker's years of experience with market conditions and trading practices in general—including an array of trading strategies—enables him or her to establish an edge (however slight) over the market. This edge is the basis for the market maker's potential wealth.

Trading Styles

Throughout the trading day, market makers generally use one of two trading styles: scalping or position trading. *Scalping* is a simpler trading style that an ever-diminishing number of traders use. *Position trading*, which is divided into a number of subcategories, is used by the greatest percentage of all market makers. As we have discussed, most market makers' positions are dictated to them by the public's order flow. Each individual market maker will accumulate and hedge this order flow differently, generally preferring one style of trading over another. A market maker's trading style might have to do with a belief that one style is more profitable then another or might be because of a trader's general personality and perception of risk.

The scalper generally attempts to buy an option on the bid and sell it on the offer (or sell on the offer and buy on the bid) in an effort to capture the difference without creating an option position. Scalpers profit from trading what is referred to as the *bid/ask spread*, the difference between the bid price and the ask price. For example, if the market on the PDQ October 30 puts is 3 (bid) − 3.38 (ask), this trader will buy an option order that comes into the trading pit on the bid along with the rest of the crowd. This trader is now focused on selling these puts for a profit, rather than hedging the options and creating a position. Due to the lack of commission paid by market makers, this trader can sell the first 3.13 bid that enters the trading crowd and still make a profit, known in the financial industry as a *scalp*. The trader has just made a profit without creating a position. Sometimes holding and hedging a position is unavoidable, however. Still this style of trading is generally less risky, because the trader will maintain only small positions with little risk. The scalper is less common these days because the listing of options on more than one exchange (dual listing) has increased competition and decreased the bid/ask spread. The scalper can make money only when customers are buying and selling options in equal amounts. Because customer order-flow is generally one-sided (either customers are just buying or just selling) the ability to scalp options is rare. Scalpers, therefore, are generally found in trading pits trading stocks that have large option order flow. The scalper is a rare breed on the trading floor, and the advent of dual listing and competing exchanges has made scalpers an endangered species.

The position trader generally has an option position that is created while accommodating public order flow and hedging the resulting risk. This type of trading is more risky because the market maker might be assuming directional risk, volatility risk, or interest rate risk, to name a few. Correspondingly, market makers can assume a number of positions relative to these variables. Generally the two common types of position traders are either *backspreaders* or *frontspreaders*.

Backspreader

Essentially, backspreaders are traders who accumulate (buy) more options than they sell and, therefore, have theoretically large or unlimited profit potential. For example, a long straddle would be considered a backspread. In this situation, we purchase the 50 level call and put (an ATM strike would be delta neutral). As the underlying asset declines in value, the put rises in value, and as the underlying asset increases in value, the call will increase in value. In order for the position to profit, the value of the rising option must increase more than the value of the declining option, or the trader must actively trade stock against the position, scalping stock as the deltas change.

The position could also profit from an increase in volatility, which would increase the value of both the call and put. As volatility increases, the trader might sell out the position for a profit or sell options (at the higher volatility) against the ones she owns. The position has large or unlimited profit potential and limited risk.

As we know from previous chapters, there is a multitude of risks associated with having an inventory of options. Generally, the greatest risk associated with a backspread is time decay. Vega is also an important factor. If volatility decreases dramatically, a backspreader might be forced to close out his position at less than favorable prices and may sustain a large loss. The backspreader is relying on movement in the underlying asset or an increase in volatility.

Frontspreader

The opposite of a backspreader, the frontspreader generally sells more options than he or she owns and, therefore, has limited profit potential and unlimited risk. Using the previous example, the frontspreader would be the seller of the 50 level call and put, short the 50 level straddle. In this situation, the market maker would profit from the position if the underlying asset failed to move outside the premium received for the sale prior to expiration. Generally, the frontspreader is looking for a decrease in volatility and/or little to no movement in the underlying asset.

The position also could profit from a decrease in volatility, which would decrease the value of both the call and put. As volatility decreases, the trader might buy in the position for a profit or buy options (at the lower volatility) against the ones he or she is short. The position has limited profit potential and unlimited risk.

When considering these styles of trading, it is important to recognize that a trader can trade the underlying stock to either create profit or manage risk. The backspreader will purchase stock as the stock decreases in value and sell the stock as the stock increases, thereby scalping the stock for a profit. Scalping the underlying stock, even when the stock is trading within a range less than the premium paid for the position, cannot only pay for the position but can create a profit above the initial investment. Backspreaders are able to do this with minimal risk because their position has positive gamma (curvature). This means that as the underlying asset declines in price, the position will accumulate negative deltas, and the trader might purchase stock against those deltas. As the underlying asset increases in price, the position will accumulate positive deltas, and the trader might sell stock. Generally, a backspreader will buy and sell stock against his or her delta position to create a positive scalp.

Similarly, a frontspreader can use the same technique to manage risk and maintain the profit potential of the position. A frontspread position will have negative gamma (negative curvature). Staying delta neutral can help a frontspreader avoid losses. A diligent frontspreader can descalp (scalping for a loss) the underlying asset and reduce her profits by only a small margin. Barring any gap in the underlying asset, disciplined buying and selling of the underlying asset can keep any loss to a minimum.

To complicate matters further, a backspreader or frontspreader might initiate a position that has speculative features. Two examples follow.

Directional Traders.   These traders put on a position that favors one directional move in the underlying asset over another. This trader is speculating that the stock will move either up or down. This type of trading can be extremely risky because the trader favors one direction to the exclusion of protecting the risk that is associated with movement to the other side. For example, a trader who believes that the underlying asset has sold off considerably might buy calls and sell puts. Both of these transactions will profit from a rise in the underlying asset; however, if the underlying asset were to continue downward, the position might lose a great deal of money.

Volatility Traders.   Volatility traders will generally make an assumption about the direction of the option volatility. For these traders, whether or not to buy or sell a call or put is based on an assessment of option volatility. Forecasting changes in volatility is typically an option trader's biggest challenge. As discussed previously, volatility is important because it is one of the principal factors used to estimate an option's price. A volatility trader will buy options that are priced below his or her volatility assumption and sell options that are trading above the assumption. If the portfolio is balanced as to the number of options bought and sold (options with similar characteristics such as expiration date and strike), the position will have little vega risk. However, if the trader sells more volatility than he or she buys, or vice versa, the position could lose a great deal of money on a volatility move.

Market Maker Trading: An Overview

In general, the market maker begins his or her assessment by using a pricing formula to generate a theoretical value for an option and then creating a market around that value. This process entails creating a bid beneath the market maker's fair value and an offer above the market maker's fair value of the option. Remember that the market maker has a legal responsibility to ensure a liquid marketplace through supplying a bid/ask spread. The trading public then can either purchase or sell the options based on market-maker listings, or it can negotiate with the market maker for a price that is between the posted bid/ask prices (based on his or her respective calculations of the option's theoretical value).

In most cases, the difference between market maker and individual investor bids and offers are a matter of pennies (what we might consider fractional profits). For the market maker, however, the key is volume. Like a casino, the market maker will manage risk so that she can stay in the game time after time and make a $1/16$ here and an $1/8$ there. These profits add up. Like the casino, a market maker will experience loss occasionally; however, through risk management, he or she attempts to stay in the business long enough to win more than he or she loses.

Another analogy can be found in the relationship between a buyer and used car dealer. A car dealer might make a bid on a used car for an amount that is less than what he is able to resell the car for in the marketplace. He or she can make a profit by buying the car for one price and selling it for a greater price. When determining the amount that he or she is willing to pay, the dealer must make an assumption of the future value of the car. If he is incorrect about how much someone will purchase the car for, then the dealer will take a loss on the transaction. If correct, however, the dealer stands to make a profit. On the other hand, the owner of the car might reject the dealer's original bid for the car and ask for a greater amount of money, thereby coming in between the dealer's bid/ask market. If the dealer assesses that the price that the owner is requesting for the car still enables a profit, he or she might buy the car regardless of the higher price. Similarly, when a market maker determines whether he or she will pay (or sell) one price over another, he or she determines not only the theoretical value of the option but also whether or not the option is a specific fit for risk-management purposes. There might be times when a market maker will forego the theoretical edge or trade for a negative theoretical edge for the sole purpose of risk management.

Before proceeding with our discussion of the market maker's trading activity in detail, let us again refer to the casino analogy. The house at a casino benefits largely from its familiarity with the business of gambling and the behavior of betters. As an institution, it also benefits from keeping a level head and certainly from being well (if not better) informed than its patrons about the logistics of its games and strategies for winning. Similarly, a market maker must be able to assess at a moment's notice how to respond to diverse market conditions that can be as tangible as a change in interest rates or as intangible as an emotional trading frenzy based on a news report. Discipline, education, and experience are a market maker's best insurance. We mention this here because, as an individual investor, you can use these guidelines to help you compete wisely with a market maker and to become a successful options trader.

Market Making As a Business

In the previous section, we addressed rather conceptually, how a market maker works in relation to the market (and, in particular, in relation to you, the individual trader). A market maker's actual practices are dictated by a number of bottom-line business concerns, however, which require constant attention throughout the trading day. Like any business owner, a market maker has to follow business logic, and he or she must consider the wisest uses of his or her capital. There are a number of factors that you should consider when assessing whether an option trade is a good or bad business decision. At base, the steps that a market maker takes are as follows:

1. Determining the current theoretical fair value of an option. (As we have discussed, the market maker can perform this task with the use of a mathematical pricing model.)
2. Attempting to determine the future value of an option. Buying the option if you think that it will increase in value or selling the option if you think that it will decrease in value. This is done through the assessment of market factors that may affect the value of an option. These factors include

    a. Interest rates
    b. Volatility
    c. Dividends
    d. Price of the underlying stock

3. Determining whether the capital can be spent better elsewhere. For example, if the interest saved through the purchase of a call (instead of the outright purchase of the stock) exceeds the dividend that would have been received through owning the stock, then it is better to purchase the call.
4. Calculating the long stock interest that is paid for borrowing funds in order to purchase the stock and considering whether the money used to purchase the underlying stock would be better invested in an interest-bearing account. If so, would buying call options instead of the stock be a better trade?
5. Calculating whether the interest received from the sale of short stock is more favorable than purchasing puts on the underlying stock. Is the combination of owning calls and selling the underlying stock a better trade than the outright purchase of puts?
6. Checking for arbitrage possibilities. Like the preceding step, this task entails determining whether one trade is better than another. In the section on synthetics, we explored the possibility of creating a position with the same profit/loss characteristics as another by using different components. At times, it will be more cost effective to put on a position synthetically. Arbitrage traders take advantage of price differentials between the same product on different markets or equivalent products on the same market. For example, a differential between an option and the actual underlying stock can be exploited for profit. The three factors to base this decision on are as follows:

    a. The level of the underlying asset
    b. The interest rate. For example, if you buy a call option, you save the interest on the money that you would have had to pay for the underlying stock. Conversely, if you purchase a put, you lose the

short stock interest that you could be receiving from the sale of the underlying stock.

   c. The dividend rate. If you buy a call option, you lose the dividends that you would have earned by actually holding the stock.

7. Finally, determining the risk associated with the option trade.

As previously discussed, all of the factors that contribute to the price of the option are potential risk factors to an existing position. As we know, if the factors that determine the price of an option change, then the value of an option will change. This risk associated with these changes can be alleviated through the direct purchase or sale of an offsetting option or the underlying stock. This process is referred to as hedging.

A Market Maker's Complex Positioning

As we mentioned earlier, the bulk of a market maker's trading is not based on market speculation but on the small edge that can be captured within each trade. Because the market maker must trade in such large volumes in order to capitalize on fractional profits, it is imperative that he or she manage the existing risks of a position. For example, in order to retain the edge associated with the trade, he or she might need to add to the position when necessary by buying or selling shares of an underlying asset or by trading additional options. In fact, it is not uncommon that once the trade has been executed, the trader will hedge the corresponding risk within seconds by taking an opposite market position in the underlying security or in any other available options. Over time, a large position consisting of a multitude of option contracts and a position in the underlying stock is established. The market maker's job at this point is to continue to trade for theoretical edge while maintaining a hedged position to alleviate risk. In the following section, we will review the basics of risk management in the form of hedging. Although market makers are the masters of hedging, hedged positions are essential for the risk management for all option traders. It will be equally important for you to understand how to use these strategies.

Profit and Hedging

Thus far, we have overviewed the logistics of the market maker's business model and have seen how it functions to both serve the trading public and the market maker simultaneously. Now we will consider how market makers work to secure their edge against the ongoing risks presented to their many positions.

An investor who chooses to invest in a particular market is exposed to the risks that are inherent in that market. The specific risk is high if the investor concentrates on one security only. The more a portfolio is diversified, the lesser the specific risk. Hedging is the most basic strategy that an investor can use in order to guard against loss. A hedge position is taken with the specific intent of lowering risk. As we have learned, option positions are susceptible to more than just simple directional price risks, and therefore, a trader must be concerned with more than simple delta neutral trading. There is risk associated with each of the variables that determine an option's value (from interest rates to time until expiration). In order to minimize the effect of these risks to an option's value, a trader will establish a position with offsetting characteristics. Just as you hedge a bet by betting against your original bet too a lesser degree, market makers try to take on complementary positions (in stock or options) with characteristics that can potentially buffer against exposure to loss. A hedge, then, is a position that is established for the sole purpose of protecting an existing position.

Determining what risks an option position might be exposed to is one of the first steps towards determining how best to hedge risk. We have learned that six risks are associated with an option position:

1. Directional risk (delta risk) is the risk that an option's value will change as the underlying asset changes in value. All other factors aside, as the price of an underlying asset decreases, the value of a call will decrease while the price of the put will increase. Conversely, as the underlying asset increases in value, a call will increases in value as the put decreases in value. Delta risk can easily be offset through the purchase or sale of an option or stock with opposing directional characteristics. Directional hedges are illustrated in Tables 10-1 and 10-2.

2. Gamma risk is the risk that the delta of an option will change. The holder of options is long gamma (backspreader) and the seller of options is short gamma (frontspreader). Sometimes referred to as curvature, gamma can be offset through the purchase or sale of options with opposing gammas.

3. Volatility risk (vega risk) is the risk that the volatility assumption used in pricing the options will change. If the option volatility rises, the value of the calls and puts will increase. The holder of any options might benefit from an increase in volatility whereas the seller might incur a loss. This risk can be offset through the purchase or sale of option contracts that have an opposing vega value. For example, we know that options decrease in value as volatility decreases.

Table 10-1 *Delta Effects*

When the Underlying Security....	Increases in Value	Decreases in Value
The Long Call will....	Increase in Value	Decrease in Value
The Short Call will....	Decrease in Value	Increase in Value
The Long Put will....	Decrease in Value	Increase in Value
The Short Put will....	Increase in Value	Decrease in Value

Table 10-2 *Position Hedges*

Option Position	Hedge Position
Long Call – Increases in value as the underlying increases in value	Short Underlying Short Call Long Put
Short Call – Decreases in value as the underlying increases in value	Long Underlying Long Call Short Put
Long Put – Decreases in value as the underlying increases in value	Long Underlying Short Put Long Call
Short Put – Increases in value as the underlying decreases in value	Short Underlying Long Put Short Call

Table 10-3 *Effects of Theta*

As Time Moves Forward...	
Underlying Security	Value remains constant
Long Call	Decreases in Value
Short Call	**Increases in Value**
Long Put	Decreases in Value
Short Put	**Increases in Value**

Therefore, selling options (that benefit as volatility decreases) might be the best hedge for a trader who is looking to offset vega risk.

4. Time decay (theta risk) is a positions exposure to the effects of a change in the amount of time remaining to expiration. We know that time moves forward and as it does, the time value of an option decreases. This exposure can be offset through the purchase or sale of options with opposite theta characteristics. The effects of time decay on an options value are illustrated in Table 10-3.

5. Interest rate risk (rho risk) is negligible to most traders. Its impact can be substantial if a position contains a large amount of long or short stock or long-term options. Decreasing the stock position, replacing stock with options is the most efficient way to reduce rho risk. Remember, longer-term options are more interest rate sensitive.

6. Divided risk can be offset through the purchase or sale of options or the underlying stock. An increase in the dividend will make the call decrease in value because the holder of the call does not receive the dividend whereas the holder of the underlying asset will receive the dividend. In this situation, it is more advantageous to own the underlying asset over owning the call. Conversely, the put will increase in value when the dividend is increased because the short stock seller must pay the dividend to the lender of the stock, which makes owning the put more desirable than shorting the underlying asset.

Table 10-4 illustrates the effects of changing input variables on an option's theoretical value.

Knowing the risks involved with options trading is the first step to successful trading while hedging these risks to create a profitable position is the second step. We have learned that there are different ways to hedge each trade, providing a market maker with the important task of determining the best hedge possible for each trade he or she executes. Determining which hedge is the best is based on knowing not only the risks of the original trade but also the corresponding risk of the hedge. Observing actual positions under a multitude of conditions is by far the best way to learn the complex nuances of options. The next two chapters will guide the reader through the fundamentals of the marketplace and setting up a trading station, giving the investor the ability to begin trading on his or her own.

Table 10-4   *Varying Market Conditions*

As market conditions change the values of ...	Rise in price of the underlying ...	Interest rates Rise ...	Volatility Rise ...	Passage of time ...	Dividends Rise ...
Long Underlying	Increase	No effect	No effect	No effect	Increase
Short Underlying	Decrease	No effect	No effect	No effect	Decrease
Long Call	Increase	Increase	Increase	Decrease	Decrease
Short Call	Decrease	Decrease	Decrease	Increase	Increase
Long Put	Decrease	Decrease	Increase	Decrease	Increase
Short Put	Increase	Increase	Decrease	Increase	Decrease

Chapter 11

The Marketplace

Introduction to Stocks

Due to the derivative nature of stock options, it is necessary to have a foundational knowledge of the key characteristics of stocks. Without fully understanding the characteristics of an underlying security, it is difficult to understand the option that is derived from it. The following section provides an overview of stock market basics that are relevant to the understanding of stock options trading. First, we will review how to access and read stock quotes. You can determine the previous and current market value of an underlying security in one of two ways: through historical or real-time stock quotes.

Historical Quotes

A quote is the bid and offer being disseminated by a market maker or broker-dealer for a specific stock or option. The highest bid and lowest offer make up the quote. We define historical quotes as any quotes that are not current. Sources for historical stock quotes range from newspapers such as *The Wall Street Journal* and *Barron's* to free online services and television financial broadcasts such as CNBC or Bloomberg. Stock quotes in the daily newspaper list where the stock opened on the day, the last trade price of the day (known as the closing price), the net change from the previous day's close, the high and low of the day, and the trading volume. (Some newspapers include the 52-week high and low as well.) Refer to the section in this chapter called Reading Stock Quotes.

There are a number of sources for free, historical, online quotes, including the Web sites www.pacificex.com, www.nyse.com, and www. marketcompass.com. These sites offer static quotes (also referred to as snapshot quotes), which typically reflect a 10- to 20-minute delay in real-time activity. These quotes can provide you with a rough indicator of where the stock is trading during the day. They are valuable for investors who are interested in stocks that are not highly volatile or for those who are interested in making long-term investment decisions.

Real-Time Quotes

While a stock's trading history is relevant to your option trading decision, stock option trades are not executed based on historical quotes. A minute can be a long time for the active equities and options trader, because prices can change significantly in the blink of an eye. Because the power of stock options is marked by the option investor's leveraged assessment of these incremental fluctuations, it is essential for him or her to have access to real-time trading quotes.

In this respect, it is not surprising that the Internet, which has the capacity to provide real-time access to trading information, is having a revolutionary effect on equities and options trading. Prior to this recent development, direct monitoring was available only to the professional investment community. Only traders on the exchanges' floor could monitor fluctuations in the value of a stock during a trading day. By contrast, today's online quote services enable private investors to monitor current quotes and trade accordingly.

Reading Stock Quotes

Newspaper Quotes.

> MICROSOFT (MSFT) 92.75 − 1.13 OPEN: 93.75 HI: 94.38 LOW: 91.50
> VOL: 95622

The first number listed, 92.75, is the closing price. Next is a positive or negative number (in this case, −1.13) that indicates how much the closing stock price was up or down from the previous day's closing price. The OPEN (93.754) refers to the price of the first trade of the day, then the HIGH (94.38) and the LOW (91.50) refer to the high and low trading prices of the day. The volume, 95622, is always listed in the hundreds. You can identify the actual volume of the day by adding two zeros to the volume number, in this case indicating 9,562,200 shares were traded that day.

Online Quote. The online quote is similar to the newspaper quote (with a few exceptions). Refer to Table 11-1 for an example. The first column, "Last," lists the last price at which the stock traded (unlike the newspaper, where this number reflects the closing price). The bid and offer represent where the specialist or market maker is willing to buy and sell the stock. The trade column shows the volume of the last trade. You can view this online quote live through a data service provider or broker for a nominal fee. You can also view this information at no charge on the Internet, but remember that the data will be delayed by 10 to 20 minutes.

The Exchanges

The stock of public companies will trade either by using the specialist system (used most prominently by the *New York Stock Exchange* (NYSE) or

Table 11-1 *Example of an Online Quote*

Symbol	Last	Chg.	BID	OFFER	Trade	Volume	Open	HI	LOW
IBM	123.13	−1.25	123.00	123.25	200	55004	122.25	123.13	121.50
MSFT	92.75	−1.13	92.63	92.87	1000	95622	94.00	94.25	91.50
CPQ	26.25	+.75	26.25	26.38	500	87551	26.50	26.50	25.38
MO	38.38	+.25	38.25	38.50	1200	62750	38.13	38.75	37.93
YHOO	146.25	−4.44	146.13	146.63	700	110760	148.50	152.38	146.13

the market maker system employed by the *National Association of Security Dealers Automated Quotation* (NASDAQ) system. Each exchange uses unique symbols to identify stocks.

An easy way to identify whether you are trading or viewing a NYSE or NASDAQ stock is by noting the number of letters in the symbol. NYSE stocks are three letter symbols or fewer, while NASDAQ stocks are four or more lettered symbols. For example, the symbol for Microsoft, which is a NASDAQ stock, is MSFT. The symbol for Compaq, which is a NYSE-listed stock, is CPQ.

The Specialist System

The NYSE is the oldest and perhaps most respected exchange in the United States. Stocks, warrants, and *American Depository Receipts* (ADRs) represent shares in foreign corporations and are all traded on the NYSE. The total capitalization of the stocks on the NYSE is larger than that of any other exchange in the world. The NYSE, sometimes referred to as the "big board," is the primary marketplace for most U.S. stocks and provides the most liquid markets in the world. The *Dow Jones Industrial Average* (DJIA) and the *Standard & Poor's 500* (S&P 500) index are both comprised primarily of stocks that are traded on the NYSE.

Traders trade big-board stocks by using the specialist system, which employs an auction system. Exchange members who are acting on behalf of the public and/or institutions announce buy and sell orders to the trading crowd. The specialist manages the auction market on behalf of a trading firm. There are more than 450 specialists on the NYSE floor who make markets in more than 3,000 stocks (most specialists manage five or more stocks). The specialist is responsible for maintaining a fair and orderly marketplace, disseminating quotes, determining the stock price based on the order flow, and matching buyers with sellers. If there are more buyers than sellers for a given stock, the specialist acts like an auctioneer—raising the price until a seller can be found. (The same situation holds true in reverse if there are more sellers than buyers.) The specialist might also accommodate the buyer from his or her own stock portfolio. The specialist actually determines the stock price based on the basic laws of supply and demand. Because the supply and demand can be lopsided (more buyers than sellers or more sellers than buyers), a stock gap can occur.

NASDAQ and the Market-Maker System

Originating in February 1971, the NASDAQ system was developed as one of the first practical applications of computer networking technology. Using computers that were networked across great distances, NASDAQ served as an electronic trading system that enabled market makers to post bids and offers on a single stock without having to be in the same physical location.

In contrast to the NYSE specialist system, NASDAQ has no individual specialist through which a stock's transactions must pass, and issues traded on the NASDAQ are correspondingly referred to as *over-the-counter* (OTC) issues. Instead, market makers compete with one another for the investors' buy and sell orders by displaying quotes that represent their own buy and sell interests. Market-making firms such as Goldman Sachs, Morgan Stanley, Knight, and Merrill Lynch commit their own capital, maintain an inventory of stock, and represent customer orders. When comparing stock that is traded on the NYSE, you will find that NASDAQ trading is less centralized. Correspondingly, stock prices can be more volatile. Each market maker is like a competing specialist. He or she sees the firm's position and the customer order flow and must make a two-sided (bid and offer) market in the stock that he or she is trading. Because there is no one specialist, the liquidity and volatility vary. It is hard to get an exact picture of the bid and offer price and their corresponding sizes. There are also auctionary markets, *Electronic Communication Networks* (ECNs), that compete with the NASDAQ market makers. The NASDAQ market makers can also trade on many of these auctionary markets. Data must be collected from multiple sources in order to maintain a fair evaluation of what is going on in the NASDAQ marketplace.

Options Exchanges

The options exchanges are different from both the NASDAQ and listed stock exchanges. Actually, they are a combination of both types of stock exchanges. The option exchanges use a competing market-maker system like NASDAQ but trade on a trading floor at a post that is similar to listed stock exchanges.

The exchange floors are divided into trading pits, each of which represents anywhere from one to 30 or more issues. Each trading pit contains a group of market makers who trade in competition with one another as either employees of a trading firm (by using that firm's capital) or as sole proprietor traders who use their own capital to trade. As members of the exchange, they have a fiduciary responsibility to provide a two-sided market (bid and ask) that represents the best possible market for public customers. As such, the market maker's high-volume trading activity serves public customers and provides depth and liquidity in the marketplace.

In providing liquid markets, a market maker can compile a large position that consists of options and stock. He or she will continually monitor and adjust this position in order to curb, or hedge, that position's risk. Market makers aim to capitalize, then, off a marginal edge that they seek to accrue as trading volume increases.

In the past, market makers have had an inside edge on the individual investor. Yet, with today's technology, educational resources, and pricing models now at the fingertips of the everyday investor, he or she can trade like the professionals. By understanding how the option exchange works, the roles of the staff and members, and order execution, the trader will have a better understanding and keener insight when making trading decisions.

Rules of the Option Exchange

In order to maintain a fair and orderly market in which the public can trade, each exchange has a constitution. The constitution covers all of the rules governing the exchange, the methods of execution, conduct on the trading floor, and the role of the market makers and brokers.

The exchanges and their members provide a marketplace in which the public can buy and sell options. The exchange provides the location, regulatory body, computer systems, and staff in order to create a public forum for trading options. The market makers actually make the option market while the brokers represent the public's orders.

The Exchange Floor Staff and Members

The option floor can be an amazing place, with hundreds of members buying and selling, screaming, and fighting for order flow. The exchange hires staff to monitor trading and to ensure an orderly marketplace. To help give the reader a better idea of what transpires on the trading floors, here is a breakdown of the exchange staff and members. Each exchange can have different terms used to describe a particular function, but the roles are similar.

The Exchange Staff

Order Book Official (OBO). The OBO is in charge of the trading post. He or she is responsible for opening and closing the issues traded in the pit, monitoring trading activity, enforcing the applicable rules, supervising staff, and filling the public orders that the firms have entrusted with the exchange's order book. He or she is an exchange employee who has no biases toward the marketplace, price of the options, market makers, or brokers. The OBO's duty is to simply maintain an orderly marketplace and are sometimes referred to as the sheriff of the pit because of their role as the enforcer of the exchange's rules and regulations.

Assistant OBO. The assistant at each trading post acts as a backup to the OBO in running the post, handling staff, and helping with clerk and market quote-terminal duties when necessary. Assistant OBOs also act as OBOs and are required to monitor the trading crowd, enforce rules, and fill public orders that the firms have left with the exchange book. In the OBO's absence, the assistant is in charge of the trading post. If the OBO is the sheriff, then the assistant OBO is the deputy.

Clerks. The clerk's role is a support role for order entry and checking as well as for assisting the market quote-terminal operator with posting quotes as necessary. Ordinarily, at least one and sometimes two or more clerks are assigned to a trading post. Their function is to assist the OBO or assistant OBO.

Market Quote-Terminal Operators (MQs or MQTOs). One of the key roles in the function of disseminating quotes is the MQTO or MQ. The MQ's role is to listen to the trading crowd and enter the highest bid and lowest offer on any option that is traded at that post. The MQ enters the quotes that are called out, and the exchange disseminates the best bid and offer worldwide. The MQ's job is difficult, because he or she is responsible for entering the correct quotes. Any errors could cost the traders in the pit a great deal of money. The MQ must understand the slang terminology on the floor, be able to differentiate between market makers and broker orders, and always disseminate the highest bid and lowest offer. The MQ is an employee of the exchange and is not biased toward the marketplace or toward members of the exchange.

Trade Match.   The trade match staff is responsible for comparing the exchange's option transaction records with the member firm (market makers and brokers) option transaction records and to resolve any discrepancies.

Trade Processing.   The trade processing staff's responsibility is to enter all option trades into the exchange's computer system, which records all trading transactions at the exchange.

Other Floor Staff.   Other important roles on the trading floor do not involve the exchange staff or members of the exchange. We will take a brief look at these roles to help give you a better idea of how the trading floor operates.

Stock Firms/Clerks

Market makers are continually hedging their positions in the marketplace. In order to hedge their positions, they need to be able to trade stock. Private stock firms that charge market makers a commission for trading stock are located around the trading floor. Each stock firm has stock clerks that stand next to the trading crowds in order to take orders and to relay them verbally to the stock firm booths.

Runners.   Other than the brokers on the floor, the most common job referred to at an exchange is the runner. This term is used although running is not permitted on the floor of the exchange. The runner relays orders and market quotes between floor brokers and firm booths. They are the lines of communication between the brokers and phone clerks.

Phone Clerks.   The phone clerk is the eyes and ears for the retail broker. These employees pass along information from the trading floor to the retail brokers. They are also responsible for receiving orders from retail brokers and reporting to them. Some phone clerks specialize in watching order flow and report back to large trading firms what is going on down on the floor. The large institutions want to keep a watchful eye over what other firms are doing. This reporting is the role of the phone clerk. He or she must assess all of his brokers' data and relay what might be of interest to the trading firms that he or she represents.

Members.   The members of the exchange are responsible for making a market (the market makers) or executing institutional or retail customer orders (the floor brokers).

Floor Brokers.   Floor brokers represent customer and firm orders and are generally paid on commission. Their responsibility is to execute their customers' or firms' orders in a timely and diligent manner.

Few brokerage firms have their own brokers on the floor. Instead, there are actually independent floor brokerage firms that represent several retail or institutional brokerage firms. These independent floor brokerage firms usually specialize in either retail accounts or the large institutional accounts. It is possible to have an independent floor brokerage firm represent several firms simultaneously (this situation is usually the case). A floor brokerage firm, for example, might represent Goldman Sachs, Smith Barney, and Bear Stearns. The advantage is that it is cheaper for the brokerage firm to contract out the business, rather than staffing an entire operation on the trading floor.

There are three types of option floor brokers: the independent floor broker, the pit broker, and the firm broker.

The independent broker pays for his or her own seat or seat lease, handles his or her own errors, and executes any array of orders from market makers, large institutional, or small retail. They usually cover only one pit or a group of pits. They also have a keen sense of what is going on in their trading crowd, and they fight for every order.

The pit broker represents an independent brokerage firm. He or she handles all orders for the firm in the particular pit to which he or she is assigned. Most floor brokerage firms that handle retail orders have pit brokers.

The firm broker represents an independent brokerage firm that usually handles the large institutional orders. They go to whereever the action is and report back to their firm as to what is going on down on the floor. They are the eyes and ears for the large institutional firms.

Analyzing the Marketplace

Analysis: Understanding Market Conditions.   The starting point for any investment strategy is your basic market outlook. The individual investor has several speculative decisions from which to choose, including the following:

- **Bullish**—The investor is speculating a rise in stock price.
- **Bearish**—The investor is speculating a decline in stock price.
- **Volatile backspread**—The investor is speculating that the stock will make a significant move in either direction but has no idea as to which direction it will move.
- **Neutral frontspread**—The investor is speculating that the stock will remain at its current level or will stay within a small trading range.
- **Uncertain**—The investor cannot make a speculative decision and should remain out of the marketplace until he or she has made a decision.

In order to speculate on a certain market outlook, the individual investor must analyze certain market data. The data that the trader decides to analyze is based on what type of trader he or she is:

- **Technical analysis**—Analyzing chart patterns and looking for trends in the market
- **Fundamental analysis**—Analyzing the company, price/earnings ratios, and so on and looking for undervalued or overvalued companies
- **Market analysis**—Analyzing market indicators and market movement (looking for market sentiment)

Technical Analysis.   As a technical analyst, the individual investor will be looking for trading ranges, supply levels, and support levels in order to make a decision in the marketplace. There is only one slight flaw in the technical-analyst technique, however: This position cannot predict practical, real-world events (such as surprise earnings, takeovers, spin-offs, CEOs retiring, cooking the books, and so on). When the individual investor or trader uses technical analysis, however, we recommend for him or her to use this strategy only as a conformation to the trader's overall sentiment. It is possible to over-analyze the market and to get lost in all of the technical analysis tools that are available. We call this situation "analysis paralysis." This situation occurs when a trader or investor is unable to make a decision because too many of the tools upon which he or she relies have generated conflicting reports. Again, use these tools as confirmation tools only.

Using a basic high/low graph is the easiest way to jump into technical analysis. The individual investor should first make his or her own decisions based on the high/low data before launching into the hundreds of analyzing tools that are available. The trader should look for a couple of patterns:

1. Where is the previous low or support?
2. Where is the previous high or supply?
3. Is the stock in a channel? What type of channel is it (bullish, bearish, or neutral)?
4. Is the stock in a wedging or flag formation?
5. Is the stock breaking out of a channel?
6. Is there a stock gap?

By looking for these basic patterns, the individual investor can now make some basic market speculation on the stock.

The two easy speculations are bullish or bearish (see Figures 11-1 and 11-2). The trader does not need any special tool to determine whether a stock is rising or declining in price. Figuring out supply and support levels are as easy as looking at a graph. We do not guarantee that the trader will be right, but he or she can make some basic determinations (such as whether the stock is at its previous low or previous high).

Figure 11-1   *Bullish outlook.*

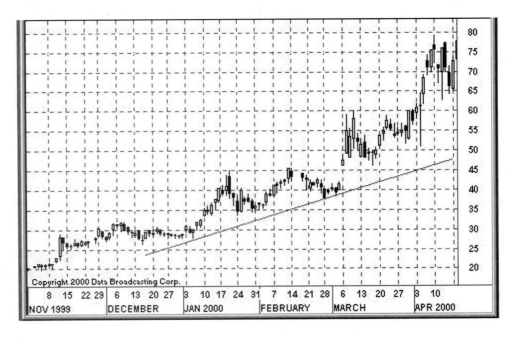

Figure 11-2   *Bearish outlook.*

You will find it a little more difficult to analyze stocks in order to determine whether they will be volatile (expected to make a big move either up or down) or neutral (unchanged or to slowly move in a small range).

A pattern that professional traders frequently look for is the wedging or flag pattern. This pattern is where a stock trading range is narrowing, with lower highs and higher lows. This situation results from either a lack of interest in the stock or the presence of a large seller and large buyer. As the stock range narrows, the volatility decreases as well. The trader is now speculating that something will happen but is uncertain of the result. He or she believes that either the buyer will step aside or the seller will create an imbalance in the stock, sending it into a dramatic swing in one direction or the other.

This pattern would result in the trader or individual investor purchasing a long straddle or other backspread-type strategy, looking to gain from the increase in the underlying volatility (see Figure 11-3).

If the trader has noticed that a wedging or flag pattern is beginning, he or she is speculating that the volatility will decrease as the stock's trading range narrows. The individual investor will probably want to implement a neutral or frontspread strategy, looking to capture the decreasing volatility in the stock.

Speculating on neutral or volatile conditions in the marketplace can be as simple as analyzing the chart and determining whether it is bullish or bearish. Many traders find it easier to speculate on volatility than direction. Bulls and bears are direction speculators, while frontspreaders and backspreaders are speculating on market volatility.

Here are some other common patterns that we look for:

- **Bottom testing**—Bullish. This situation occurs when a stock has found a support level and has continued to bounce off the lows. This situation is usually an indication of a low and support, and many

Figure 11-3 *Backspread-type strategy*

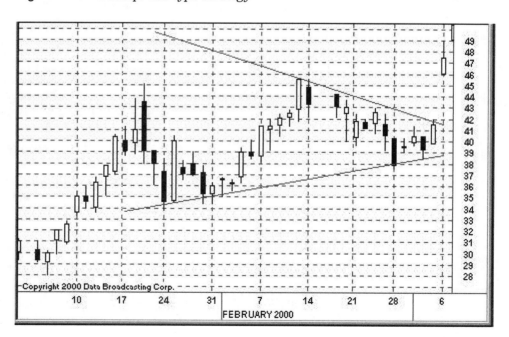

Figure 11-4 *Bottom testing.*

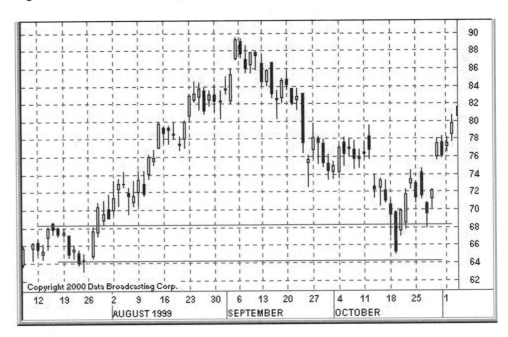

investors are interested in owning stock at this price. This situation
creates a group consensus that the stock is cheaply priced and is a
worthwhile purchase at these levels (see Figure 11-4).

- **Gap up**—Bearish. Stocks sometimes gap up because of speculation on
  an event, news, rumors, takeovers, and so on. If the gap is unfounded,
  meaning that it is speculative, there is a good chance that it will pull
  back. The stock loses momentum in the short term, and sellers step in
  —believing that the gap up was unwarranted. This situation has hap-
  pened frequently with many dot-com companies, only to fall back to
  their previous levels (see Figure 11-5).
- **Gap down**—Bullish. This situation is the exact opposite of a gap up.
  The stock has dropped significantly based on an event, and if this
  event is unwarranted or the gap is extreme, there is a good chance
  that it will rebound and fill the gap. This situation happens frequently when a company announces bad earnings ahead of time. The
  stocks are sometimes oversold and eventually rally back to their previous levels. Remember that in both gap situations, if the stock warrants the gap a rebound strategy will not be effective. You need to
  evaluate the reason for the gap (see Figure 11-6).
- **Topping**—Bearish. The stock has lost its momentum to the upside
  and is looking to reverse. This situation happens in a short-covering
  rally or short squeeze. When the shorts are done covering their
  losses, they reduce their buying pressure—thus slowing down the
  momentum. Chances are that the stock will fall dramatically (see
  Figure 11-7).

Figure 11-5   *Gap up.*

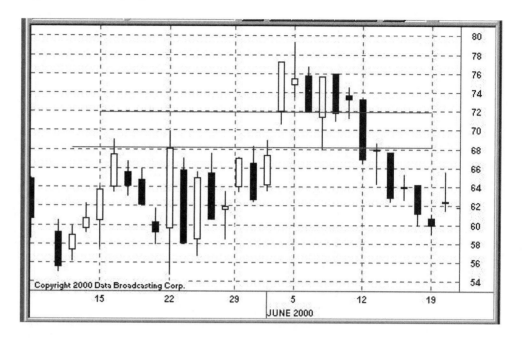

Figure 11-6   *Gap down.*

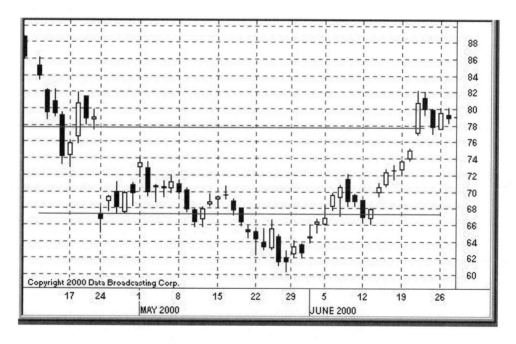

Technicians have defined many patterns in the charts that they study; the preceding are only a handful. Although some technical analysts rely on charts to make investment decisions, it is wise to leave this to the technicians. Your time may be better spent investing in a company from the inside out, that is, focusing on the value of a company.

.Figure 11-7   *Topping.*

Fundamental Analysis

The study of a company from the inside out is known as *fundamental analysis*. When determining the value of a company, an investor must look at a company's internal workings, as well as its business environment and competition. The fundamentals of a company give an investor an idea of what each share represents: a percentage ownership of an actual business. Each share of stock is tied to the performance of the underlying business. Although the dotcom mania has made it appear that valuation is no longer a concern, the eventual fallout will separate the performers from the faux-formers. Finding the needles in a haystack becomes an ever-increasing task in such a frenzied environment. It is important that investors become familiar with the steps used in evaluating a company. Some helpful guidelines may be useful.

When determining the value of a company, it is important to investigate the following:

1. Is this a company that is strong and growing?
2. Is the company's stock priced to reflect its earning potential?

In order to answer these questions, an investor should take the following into consideration:

1. The company's P/E ratio (price to earnings ratio), which compares the stock price to the earnings per share. For example, assume that Assume PDQ Co. sells for $50.50 per share and has earned $5.50 per share this year: $50.50 = 10 times $5.50. PDQ stock sells for 10 times earnings. P/E = current stock price divided by trailing annual earnings per share *or* expected annual earnings per share.

2. *Return on equity* (ROE) is an indicator of profitability. The ROE is determined by dividing net income for the past 12 months by common stockholder equity (adjusted for stock splits). The result is shown as a percentage. Investors use ROE as a measure of how a company is using its money.

3. Profit margin is another indicator of a company's profitability. The company's profit margin is the ratio of earnings available to stockholders to net sales. The profit margin is determined by dividing net income by revenue for the same 12-month period. The result is shown as a percentage.

Using fundamentals will help you determine whether a company's shares are a buy or sale at their current price. At first glance, an investor may think that a stock that is trading $50 per share is more attractive than a stock currently trading $250 per share. This is a common misconception; the $50 stock may be overvalued, whereas the $250 dollar stock may be undervalued at its current price.

Obtaining the information needed to make an educated assessment of a publicly traded company's valuation is simple and *free*. You can call the company's Investor Relations department, and they can provide you with an investor information package that will contain the most recent

- Press releases
- 10-K (annual report that provides a comprehensive overview of a company's state of business)
- 10-Q (quarterly report)
- Analysts' reports (they also can provide you with the dates of earnings announcements and shareholder meetings)

If you want the information immediately or are requesting information from a number of companies, you can go to the company's Web site. Most companies provide the preceding information online.

Examining a stock's chart and a company's fundamentals is key to determining a company's stock-price history and value. Assessing the condition of the overall market is just as important, however. Many indices will help you assess market volatility and value. As we have discussed, one of the most important factors in determining whether to buy or sell is market volatility. Using the CBOE's *Volatility Index* (VIX) is the best way to get a sense of overall market volatility.

CBOE Volatility Index—VIX

The VIX is a measure of the level of implied volatility in index options and is used to assess the volatility of the U.S equity market. The VIX index is calculated by taking a weighted average of the implied volatilities of eight OEX calls and puts having an average time to maturity of 30 days and is used by some traders as a general indication of index option implied volatility. Because the VIX uses near-term options to measure implied volatility, it should not be used as an indicator of long-term implied volatility. Many traders use the index as a gauge of anxiety in the market.

The VIX is generally used as a contra-indicator. Many traders use the VIX to predict market direction, with a low VIX indicating a bullish sentiment and a high VIX being a bearish indicator. The logic of this view is as follows. A high VIX value usually correlates to increased put buying. These puts provide downside protection, which reduces selling pressure. Conversely, a low VIX indicates lighter than normal put buying. This would increase selling pressure in a declining market. Although this sentiment used to be widely held, there is a running debate as to whether the VIX is a valid indicator of volatility in the broader market because volume in OEX options (options based on the S&P 100) has declined significantly over the past few years.

Similarly, option volatility in equity issues increases as public and institutional buying increases in the options. It is, therefore, prudent for a stock trader to be aware of increases and decreases in that stock's option volatility, not just the volatility of the specific underlying stock. Option volatility is a good indicator of future volatility in the underlying whereas the volatility of the underlying is generally a historical view of volatility.

The VIX decreases when the volatility of the market remains rather low. For instance, if the stock market is slowly rising, slowly declining, or remaining unchanged, the volatility of the marketplace is declining. The market might still move and the VIX might decrease, but the key word here is *slowly*.

When the VIX is rather low, this situation is usually an indication of a correction in the marketplace—whether positive or negative. Usually, it is an indicator of a negative correction, because most individuals are long stock and will have to sell stock.

As the VIX increases rapidly, this situation will coincide with the market correction. As the VIX slows in momentum, this situation indicates that volatility in the marketplace is stabilizing and that it will begin to decrease. Because corrections are usually negative, the VIX slowing and decreasing is usually an indication of a market bottoming and the end of the correction.

We can see a couple of excellent examples of the VIX and its relationship to the market during the "Asian flu" of 1998, which started a global correction. During the initial phases of the Asian flu, the U.S. market continued to rise as the VIX declined. It was not until the global crisis reached the shores of South America that the U.S. market felt its wrath and the market began its correction. The VIX skyrocketed as the *Dow Jones Industrial Index* (DJIA) and other broad-base indices dropped in price.

Many market makers and professional traders kept a close eye on the VIX during this period, realizing that it would be the first indication of a market correction. As long as the VIX was low, no one was buying calls and puts. Institutions, hedge funds, and money managers began purchasing options for protection against a volatile event or in the event of a crash. The VIX started to rise dramatically. This indicator was the first sign that the professionals were concerned.

You can use regular technical analysis to analyze the VIX. As options traders, we recommended for this indicator to be closely watched, because it shows the market's implied volatility. A graph of the VIX is seen below (see Figure 11-8).

Put-to-Call Ratio

The put-to-call ratio measures the amount of puts being purchased versus the number of calls purchased. Many believe that this indicator shows market sentiment. Some believe that when the put volume is larger than the call volume, the market will decline. Some believe that this ratio indicates a bottom in the marketplace.

There are two major problems when analyzing the put-to-call ratio. The first concern is that it is almost impossible to know who is on which side of the trade. For instance, is it the market makers buying the puts and the customers selling them, or are the market makers selling the puts and the customers are buying them? This situation alone makes it hard to determine market sentiment. The second problem is that we really do not know what the customer, market maker, or institutional

Figure 11-8 *Volatility Index (VIX).*

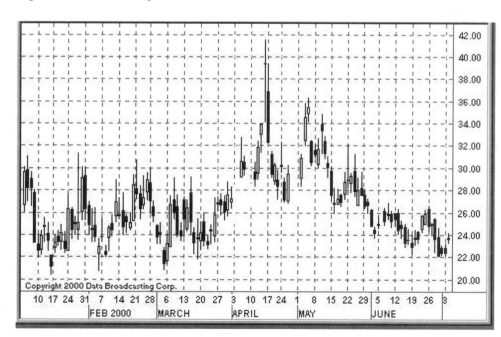

stock position is. Are they buying speculative puts, or are they purchasing puts against an existing long stock position or long portfolio position? Are they buying speculative calls or selling calls against long stock, creating the covered call?

Then, there is the whole aspect of synthetics. Buying puts is bearish, but buying puts and stock together is a synthetic long call (which is bullish). Buying calls is bullish, and buying calls and selling short stock is a synthetic long put (which is bearish).

The put-to-call ratio cannot tell us the two major ingredients that are needed to make a valuable indicator. How is the buyer or seller of options hedging his or her position?

The put-to-call ratio can only indicate whether more puts are being purchased than calls. This information can be useful in that it might offer a brief glimpse as to market sentiment where the ratio is concerned. Among professional market makers, this information is seldom watched or analyzed because of two simple reasons.

1. We do not know whether the customer is buying or selling.
2. We do not know how the customer is hedging the trade.

Indices

Learning to read stock indices is also an important part of assessing the market for stock option trading. A stock index is a composite of several stocks that can provide an effective means for evaluating and analyzing certain sectors of the market. All indices provide an indication of how the stocks that they represent fared for a given trading day. Some stocks in an index might represent a particular sector of the market (for instance, the oil, semiconductor, pharmaceutical, or service industries). Others, like the DJIA, represent an index of activity for a more random selection of large, credit-worthy, or blue-chip companies.

Because no one index can represent the market activity as a whole, it is important to learn how to read a number of indices in order to make an overall assessment of the trading day. Having said that, however, a disproportionate significance tends to be given to certain indices. For example, although it represents only 30 stocks (albeit important stocks), the DJIA receives considerable attention from the trading public. For this reason, the DJIA has a great psychological influence over U.S. and international trading (see Table 11-2).

Weighting Indices

You must understand how indices are weighted, because the movement of one stock in a particular index can have a dramatic effect on the overall index. Indices are weighted according to different characteristic properties. Here, we will discuss both capital-weighted indices and price-weighted indices.

Table 11-2 *Common Indices*

Symbol	Description	Price	Change	%CHG
INDU	Dow Jones Industrial	10531.09	–123.58	–1.17
TRAN	Dow Jones Transportation	3453.33	–20.47	–.59
UTIL	Dow Jones Utility	328.48	1.05	.32
COMPX	NASDAQ Composite	2380.90	–72.76	–3.06
SPX	Standard & Poor's 500	1284.40	–22.25	–1.73
OEX	Standard & Poor's 100	647.45	–10.94	–1.69
XAL	Airline Index	166.96	.73	.44
AUX	Automotive Index	333.72	1.81	.54
BKX	Banking Index	822.44	–30.85	–3.75
XCI	Computer Index	841.23	–26.92	–3.20
XAU	Gold & Silver Index	60.40	–2.11	–3.49
NDX	NASDAQ 100 Index	1999.04	–61.55	–3.08
XOI	Oil Index	502.86	–3.51	–.70
RUT	Russell 2000	434.45	–5.94	–1.37
SOX	Semiconductor Index	373.28	–21.75	–5.83

*List of other indices can be found in the appendix.

Capital-Weighted Indices.   Capital-weighted indices are based on the capitalization of each stock. Capitalization offers an indication of the company value in question based on the number of outstanding shares (the total number of shares available for trading) and the current stock price. To calculate the capitalization of a stock, take the number of outstanding shares (also known as the float) and multiply it by the current stock price. The overall index price, then, is the average capitalization of all of the stocks that make up the index. Refer to the following formula:

Market capitalization for a stock = float × stock price

Here is an example. Stock ABC is currently priced at $42 and has a float of 70 million shares. Its market capitalization is $42 × 70 million, which equals $2.94 billion.

This average will usually be an extremely high number—sometimes in the billions. To make the underlying price an easier number to work with, we use a divisor to knock off the extra zeros and/or to create a more manageable index base line. For instance, if we had an average capitalization in our index of $6,830,000,000 and we wanted our index to start at $1,000, our divisor would be $6,830,000. Performance in that index will then fluctuate around this base-line index. Furthermore, the divisor will be modified in order to ensure this base line's continuity when the float of a stock in the index is changed. For example, if a stock in an index issues new shares, the divisor is adjusted in order to reflect market continuity. If the divisor were not changed, you would see a price change in the index before the market opens. Establishing this continuity keeps the index price adjusted in order to reflect the marketplace.

Not surprisingly, heavily weighted stocks within an index can have a disproportionate influence on the overall index price. The stock that has the highest capitalization will affect the index the most. For instance, a stock might have the lowest price in the index, but if it also represents the largest market capitalization, this stock would be the most heavily weighted stock in the index.

Here is an example. ABC and XYZ are both trading in the same index. Stock ABC is currently priced at $42 and has a float of 70 million shares. Its market capitalization is $42 × 70 million, which equals $2.94 billion. Stock XYZ is currently priced at $123 and has a float of six million shares. Its market capitalization is $123 × six million, which equals $783 million. The total market capitalization of both ABC and XYZ is $3.723 billion.

The index starts at $1,000, so the divisor is $3,723,000 (knocking off those extra zeros). A one-poing move in ABC equals $70 million in market capitalization, which equals an $18.80 move in the index. A one-point move in XYZ equals $6 million in market capitalization, which equals a $1.61 move in the index.

Although it is trading at a lower price, ABC has a larger influence on the capital-weighted index because of the larger market capitalization. As you can see in this case, the stock price has less of an effect than the market capitalization of that stock.

Price-Weighted Indices. Price-weighted indices are based on the price of each stock in the index. The index price is the average price of all stocks in the index divided by a specified divisor in order to create continuity in the index. In this case, the divisor is used to create an equal distribution of stock in a price-weighted index.

For example, Stocks ABC and XYZ are trading on a price-weighted index. Stock ABC is currently $42. Stock XYZ is currently $123. The average is ($123 + $42)/2, which equals $82.5.

We would like to start the index at $1,000:

$$\frac{\$1,000}{\$82.5} = \$12.121 \quad \$82.5 \times 12.121 = \$1,000$$

12.121 would be the divisor. A one-point increase in ABC would affect the index by 3.547:

$$\frac{\$43}{12.121} = \$3.547$$

A one-point increase in XYZ would affect the index by 10.230:

$$\frac{\$124}{12.121} = \$10.230$$

As you can see, the stock that has the higher price is the most heavily weighted and therefore has more of an impact on the index. In addition, as with capital-weighted indices, if a stock splits in a price-weighted index, the divisor is changed in order to reflect an equal distribution of stock throughout the index.

Using Indices

Indices are a sound indicator as to how a particular sector of the market is doing. Frequently, investors watch the DJIA or the NASDAQ composite (which are both consistently on the news, reflected in every newspaper, and known by everyone—even those who are not in the market). The DJIA, however, is a composite of only 30 stocks—and unless the investor has a position in a stock that is in the DJIA, it has little relevance to his or her position. Because the NASDAQ composite is a broad-based index, it might not reflect an accurate correlation to the individual's stock position.

The DJIA and the NASDAQ composite, which has become a popular indicator of late, are indices that are more psychological and can create false sentiments as to an individual position. There are many other indices in the marketplace that can give an investor a better market outlook on a particular stock.

Market makers and institutional traders frequently watch specific indices in order to see how their particular stock is performing. If the individual investor is trading a semiconductor stock such as AMD, INTC, or AMAT, the *Semiconductor Index* (SOX) will reflect a more accurate picture of how that semiconductor stock is performing as compared to its corresponding sector.

Because large institutional firms, hedge funds, and mutual funds are moving stock frequently from one sector to another, it is important to watch how that sector is performing. The broad-based indices or DJIA will not reflect this situation. Especially now that the DJIA is made up of a variety of stocks, it does not really correspond to any sector other than itself.

Two main strategies used by larger funds are looking for stocks that are overperforming or underperforming as compared to their sectors. Of course, it is important to note that some stocks might not perform well as others in their sectors due to news or some other volatile event. Generally, people believe that if one stock in a particular sector reports earnings or news that reflect their sector, the rest will follow. A perfect example is when the price of memory chips fell dramatically in 1996–1997. MU sold off significantly, and shortly thereafter, many other stocks in the sector followed suit. This situation usually reflects a large order flow leaving a sector that is believed to be doing poorly (whether in the short term or long term) and looking for greener pastures. Although the individual investor might not own MU but owns another stock in that sector, knowing that it is in the SOX and knowing how it affects the SOX underlying price is crucial. The SOX index is subsequently sold off.

The investor must pay attention to four indices when trading options and stock (see Table 11-3).

The sector index will vary based on which stocks the individual investor is trading. If he or she is trading airline stocks, then he or she might watch the airline index (XAL). If he or she is trading automotive stocks, then he or she might watch the automotive index (AUX). There is a corresponding index for each sector. Appendix C has a list of common indices.

Table 11-3 *Four Important Indices*

Sector Index	To see how the investors stock is doing compared to the rest of the sector
VIX Index	For general market volatility sentiment
NASDAQ Composite / broad based index	For broad based market sentiment
Dow Jones Industrial (INDU)	For psychological market sentiment

Chapter 12

Getting Started

Introduction

In this section, we will discuss methods of executing stocks and options, order types, selecting a broker and a data service provider, and building a trading station.

Trading Stock

Many of the strategies that we have discussed in this book cover the use of the underlying security. In Chapter 10, "Market Making," we discussed the marketplace and how the specialists and market makers set the marketplace and trade in the market. We will now cover how to execute stock in the marketplace. The methods that we discuss here are commonly referred to as direct access. These are the methods and systems that *Direct-Access Traders* (DATs) (more commonly referred to as day traders) use to execute their stock positions. These methods are made available through many brokerage firms and are an important part of any trader's arsenal. We will also discuss the pros and cons of the various systems.

Executing New York Stock Exchange (NYSE) Orders

In Chapter 11, we discussed the function of a specialist. We learned how a specialist sets the market and trades with the public. Because there is only one specialist for any particular stock on an exchange, there is no need for multiple methods of execution or secondary market systems (as found with trading NASDAQ issues). This situation makes executing listed stock simple. You can trade listed stocks either directly or through your broker. In order to trade a NYSE/listed stock directly, your brokerage firm must give you access to *Designated Order Turnaround* (DOT) or to SuperDOT. (Access is available only if you are affiliated with a licensed broker-dealer; in other words, if you have a trading account with a brokerage firm or have your own broker-dealer license.) DOT is an electronic execution system for listed stocks. The system is similar to an e-mail system in that it can send your order directly to the specialist's post. You can also check the status of your order by using this system. When placing an order on DOT, you must include 1) the price at which you are willing to buy or sell shares and 2) the amount of shares that you are willing to buy or sell (also known as the size). The DOT system is a direct-access system because it bypasses the retail broker and gives the trader direct access to the exchange and specialist who is making a market in that stock. Several brokerage firms offer the DOT system to their customers. If you plan on trading a listed stock, make sure that you have access to the DOT system. The system is straightforward, and everyone can use it to participate. The DOT system offers limit order protection and offers instantaneous access to the specialist. The listed exchanges are the oldest exchanges in the world and remain successful because of their simple and clean methods of executing stock. As technology increases, you might see more electronic systems such as DOT implemented on the listed exchanges. At this writing, the *Pacific Exchange* (PCX) created a partnership with Archipelago—thus creating the first fully electronic listed exchange in the United States. Archipelago will merge many of its electronic execution systems and *electronic communication networks* (ECNs) with PCX, enabling the customers more access to the marketplace at lower costs and increasing the speed of execution. We are sure that this technology is the tip of the iceberg in the new electronic listed exchanges, and other exchanges will probably follow a similar course.

Executing NASDAQ Stock

The NASDAQ is a complicated marketplace for two reasons. First, the NASDAQ marketplace has groups of market makers competing. Second, there are several methods of viewing and executing in the NASDAQ marketplace. This situation creates new challenges for the individual investor. In order to trade a NASDAQ or *over-the-counter* (OTC) issue effectively, you need to be able to monitor the current market price, watch the activity of the market makers, and determine both the depth of the market and the trading momentum. To do so, you have to be able to view the market. The NASDAQ exchange offers a firewall hierarchy of three different levels of access for viewing the market and several methods of trading.

NASDAQ Levels. With the explosion of online trading and day trading, NASDAQ Level II has become a household word. Many individuals do not understand what it is, but they feel that they need it in order to make money in the marketplace. Remember that data is only information, and you still need knowledge in order to analyze the data.

Level I. NASDAQ Level I provides the viewer with a composite of the highest bid and the lowest offer among the market makers. These figures are also referred to as the quote or inside market. This technique is the most common method of viewing a NASDAQ stock quote. All investors have access to Level I quotes. Level I quotes are free (if delayed) and can be viewed at variousWeb sites. When your broker gives you a quote over the phone, he or she is giving you a Level I quote. The chart in the Online Quote section (earlier) is an example of a Level I quote.

Level II. NASDAQ Level II disseminates the names of all of the market makers and ECNs (ECNs are described later in this section) who make bids and offers on a particular security. Level II is also known as "the street." All professional traders, firms, and brokers use Level II to assess the buyers and sellers, the momentum of the stock, and the depth and liquidity of the market (see Table 12-1).

Recently, a number of online brokerage firms and data providers have made Level II available to individual investors. Level II availability has spurred the current growth of day trading. For the first time in history, the individual investor has both the capacity to see who is making the market in a NASDAQ stock and the ability to execute an order directly with the market makers. These practices are referred to in the individual retail investor community as DAT or *Electronic Direct-Access Trading* (EDAT).

Reading Level II. NASDAQ Level III is the same as Level II. The online retail community has used the term Level III to describe the mysterious system that allows market makers to post their bids and offers to trade in the NASDAQ arena. The NASDAQ Level III is actually the Enterprise Wide Network (EWN II) system, which is the backbone of NASDAQ. It is the world's largest closed network system (extranet) designed by NASDAQ and MCI WorldCom. The system allows the market makes to interface into the virtual world of NASDAQ. Retail customers view a modified version of the EWN or Level III system through Level II.

The top line of the table represents the Level I (L1) quote, reflecting the highest bid and the lowest offer (in the gray box across the top). Below the gray box is a list of four-letter symbols representing the different market makers and ECNs that are making bids and offers on the stock. Currently, there are six bidders of stock for $72\,^5/_{16}$ (the highest bid). On the top line, INCA represents the Instinet ECN; and below that there are several market makers who are also bidding for stock: BEST, SBSH, MLCO, GSCO, and another ECN—REDI. There are seven sellers of stock at $72\,^3/_8$: ISLD, INCA, BRUT, REDI, BEST, DBKS, and ARCA. The colors help visu-

Table 12-1 *NASDAQ Level III*

alize the depth of the marketplace. This layout helps you assess buying and selling pressure by determining how many buyers and sellers there are for a particular issue. The last column is the Time and Sales report, which reflects all trading activity in that particular issue.

Executing NASDAQ Orders

There are three executing systems for NASDAQ or OTC issues: SOES, SelectNet, and ECN. Each system has its own advantages, and you should become familiar with (and have access to) all three. You will find times when one particular execution system works better than another.

SOES. SOES stands for Small Order Execution System. The SOES system enables the trader to execute an order on the bid or offer of a particular market maker (Level II). This procedure is done through an electronic direct-access brokerage firm. The individual investor will receive software from his or her brokerage firm or access his or her account through the brokerage Web site, where he or she is able to place the order.

The SOES order provides for the automatic execution of your order. This system is also known as auto-execution. When using the SOES system, you can get your order instantaneously filled. This system is available to the non-professional trading public only. To limit the ability of professional traders to take advantage of price discrepancies, registered NASDAQ broker-dealers cannot use the system.

Here are some characteristics of SOES:

1. Auto-execution up to a specific number of shares, depending on the liquidity of a particular stock (with a 1,000 share maximum)
2. A five-minute time interval restriction between orders in the same stock. This rule is in place to protect the market maker from investors who might take advantage of the rapid execution.
3. Short sales require a plus tick in the stock. This rule is to reduce selling pressure in a declining market and is applied to all stocks in an effort to protect the market in a crash scenario.
4. The market maker is required to buy or sell shares of a stock issue in which he or she is making a market and trade at least the amount being posted in large, capitalized stocks.

Here are some advantages and disadvantages:

1. The advantage of SOES to the individual investor is the rapid execution of the trade. This method is the fastest method of trading a NASDAQ stock with a guaranteed fill.
2. The disadvantage is the limited number of shares per execution and the five-minute interval between transactions.
3. The rules and characteristics of the SOES system change frequently. Contact your broker to find out whether any rules or characteristics of the system have changed before you trade any orders via the SOES system.

SelectNet. SelectNet serves as a means for the rapid routing of orders to market makers. This system has replaced the telephone—which, prior to the development of SelectNet, was the only means by which to trade with market makers. SelectNet enables a trader to send a bid or offer over NASDAQ directly to a market maker who is making the market in a particular issue. The market maker then decides to trade all or any part of your order. You can choose to send the order to all market makers who are making a market on a particular issue, or you can "preference" a selected market maker. Traders might want to select a particular market maker who they feel honors the markets in which they are disseminating (and/or returns filled information promptly).

Here are some advantages and disadvantages to this system:

1. The advantage of SelectNet to the individual investor is that it enables him or her to choose which market maker with which he or she wishes to trade. This method is also faster than calling your broker, who would have to either SelectNet for you or call market makers directly in order to fill your order.

2. There are, however, three shortcomings to using SelectNet. First, market makers are not obligated to trade with you if they can show that they have already traded at that price. Second, SelectNet does not offer any limit order protection. If you place a SelectNet order and select a certain market maker, the stock could be trading elsewhere at your limit price—and you would not be guaranteed a fill. Lastly, SelectNet orders are not disseminated. SelectNet only displays your order to the market maker(s) whom you have referenced. Someone out there might be willing to buy or sell the stock to you for your price, but if you have not selected to show him or her the offer, then he or she will never know that your offer was available.

ECN. ECNs are not stock exchanges; rather, they are proprietary network systems that enable investors to trade OTC stocks. All ECNs are open to retail investors so that they can trade any OTC stock, and some enable investors to trade listed stocks. There are currently 10 ECNs, although as the demand grows, more ECNs will be formed. Note that some ECNs enable 24-hour trading, while others are only open during market hours.

ECNs represent an auction-based marketplace that enables individual investors to place orders that are available to everyone who is currently watching the particular ECN. An ECN can list many bids and offers on any particular stock. Each stock that is trading on an ECN has its own auctionary online room where all of the bids and offers are displayed. Although the ECN market might not reflect the same market on Level II, it directly competes with Level II. An ECN system might have the best market at any particular time, making the ECNs a viable alternative place in which to trade stock. You can see most ECN systems if you are watching Level II.

Examples of ECN systems are Instinet, Island, Archipelago, and REDI. We will now examine two major ECN systems: Instinet and Island.

The former caters principally to inter-institutional trading, and the latter caters mainly to retail customers.

Instinet. Instinet (Institutional Net) was the first ECN. It was developed so that institutions could bypass brokers by displaying bids and offers directly to one another. In the mid-1970s, Instinet opened its doors to brokerage firms, enabling them to participate as active buyers and sellers alongside the institutional firms. Today, access to Instinet for trading is limited to member institutions, brokerage firms, and licensed broker-dealers. Recently, some brokerage firms have given retail customers limited access to Instinet. You should contact your brokerage firm to find out what kind of access you might have to Instinet. The symbol for Instinet on Level II is INCA.

Instinet handles both NASDAQ and listed issues. The Instinet Book (referred to as the Box) is where all of the orders on Instinet are placed. The Instinet Book is available for trading NASDAQ and listed stock 24 hours a day. The exact price and size must be submitted.

Hiding Orders on Instinet. There are various levels of disclosure available for Instinet trades. Not all bids and offers on Instinet are disseminated to Level II. Therefore, you can hide your orders so that only other Instinet users can see them. Hiding orders is advantageous, because you might not want to show your true intention or order size and scare off potential buyers or sellers. You can also hide the exact size of your order in the Instinet Book by disseminating your bid in smaller blocks of shares. If you are trying to buy 10,000 shares for a designated price, you can hide your volume to reflect only 1,000 shares at a time. Once 1,000 shares are filled, another 1,000 shares will pop up. This method is a great way to hide a large bid or offer, but keep in mind that others might realize what you are doing.

Island (ISLD). Island was introduced in 1996 and was the first ECN to give access to the retail customer. A retail customer cannot only watch the order flow on the Island Book, but he or she can also participate directly. The Island Book market is similar to the Instinet Book market in that orders have to disseminate price and volume. Furthermore, the Island Book can be accessed on the Internet with any standard browser. Offering a great alternative to the retail customer, Island has become the second most popular next to Instinet, which is the largest ECN.

Here are some advantages and disadvantages of ECNs:

1. In general, the main advantage to trading by using ECNs is that they enable individual investors to compete with market makers on NASDAQ Level II by bettering the market or by making their own disseminated market. Individual investors no longer have to trade with market makers. The investor also can see the exact size and price of each order placed on the ECN.
2. The main disadvantage with ECNs is that in using them, you are not guaranteed that your stock will trade. Because there are no market

makers who are making markets on an ECN, no one is required to buy or sell shares of stock. You might see a stock on an ECN that has only offers and no bids. Similarly, ECNs do not have that many clients or investors participating, which makes stocks more volatile and further contributes to the problem of limited liquidity. Another disadvantage of ECNs is that there are so many of them. A stock might be trading at a price that interests you, but unless you have access to that ECN, you cannot trade it. Finally, ECN systems usually charge a fee in addition to the broker's commission.

Other ECNs. There are currently 10 ECNs that are available to the retail investor, and the future will evidently bring more. The main issue with these other ECNs is liquidity. If there is little liquidity, the whole concept of the ECN is moot. No liquidity equals no trades and increased volatility. One of the main problems with ECNs is that they are self-contained auctionary markets and cannot speak to one another. In other words, volume is divided between several ECNs, and no one ECN will always have the best market or enough volume. Currently, the leaders in the ECN community are Instinet (INCA), Island (ISLD), and Archepelago (ARCA).

Recently, the PCX has partnered with Archepelago. This partnership will bring the advantage of using ECN into the world of listed stocks. The future will be an interesting one, because ECNs will play an ever-important part as financial-trading instruments. The PCX-Archepelago partnership is only the beginning, so expect to see ECN-type systems for other financial products (such as bonds, options, futures, and others). As long as there is liquidity, there is room for ECNs.

Options Execution

We discussed the fundamentals of trading NASDAQ and listed stocks. Now, we will discuss methods of executing option orders.

The options trading floor is still an open-outcry system, but technology is changing rapidly. Many orders are still executed the old way (floor execution), with hand signals, screaming, and paper and pencil. As this style of trading gives way to faster methods of execution, brokerage firms can pass along savings by bypassing the staff that is needed to execute orders in the traditional floor-execution method.

The option exchanges of today are actually hybrids of an open-outcry system and a fully electronic execution, as with NASDAQ. As far as electronic execution, the auto-exchange system of the trading floor is fully automated—involving only the investor and the exchange computer systems. This system eliminates the need for floor and retail brokers.

Let's walk through the three methods of executing an options order—from the traditional floor execution to the extremely fast fully automated system.

Floor Execution. The most common way to trade options is to phone your broker, who will then send your request to the trading floor (where the order will be given to a floor broker). A floor broker is an individual who executes orders on a commission basis on the trading floor of an exchange. The floor broker will then announce the order in the trading pit, where the options on that specific issue trade. Open-outcry bidding for the order ensues among the market makers who are in the pit. Open outcry is a method of trading in which the floor broker calls out the specific details of a buy or sell order so that the information is available to all of the traders in the trading crowd. If your order is a market order and states that you are willing to pay (sell) the ask/offer (bid) listed by the market maker, your order will be executed (traded) right away and the broker will contact your brokerage firm to notify you. The option contract(s) will then be placed in your trading account, where you will have an open position (an existing position that has not yet been closed out). In order to close out the position, you must either 1) sell the option(s) that you bought, 2) buy back the option(s) that you sold, or 3) exercise your option(s), thereby converting your position into a position in the underlying security.

Phone Orders. Placing phone orders has almost become outdated. This process generally takes a long time to execute by today's standards because of all of the individuals who are involved.

Step by step, here is the process:

- The customer calls his or her broker in order to place an order.
- The broker calls the phone clerk on the trading floor.
- The phone clerk hands the order to a runner.
- The runner runs the order to the floor broker.
- The floor broker asks for the market and trades the order.
- The floor broker hands the filled order back to the runner.
- The runner runs the completed order back to the phone clerk.
- The phone clerk calls the retail broker to tell him or her that the order is filled and at what price.
- The retail broker calls the customer to let him or her know that the order is filled and at what price.

As you can see, there are many people in the middle (which slows down the process), and communication becomes important. If anyone in the chain forgets something or misunderstands something, the order can be executed incorrectly.

Electronic Floor Broker Execution

If you are trading electronically through one of the online brokerage firms, then you might be entering your order and sending it directly to one of the option exchange's floor brokers—thereby bypassing the long, involved process of sending the order over the telephone. This type of execution is faster and cheaper, and we advise you to investigate it if you have not already. Importantly, the direct access to the trading floor afforded by electronic orders gives the individual investor an advantage of fast executions. Through this method, you can execute an order faster than the traditional method, and your order is instantly in the trading crowd on the options floor. The floor broker has the order and can execute it without relaying information back to a retail broker through a chain of people (from the runner to the phone clerk).

You use a computer to place electronic orders. There are several ways in which electronic orders are placed:

- The customer places an order on his or her computer through his or her online brokerage firm.
- The order goes directly to the floor broker, who then executes the order and sends back the results via his or her hand-held computer.

As you can see in this situation, the phone clerk, runners, and retail broker were all eliminated. Electronic execution has become quite fast.

Auto-Execution

The automatic execution system has bypassed all individual order handling. In fact, the floor broker is not even involved. Auto-execution is the fastest method of execution and enables the individual investor to participate directly in the marketplace. The customer is now directly trading with the market maker as if he or she were actually in the trading pit. Open outcry is typically slower then the click of a mouse and limits the market maker's ability to trade with the same efficiency that is now available to the public. The public actually has an advantage by the simple speed of execution. In some cases, the public customer can execute his or her order faster than the market maker can update his or her market.

Because this method has become a more viable way of trading, professional options market makers have been leaving the floor to pursue this method of execution. This system bypasses everyone, including the market makers. The trader has direct access to the marketplace. He or she can better the market by placing a higher bid or a lower offer, enabling the trader to actively compete with the market maker. They can trade on the market maker's bid or offer and receive an instantaneous fill. Using the auto-execution system provided by the different exchanges, this method of trading options is as fast as trading NASDAQ stocks. The auto-execution system has brought the capabilities of NASDAQ trading to the options arena and has made it available to retail customers.

Systematic execution occurs as follows:

- The customer places an order on his or her computer.
- The order is sent to the exchange and is executed automatically with the market maker or public order (if the customer is paying the offer or selling the bid).
- If the order is away from the current market price, it is placed in the exchange's order book to be executed by the exchange electronically when the market price meets the customer's order price.

This method of execution is almost instantaneous. Several brokerage firms have this feature in place in order to enable their customers to directly place the order in the marketplace. Because there are no other individuals involved, the price of execution has dropped to $2 a contract.

Order Types. There are several types of orders in the marketplace. Each has a specified set of parameters and is designed for certain market conditions. All orders that are sent to the marketplace are assumed to be day orders unless otherwise noted.

All-or-None (AON) Order. An AON order requires the order to be executed in full or not at all. A partial trade will not be accepted with this type of order. If, for example, an order to buy 100 contracts enters the trading pit and the crowd will only fill half of the order at the requested price, then order will not trade at all. This order can be entered as a GTC (or good-until-canceled) order.

Day Order. This type of order instructs the broker to cancel any remainder of the order at the close of the trading day. The order is good for the day in which it is entered. All orders are entered as either DAY or GTC orders.

Market (MKT) Order. A market order is simply an order to buy or sell a specified number of shares of stock or option contracts for the best available price at the time that the order is entered. This order type will generally not contain a specified price, which means that the broker will attempt to obtain the best price available. The risk when placing this type of order is that the customer might be filled for a price that is nowhere near the price that he or she assumed that he or she would receive. There are times in active markets when prices fluctuate a great deal and the investor is at risk of being filled at the market price, regardless of what it is. The benefit of this order type is the immediacy of the execution. A market order will be filled quickly and without hesitation.

Stop Orders. Stop orders are the traditional method of taking a limited loss or locking in a gain if the stock sells off. A stop order is a price-triggered sell order. If the investor or trader has purchased a stock for $40 but wants to set a limited loss to his or her position of $2, he or she would put in a stop order at $38. This order would tell the broker that he or she wants to sell the stock if it trades at $38 and will take a limited loss of $2 on his or her long stock. The stop order is triggered when the stock price declines to $38 and the stock is sold for $38. There are no guarantees when using a stop order.

There are two basic types of stop orders: the limit-stop and market-stop. The previous example is a stop-limit order; a sell order is placed for $38 when the stop order is triggered. A market-stop order has the same triggering method of the limit-stop. The sell order is a market order, not a limit order. The main difference is that the limit-stop is not guaranteed to be sold for the limit price, while the market-stop is guaranteed a fill (but at a market price).

The main problem with stop orders (whether limit-stop or market-stop) is that they are ineffective if the stock gaps down through the stop-order trigger price. In addition, if the stock trades down to the stop loss point, sells out your stock position, and then the stock rebounds, you are out of the stock at the lower price. In effect, you have lost execution control of the stock while your stop order is in place.

Because of these two main drawbacks, stop orders offer limited risk protection with their own risk profile: the gap risk.

Options are another tool that you can use in a similar fashion to stop orders in order to alleviate the gap risk.

Immediate-or-Cancel (IOC) Order. This order type requires any part of the order to be executed or the order is cancelled. This cancellation happens immediately in the marketplace in order to avoid a volatile situation.

Fill-or-Kill (FOK) Order. This order type requires the order to be executed completely or not at all, just as an all-or-none order. In this case, however, if the order cannot be filled in its entirety as soon as it is announced in the trading crowd, it is to be killed (or canceled) immediately.

Good-until-Cancelled (GTC) Order. This type of order is a limit order that remains in effect until it is either executed (filled) or cancelled. This order will not expire at the end of the day like a day order (which expires if not executed by the end of the trading day). A GTC option order is an order that, if not executed, will automatically cancel upon expiration of the option.

Limit Order. A limit order is an order that sets a specific price (limit price) that is at or better than the current market price. It might be a day or a GTC order. If no price is indicated, the order is a market order by default.

Market-on-Close (MOC) Order. An MOC order is an order type that requires an order to be executed at or near the close of trading day on the day in which the order is entered. An MOC order, which can be considered a type of day order, cannot be used as part of a GTC order.

Market-if-Touched (MIT) Order. This order type is entered as a limit order, which means that once the price trades at the limit price, the order turns into a market order. This order is generally used as a stop-loss order and can be entered as either a DAY order or as a GTC order. Once the limit price is reached, the order will fill without being traded through as it becomes a limit order.

Contingency Orders. You can place contingencies on your option orders. If you only want to execute the order if the stock is trading at a certain price, you would consider a contingency order. You can place a contingency between two orders. If one order is filled, you can trade the other order. The contingency is up to the customer who is placing the order.

Brokers are weary of contingency orders and usually do not like to handle them. Make sure that you talk to your broker before trading contingency orders to find out his or her policy for handling them.

Not Held (NH) Orders. When an order is placed as an NH order, you are giving the floor broker discretion as to how and when to fill the order. The NH order simply indicates that the broker does not owe the customer a fill if the order trades at the customer's limit. This order is placed if there is a situation in which the customer wants to rely on the floor broker in order to receive the best possible fill in a volatile situation. Remember that the floor broker sees everything that is happening on the floor. If there is a trade at your limit price, you are *not* due a fill if the broker decided not to trade it. The broker is making the decision as to when and how to fill it based on the market situation. Usually, NH orders are larger orders of 50 contracts or more, because the broker has to actively watch most of them and must refuse NH orders of smaller size.

Trading Accounts

Individual investors can open trading accounts through a number of brokerage firms. Because each firm varies in the types of services and execution systems that it uses, it is important to investigate the types of services that are offered and determine whether they supply the access to information, education, and execution that you require in order to trade. There are two basic types of brokerage services offered to the retail customer:

- **Discount brokerage**—These types of accounts generally offer little to no recommendations and/or hand-holding. Investors are on their own and make their own trading decisions.
- **Full-service brokerage**—This brokerage company will offer recommendations and news to its investors. This brokerage generally offers investment advice and has a licensed broker who is assigned to your account. This broker will contact you with advice and market research. For this service, the investor generally pays a much larger commission and/or is required to have a large amount of capital in his or her trading account.

There are two basic types of accounts that retail investors can set up with a broker:

- **Cash accounts**—Cash accounts are basic accounts through which an investor can buy and sell stocks and options. Each trade is paid for in full on or before the settlement date, which is three business days after the transaction date for securities and same day for options.
- **Margin accounts**—The broker is granting the investor a line of credit up to a specific limit. Through a margin account, investors can buy stocks and options on credit—paying only part of the purchase

price up front. The brokerage company, which charges interest on the loan, pays for the balance of the transaction. In margin accounts, the securities are held by the broker in order to secure the loan. Therefore, if the value of the investment falls below a certain threshold, the broker could make a margin call. A margin call is a demand for the immediate deposit of cash into the account. If the funds are not deposited into the account, the brokerage company can sell the securities in order to cover the balance. Securities regulators determine the allowable margin rate, and although it might vary somewhat from firm to firm, it cannot exceed the amount allowable by law.

Short Selling.   Some accounts, including margin accounts, might enable short selling—the selling of a security that the seller does not own. Margin requirements for short selling differ from margin requirements for long (owned) positions. In short selling, a minimum credit balance must be maintained in the account in order to cover the risk associated with the sale. The credit balance is based on the market value of the securities being shorted, but the minimum balance is always greater than 100 percent of the market value (because additional cash is required). The proceeds of the sale are credited to the seller's account. In addition to the amount credited to the account for the sale, the investor must put up an additional amount of margin in order to ensure that if the stock increases in price, he or she will have available assets to cover the loss. For example, if an investor sells 100 shares of XYZ short at $50 per share, the investor is required to keep $7,500 in the account (the $5,000 received for the short sale, plus up to an additional 50 percent margin amount).

The Exercise/Assignment Process

The *Options Clearing Corporation* (OCC) handles the exercise/assignment process for all U.S.-traded stock options. The OCC is the largest clearing organization in the world for financial derivative instruments. The OCC is the regulatory body under the jurisdiction of the *Securities and Exchange Commission* (SEC) and the issuer of all exchange-listed options contracts. In effect, the OCC is the buyer to every clearing member who represents a seller and the seller to every clearing member who represents a buyer. This system ensures that regardless of default by any customer or trader, the options issued are guaranteed by the OCC and will stand. Seller and buyer, therefore, do not have to depend on one another. In addition, the OCC keeps a record of open interest (the total number of derivative contracts traded that have not yet been liquidated either by an offsetting transaction or exercise) of all listed option contracts. In other words, the OCC maintains records that indicate which member firms are long options and which member firms are short options—information that they use in the exercise/assignment process.

For example, if the option holder decides to exercise the option (buying stock in the case of a call and selling stock in the case of a put), he or she must contact his or her broker in order to submit an exercise notice. The notice must be submitted before the end of the trading day in order to exercise as effective that trading day. The brokerage firm then notifies theOCC. The exercise of a contract requires the following procedure:

1. The OCC randomly selects a member firm that is short the option contract being exercised.
2. The OCC notifies the firm that it has been assigned the contract.
3. The member firm that is short must then deliver the underlying stock in the case of a short call (or, in the case of a short put, it must pay for the received delivery of stock).
4. To do so, the assigned member firm selects one of its customers who are short that option contract for assignment. (Each member firm has its own standard for selecting customers for assignment.) The selection process must be approved by the exchange and by associated regulatory bodies. The two most common methods are random selection or a first-in/first-out basis.
5. The customer who is selected by the member firm must now meet the assignment by delivering stock (short call), or he or she must pay for the received delivery of stock (short put). The process of calling stock away and putting stock to the assigned-upon exercise is called conversion. Like its name implies, conversion involves the conversion of an option into a stock position.

In the case of a short put, the assigned customer has the stock put to him or her and must pay for delivery of the stock. Conversely, in the case of a short call, the assigned customer's stock is called away. The customer must deliver the stock and will have several methods available for doing so. If the customer is currently long the stock, he or she can deliver it out of his or her own inventory. If he or she is not currently long the stock, he or she must still make the delivery by either going short stock (if short stock is available) or by buying the stock in the open marketplace.

> **NOTE**
>
> Make sure to learn your broker's policy for exercising options.

The methods of standardization and forum for trading option contracts have evolved through the history of option trading. The evolution has been a slow and arduous one, however. Option trading has become one of the fastest-growing arenas for the individual investor. Stock option trading has evolved into a full-blown industry, with options now trading on more than 50 exchanges worldwide. Let's now discuss the characteristics of stock options.

Trade Station

The individual investor must choose the right execution platform for his or her own style of trading. By having the right execution platform, the individual investor will not only save time and money—but he or she will also have access to the information that is needed. A trader or an investor will find it frustrating when trying to implement a strategy and not being able to, simply because he or she is using the wrong tools and does not have access to the information that he or she needs.

When building a trading station for the office or home, you need the following items:

1. A quiet room away from distractions. Trading is a business and needs to be treated as such, whether trading from home or at a trading office. Avoid unnecessary distractions.
2. A proper desk and comfortable chair. You want to be comfortable while trading, so make sure that you have a desk that is the proper height and a chair that has good support. We suggest setting up the desk in front of a window or anywhere away from the wall. This setup enables the trader to look up away from the monitor with increased depth of field. This action alleviates eye strain by creating a depth of field.
3. A computer. The computer does not have to be the fastest or the best computer available. We suggest using a Windows-based machine, due to the available trading software. Monitors have been coming down in price, and we suggest purchasing two monitors with a dual monitor card. This setup enables the trader to monitor the market, surf the Web, and execute positions without having to flip between screens. The individual investor must decide on how the rest of the computer needs to be configured. Remember the speed of your data, and know that execution is not determined by the processor speed of your computer. Suggest a Windows operating system, dual monitors, and higher *Random Access Memory* (RAM).
4. A connection. This connection will determine how fast the computer receives data and the speed of execution. A DAT will need a fast connection speed, while an investor could settle for a regular phone connection.

   a. A 56K modem (for investors)
   b. A *Digital Subscriber Line* (DSL)/cable/satellite—This equipment enables fast home connection and is ideal for DATs, technical traders, and position traders.
   c. A T1/T3 line. This equipment is a must for trading firms.

Set your budget for building your trade station. Do not go broke setting up your trading station, however—because the money can be better spent on trading itself.

The Brokers and Brokerage Firms

Deciding on a brokerage firm is a major decision for the individual investor. The first decision to make is, do you want a full-service brokerage firm, a discount brokerage firm, or a direct-access brokerage firm? One is not better then the other, and what is important is that the firm and the broker fit within the individual investor's trading style (see Table 12-2).

Table 12-2 *Choosing a Broker and a Brokerage Firm*

Trading Style	Full Service Brokerage	Discount Brokerage	Direct Access Brokerage
Investor	Yes	Yes	Yes
Direct Access Trader	No	No	Yes
Technical Trader	Yes	Yes	Yes
Position Trader	Yes	Yes	Yes

There are several important questions to ask a brokerage firm before opening an account with them. Because all of the exchanges are competing with one another, it is important for the individual investor to get the best price. Ask the brokerage firm how it routes its order flow, and ask to see whether it routes based on payment for order flow. Payment for order flow is simply market makers paying brokerage firms to send their stock or options orders to them. This technique is a cost-saving method for the brokerage firm, which usually passes the savings on to the client (unfortunately, however, it does not guarantee the best price for the customer). The trader should have the choice of where and how he or she wants the order executed. Also ask what the average execution time is for stock and options orders.

Questions to Ask Brokerage Firms

Option Questions.

1. Do they have access to all five options exchanges?
2. Do they enable you to view the options markets on all five exchanges?
3. Do they enable you to choose on which exchange you want to execute your option order?

Stock Questions.

1. Do they offer SelectNet?
2. Do they offer access to multiple ECNs, and to which ones?
3. Do they offer access to SOES?
4. Do they offer access to DOT or SuperDOT?

Then, ask them to expound on other advantages that they might offer to the individual investor.

At this writing, we found only three direct-access brokerage firms that gave the investor the access to view the option markets on all five exchanges and that gave them the choice of where to route his or her options order. These brokerage firms are as follows:

- Preferred Capital Markets
- Mr. Stock
- Interactive Brokers

As individual investors become educated as to the benefits of options, more brokerage firms will give more access to the multiple option exchanges.

When the individual investor decides what type of trader he or she would like to be, the investor must then decide whether he or she wants to trade directly within the marketplace or whether he or she would like to have the comfort of trading with a knowledgeable broker. The DAT has no choice in the matter and usually does not have a broker, because this style of trading requires the DAT to trade directly with the market (hence the name direct-access trader). As for other styles of trading, whether it is investing, technical, or position trading, the trader has a choice and can use a broker. There is no right answer to this question; rather, it is only relevant to the comfort zone of the individual investor.

If the individual investor decides to use a broker, he or she should investigate the broker. The broker plays a crucial role and is responsible for executing your trades. Before, online trading investors had no choice but to use a broker; therefore, brokers were only required to know how to execute the trades. Now, brokers are competing with online brokerage firms and need to offer something more than just brokering tickets. Many brokerage firms have realized the value of education on the use of the many products that are available to the individual investor and are educating their brokers to help individual investors. Here are some questions that we suggest you ask a broker to help decide whether he or she will be able to handle technical or position trader questions. Remember, he or she will be part of your team, and you want to make sure that he or she understands what your goals are and your level of knowledge.

We first suggest telling the broker what style of trader you are (whether you are an investor, technical, or position trader). Then, ask the broker some questions:

1. Does he or she understand the four market outlooks?
2. Is he or she knowledgeable about synthetics and their use?
3. Does he or she know about intrinsic versus extrinsic values?
4. Can he or she route order flow to the exchange of your choice?
5. Does he or she understand most or all of the Greeks?
6. Does he or she understand the strategies that you wish to employ?
7. How long has he or she been a broker?
8. Can he or she offer alternative strategies based on your market outlook?
9. Does he or she understand risk management?
10. What style of trader would he or she be?

Always be polite to the broker, because he or she will be a valuable part of your team. It is important for you to make sure that this person is someone with whom you are comfortable working.

Data Providers

After the investor has chosen what type of trader he or she is and which brokerage firm will best suit his or her needs, then the next step is to decide whether he or she needs a data provider (and if so, which one?). See Table 12-3.

Many data providers are available, and for the most part, they all offer the same data. What the individual investor needs to decide is three important items:

1. Does the data provider offer the data that you need?
2. Do you feel comfortable with the look, feel, use, and integration into your trading station?
3. Is the price within your budget?

Some data providers have built relationships with direct-access brokerage firms in order to offer a more complete and compelling package. Perhaps the brokerage firm that you decided to use has an affiliation with data providers that will offer an integrated package. This situation adds two key characteristics for the individual investor: one, an integrated package; and two, cost-effectiveness. A data provider might offer a discount to investors who have a trading account at a certain brokerage firm.

We constantly review data providers and can recommend any of the following:

Esignal (DBC)
AT Financial
Track Data
Quote.Com

Table 12-3 *Selecting a Data Provider*

Type of trader	Data Provider	Quotes	Level II	Charts	Chart Analytics	News	Options Quotes	Greeks
Investor		YES*		YES*		YES*	YES*	
DAT	YES	YES	YES	YES		YES		
Technical	YES	YES		YES	YES	YES	YES	
Position	YES	YES		YES	YES	YES	YES	YES

*The investor does not need a data provider, but if he or she decided to use one, the asterisk (*) indicates what he or she would need.

The individual investor must decide upon the broker with which he or she will be most comfortable.

Software. An individual investor might be interested in purchasing options-analyzing software. Some data providers provide options analysts, so this software would be redundant. The software is used to analyze option strategies and to measure risks and rewards. These programs range in price from $100 to $5,000. You should find one that is easy to use and that fits within your budget.

The best software available in the marketplace is Microsoft Excel. Its only limitation is the investor's creative imagination. Some data providers (such as E-signal) offer Excel data feeds and spreadsheet layouts for those who want to watch the market data live in their Excel spreadsheet. This software offers the advantage of changing the layout, calculating your own strategies, looking for pricing discrepancies, and building your own screeners.

Appendix A

Order Types

All-or-None (AON) Order
Day Order
Market Order (MKT)
Stop Orders
Fill-or-Kill (FOK) Order
Good-Until-Canceled (GTC) Order
Limit Order
Market-on-Close (MOC) Order
Market-if-Touched (MIT) Order

All-or-None (AON) Order

An AON order requires the order to be executed in full or not at all. A partial trade is not accepted with this type of order. If, for example, an order to buy 100 contracts enters the trading pit and the crowd will only fill half of the order at the requested price, then the order will not trade at all. This order can be entered as a *good-until-canceled* (GTC) order.

Day Order

This type of order instructs the broker to cancel any remainder of the order at the close of trading that day. The order is good for the day on which it is entered. All orders are entered as either DAY or GTC orders.

Market Order (MKT)

A market order is simply an order to buy or sell a specified number of shares of stock or option contracts for the best available price at the time that the order is entered. This type of order will generally not contain a specified price, which means that the broker will attempt to obtain the best price available. When buying, this offer will be the best; when selling, this bid will be the best.

The risk when placing this type of order is that the customer might be filled for a price that is nowhere near the price that he or she assumed. There are times in active markets when prices fluctuate a great deal and the investor is at the risk of being filled at the market price, regardless of what that price is. The benefit of this type of order is the immediacy of the execution. A market order will be filled quickly and without hesitation.

Stop Orders

Stop orders are the traditional method of taking a limited loss or locking in a gain if the stock sells off. A stop order is a price-triggered sell order. If the investor or trader has purchased a stock for $40 but wants to set a limited loss for his or her position of $2, he or she would put in a stop order at $38. This order tells the broker that he or she wants to sell the stock if it trades at $38 and take a limited loss of $2 on his or her long stock. The stop order is triggered when the stock price declines to $38, and his or her stock is sold for $38. There are no guarantees when using a stop order.

There are two basic types of stop orders: the limit-stop and the market-stop. The previous example is a stop-limit order. A sell order is placed for $38 when the stop order is triggered. A market-stop order has the same triggering method of the limit-stop, and the sell order is a market order (not a limit order). The main difference is that the limit-stop is not guaranteed to be sold for the limit price, while the market-stop is guaranteed a fill but at a market price.

The main problem with stop orders (whether limit-stop or market-stop) is that they are ineffective if the stock gaps down through the stop-order trigger price. In addition, if the stock trades down to the stop loss point, sells out your stock position, and then the stock rebounds, you are out of the stock at the lower price. In effect, you have lost execution control of the stock while your stop order was in place.

Because of these two main drawbacks, stop orders offer limited risk protection with their own risk profile: the gap risk.

Options are another tool that you can use in a similar fashion in order to stop orders and alleviate the gap risk.

Fill-or-Kill (FOK) Order

This type of order requires the order to be executed completely or not at all, just as an AON order. In this case, however, if the order cannot be filled in its entirety as soon as it is announced in the trading crowd, it is to be killed (canceled) immediately.

Good-Until-Canceled (GTC) Order

This type of order is a limit order that remains in effect until it is either executed (filled) or cancelled. This order will not expire at the end of the day like a day order does (a day order expires if not executed by the end of the trading day). A GTC option order is an order that, if not executed, will automatically cancel upon expiration of the option.

Limit Order

A limit order is an order that sets a specific price (limit price) that is at or better than the current market price. It might be a day order or a GTC order. If no price is indicated, the order is a market order by default.

Market-on-Close (MOC) Order

This type of order requires an order to be executed at or near the close of a trading day on the day in which the order is entered. An MOC order, which can be considered a type of day order, cannot be used as part of a GTC order.

Market-if-Touched (MIT) Order

This type of order is entered as a limit order that, once the price trades at the limit price, turns into a market order. This order is generally used as a stop-loss order and can be entered as either a day order or as a GTC order. This action ensures that once the limit price is reached, the order will fill without being traded through as it becomes a limit order.

Appendix B

Strategy Formulas

Married Put
Protecting Unrealized Profit
Covered Call Potential
Bull Spread (Long Call Spread)
Bull Spread (Short Put Spread)
Bear Spread (Long Put Spread)
Bear Spread (Short Call Spread)
Ratio Bull Spread (Long)
Ratio Bull Spread (Short)
Ratio Bear Spread (Long)
Ratio Bear Spread (Short)
Long Straddle
Short Straddle
Long Strangle
Short Strangle
Long Butterfly
Short Butterfly
Long Iron Butterfly
Short Iron Butterfly
Long Condor
Short Condor
Risk Collar/Fence (Risk Conversion)
Risk Collar/Fence (Risk Reversal)

Married Put

$$(\text{stock price} - \text{strike price}) + \text{put price} = \text{maximum loss}$$

Protecting Unrealized Profit

$$(\text{strike price} - \text{put price}) - \text{initial stock purchase} = \text{unrealized profit}$$

Covered Call Potential

$$(\text{call price} + \text{strike price}) - \text{stock price} = \text{covered call potential}$$

Bull Spread (Long Call Spread)

$$\text{difference between strike prices} - \text{debit paid} = \text{maximum profit}$$

(The debit paid is the maximum loss.)

Bull Spread (Short Put Spread)

$$\text{difference between strike prices} - \text{credit} = \text{maximum loss}$$

(The credit received is the maximum profit.)

Bear Spread (Long Put Spread)

$$\text{difference between strike prices} - \text{debit paid} = \text{maximum profit}$$

(The debit paid is the maximum loss.)

Bear Spread (Short Call Spread)

difference between strike prices − credit = maximum loss

(The credit received is the maximum profit.)

Ratio Bull Spread (Long)

A short call spread plus a long OTM call

Ratio Bull Spread (Short)

A long call spread plus a short OTM call

Ratio Bear Spread (Long)

A short put spread plus a long OTM put

Ratio Bear Spread (Short)

A long put spread plus a short OTM put

Long Straddle

strike price − (call price + put price) = low break-even point
strike price + (call price + put price) = high break-even point

Short Straddle

strike price − (call price + put price) = low break-even point
strike price + (call price + put price) = high break-even point

Long Strangle

OTM put strike price − (OTM call price + OTM put price) = low break-even point
OTM call strike price + (OTM call price + OTM put price) = high break-even point

Short Strangle

OTM put strike price − (OTM call price + OTM put price) = low break-even point
OTM call strike price + (OTM call price + OTM put price) = high break-even point

Long Butterfly

buy one + sell two + buy one = total debit

Short Butterfly

sell one + buy two + sell one = total credit

Long Iron Butterfly

sell ATM straddle − buy OTM strangle = receive a credit

Short Iron Butterfly

buy ATM straddle − sell OTM strangle = total debit

Long Condor

buy one + sell one + sell one + buy one = total debit paid

Short Condor

sell one + buy one + buy one + sell one = credit received

Risk Collar/Fence (Risk Conversion)

long underlying security = purchasing OTM put + selling the OTM call

Risk Collar/Fence (Risk Reversal)

short underlying security = purchasing OTM call + selling the OTM put

Appendix C

Indices

Sector Indices
Broad-Based Indices
Foreign Market Indices

Sector Indices

Airline index: XAL

Automotive index: AUX

Biotech index: BGX

Banking index: BIX

Chemical stock index: CEX

Computer and technology index: XCI

Computer software index: CWX

Consumer stock index: CMR

Drug index: DRG

Gaming index: GAX

Global telecommunications index: GAX

Gold and silver stock index: XAU

Health care index: HCX

Internet index: INX (Chicago Board of Exchange) and IIX (American Stock Exchange)

Oil stock index: XOI

Phone index: PNX

Real Estate Investment Trusts (REITs) index: RIX

Retail stock index: RLX

Semiconductor index: SOX

Technology index: PSE (Pacific Exchange) and TXX (Chicago Board of Exchange)

Telecommunications index: XTC (American Stock Exchange) and TCX (Chicago Board of Options Exchange)

Transportation stock index: TRX

Utility stock index: UTY

Broad-Based Indices

Big cap index: MKT

Major market index: XMI

Mid-cap 400 index: MID

NASDAQ-100 index: NDX

New York Stock Exchange (NYSE) composite index: NYA

Russell 2000 index: RUT

Standard & Poor's 100 (S&P 100) index: OEX

S&P 500 index: SPX

Small cap 600 index: SML

Top 100 index: TPX

Wilshire small cap index: WSX

Foreign Market Indices

Eurotop 100 index: EUR

FTSE-100 (London) index: FSX

Israel index: ISX

Japan index: JPN

Latin index: LTX

Mexico index: MEX

Nikkei 300 (Japan) index: NIK

> **NOTE**
>
> There are many other indices, and new ones are constantly being added. We have listed some of the most common indices. Frequently, stocks are added and removed from these indices; check with your broker, exchange, or data service provider for a current list of stocks that comprise an index.

Appendix D

Expiration Cycles

There are always two near-term and two far-term months available. The most recently added expiration month is listed in bold. This new expiration month is added on the Monday following the third Friday of the month. These tables do not include LEAPS. LEAPS (long-term options of one to three years) expire in January of the LEAPS' specific year.

Table D-1 *January Cycle*

Current Month	Available Months			
JAN	JAN	**FEB**	APR	JUL
FEB	FEB	**MAR**	APR	JUL
MAR	MAR	APR	JUL	**OCT**
APR	APR	**MAY**	JUL	OCT
MAY	MAY	**JUN**	JUL	OCT
JUN	JUN	JUL	OCT	**JAN**
JUL	JUL	**AUG**	OCT	JAN
AUG	AUG	**SEP**	OCT	JAN
SEP	SEP	OCT	JAN	**APR**
OCT	OCT	**NOV**	JAN	APR
NOV	NOV	**DEC**	JAN	APR
DEC	DEC	JAN	APR	**JUL**

Table D-2 *February Cycle*

Current Month	Available Months			
JAN	JAN	FEB	MAY	**AUG**
FEB	FEB	**MAR**	MAY	AUG
MAR	MAR	**APR**	MAY	AUG
APR	APR	MAY	AUG	**NOV**
MAY	MAY	**JUN**	AUG	NOV
JUN	JUN	**JUL**	AUG	NOV
JUL	JUL	AUG	NOV	**FEB**
AUG	AUG	**SEP**	NOV	FEB
SEP	SEP	**OCT**	NOV	FEB
OCT	OCT	NOV	FEB	**MAY**
NOV	NOV	**DEC**	FEB	MAY
DEC	DEC	**JAN**	FEB	MAY

Table D-3 *March Cycle*

Current Month	Available Months			
JAN	JAN	**FEB**	MAR	JUN
FEB	FEB	MAR	JUN	**SEP**
MAR	MAR	**APR**	JUN	SEP
APR	APR	**MAY**	JUN	SEP
MAY	MAY	JUN	SEP	**DEC**
JUN	JUN	**JUL**	SEP	DEC
JUL	JUL	**AUG**	SEP	DEC
AUG	AUG	SEP	DEC	**MAR**
SEP	SEP	**OCT**	DEC	MAR
OCT	OCT	**NOV**	DEC	MAR
NOV	NOV	DEC	MAR	**JUN**
DEC	DEC	**JAN**	MAR	JUN

Appendix E

Fractions to Decimal Conversion Chart

Table E-1 *Fractions to Decimal Conversion Chart*

32nd	16th	8th	4th	1/2	Decimal
1/32					0.03125
	1/16				0.0625
3/32					0.09375
		1/8			0.125
5/32					0.15625
	3/16				0.1875
7/32					0.21875
			1/4		0.25
9/32					0.28125
	5/16				0.3125
11/32					0.34375
		3/8			0.375
13/32					0.40625
	7/16				0.4375
15/32					0.46875
				1/2	0.5
17/32					0.53125
	9/16				0.5625
19/32					0.59375
		5/8			0.625
21/32					0.65625
	11/16				0.6875
23/32					0.71875
			3/4		0.75
25/32					0.78125
	13/16				0.8125
27/32					0.84375
		7/8			0.875
29/32					0.90625
	15/16				0.9375
31/32					0.96875

Appendix F

The Options Clearing Corporation (OCC)

Introduction
Stock Options Exchanges

Introduction

The OCC is the guarantor of all exchange-traded options. Additionally, the OCC oversees the obligation to fulfill exercises.

When the holder of an option wants to exercise that option, he or she contacts the brokerage firm, which in turn contacts the OCC. The OCC then randomly selects a brokerage firm with customers who have sold that option contract. That brokerage firm then notifies one of those customers that he or she must satisfy the terms of the option. The brokerage firm can select its customer either by random selection or on a first in, first out basis. Because selling an option can result in a substantial liability for the seller, strict margin requirements are imposed on sellers. This margin requirement acts like a performance bond in order to assure option buyers that they will be fully satisfied should they exercise an option.

The Options Clearing Corporation
440 S. LaSalle St.
Suite 2400
Chicago, IL 60605 USA
1-800-537-4258

Stock Options Exchanges

American Stock Exchange (AMEX)
Derivative Securities
86 Trinity Pl.
New York, NY 10006 USA
1-800-843-2639

Chicago Board of Options Exchange (CBOE)
400 South LaSalle Street
Chicago, IL 60605 USA
1-800-678-4667

International Securities Exchange (ISE)
60 Broad Street
New York, NY 10004
212-943-2400

Pacific Exchange (PCX)
Options Marketing
115 Sansome St., 7th Floor
San Francisco, CA 94104 USA
1-800-825-5773

Philadelphia Stock Exchange (PHLX)
1900 Market St.
Philadelphia, PA 19103 USA
1-800-843-7459

_____ Appendix G

_____ Intrinsic and Premium Formulas

Introduction

The intrinsic value of an option corresponds to the relationship between the option's strike price and the current price of the underlying asset. The intrinsic value is the amount that an option is *in-the-money* (ITM). *Out-of-the-money* (OTM) options have no intrinsic value.

Call Intrinsic Value

current stock price − strike price = call intrinsic value

Put Intrinsic Value

strike price − current stock price = put intrinsic value

All options include premiums or values over and above the option's intrinsic value. Premium values vary based on three factors: the market anticipation of the volatility of the underlying security; the time remaining until the option's expiration; and current interest rates. (Premium value is also known as time value or extrinsic value.)

Call Premium Value

call option price − call intrinsic value = call premium value

Put Premium Value

put option price − put intrinsic value = put premium value

Appendix H

The Black-Scholes Model

Introduction
The Binomial Model

Introduction

Fischer Black and Myron Scholes were the founders of the Black-Scholes model for pricing an option. It was one of the most significant accomplishments in financial instruments. This model tries to evaluate the fair value of an option. If the model performs as it should, the option's market price will equal the theoretical fair value. The mathematics of their derivation is quite complex. Interested readers can find it in the original paper, Black-Scholes (1973), and the books by Hull (1993).

The Black-Scholes model was developed to value European-style options on shares of stocks.

The Black-Scholes model is used to calculate a theoretical call price (ignoring dividends that are paid during the life of the option) by using the five key determinants of an option's price:

1. Stock price
2. Strike price
3. Volatility
4. Time until expiration
5. Short-term (risk-free) interest rate

The Binomial Model

The binomial approach is a discrete valuation model for European/American-style options on derivative securities. This approach was first suggested by William Sharpe in 1978. This methodology is normally associated with the paper by John Cox, Stephen Ross, and Mark Rubinstein that was published in 1979, however. The binomial approach (also known as the lattice approach) can be used to value a wide range of general derivative securities and to obtain an exact formula by taking the limit in which the binomial tree converges to a continuum. As proposed by Cox, Ross, and Rubinstein, this method divides the time until option maturity into discrete intervals.

This model is used by option market makers in American-style options. The model is as follows:

$$C_{Bi} = f(S, O^2, X, T, r_1, u, d, n)$$

Appendix I

Quiz Answers

Chapter 2 Quiz Answers

1. The two types of options are:

   a. calls
   b. puts

2. The established price at which the purchase (in the case of a call) or sale (in the case of a put) of the underlying security will occur upon exercise of the option contract is known as the strike/exercise price.

3. The date on which the right to exercise an option ceases to exist is known as the expiration date and generally falls on the third Friday of the month.

4. One stock option generally represents 100 shares of the underlying asset.

5. The seller of an option is referred to as the option writer.

6. The owner of a put option has purchased the right to sell the underlying asset for the designated strike price for a specified period.

7. The two styles of options are:

   a. American
   b. European

8. Options that have more than one year until expiration are typically referred to as a LEAP.

9. The measure of the number of outstanding option contracts is the open interest.

10. The seller of a put is obligated to purchase the underlying security in case of assignment.

Chapter 3 Quiz Answers

1. If you are bearish on the market, you might short the stock.

2. A short stock position has unlimited risk.

3. The buyer of a call has as much of the profit potential as the owner of the underlying stock but has significantly limited the risk of loss.

4. The purchase of a call will result in a deficit to the trader's account.

5. A long put position gives the holder the right to sell the underlying security for a specified amount until the expiration of the option.

6. A short call position has unlimited risk.

7. The graph of a long April 50 call will bend at the 50 strike.

8. A long put position will increase in value as the underlying security decreases in price.

9. A profit/loss graph helps a trader visualize the risks and rewards associated with a position.

10. The risk involved with the purchase of an option is the premium/
purchase price of the option.

11. In the following figure, we are long two March 50-level calls for $3.

Black line = long 2 March 50 calls for $3.
Gray line = long 2 March 50 calls for $3 with 21 days to expiration.

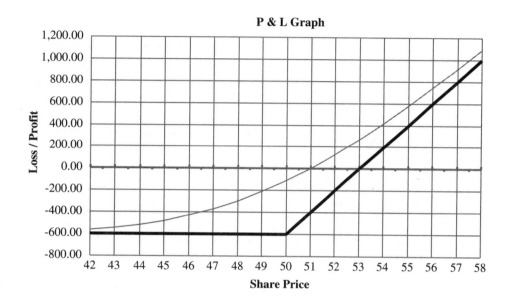

($3 × 100 = $300) upon expiration.

Chapter 4 Quiz Answers

1. A call option is said to be ITM when the underlying security is trading for more than the option's strike price.

2. A put option is OTM when the strike price is less than the current
price of the underlying security.

3. The amount that an option is ITM is referred to as the intrinsic value.

4. Strike price − current stock price = put intrinsic value

5. The price of an option is the sum of its intrinsic and extrinsic values.

6. The variables that influence the extrinsic value of an option are:

    a. time until expiration
    b. interest rates
    c. volatility
    d. any applicable dividends

7. The fair or theoretical value of an option can be calculated by using
an option pricing model.

8. The six factors used in determining the price of an option are

    a. The price of the underlying stock
    b. The option's strike or exercise price
    c. The time until expiration of the option
    d. The applicable interest rate
    e. The anticipated volatility of the price movement of the underlying asset
    f. Dividends (where applicable)

9. The greater the amount of time remaining until an option's expiration, the greater the time premium.
10. The higher interest rates, the higher the value of the calls.
11. Volatility is a measure of the speed and magnitude at which the underlying asset's price changes.
12. The portions of a company's profits that are paid back to its shareholders are the dividends.
13. The value of a stock will be discounted by the amount of the dividend on the ex-dividend date.
14. As the underlying asset increases in value, the value of a call (with all other variables remaining constant) will increase in value.
15. OTM and ATM options have no intrinsic value.

Chapter 5 Quiz Answers

1. Volatility, as indicated by the marketplace, is known as implied volatility.
2. The spread is difference between the bid and offer prices.
3. An increase in volatility increases the price of calls and puts.
4. Normal distribution is generally described by two characteristics:

    a. Its mean
    b. Its standard deviation

5. Approximately 95.4 percent of all occurrences will fall within ±2 standard deviations.
6. The average return is commonly referred to as the expected return.
7. As volatility decreases, the value of options will generally decrease.
8. Weekly volatility = annual volatility / the square root of 52
9. The mean of the mean can be used to describe standard deviation.
10. Historical volatility is a measure of actual price changes in an underlying asset over a specific period in the past.

Chapter 6 Quiz Answers

1. The relationship between a change in the price of the underlying asset and the price of the option is referred to as the option's delta.
2. Rho is a measurement of how a change in interest rates will affect the value of the position.
3. Omega measures the leverage of an option.
4. ITM options have deltas approaching $+100$ for calls and -100 for puts.
5. The delta of an OTM option will move towards zero as the likelihood of the option finishing ITM decreases as time decreases.
6. Gamma is commonly referred to the curvature of an option.
7. Rho is a positive number for calls and a negative number for puts.
8. Vega tends to be greater for ATM options and less for ITM options and OTM options.
9. As the time until expiration increases, vega increases. As the time until expiration decreases, vega decreases.
10. A positive delta position benefits from an increase in the price of the underlying asset.
11. An option's delta increases by the amount of the gamma when the underlying asset increases by one point.
12. As a value, theta helps a trader determine the effects of time on his or her overall option position.
13. If a call option delta is .50 and its gamma is .08, then a one-point increase in the underlying asset will result in an increase of .08 to the delta (which will increase to .61).
14. An ATM option typically has a delta of about $+50$ for calls and -50 for puts.
15. A long call and a short put both have a positive delta.

Chapter 7 Quiz Answers

1. Long call + short put = synthetic long stock
2. Short call + long put = synthetic short stock
3. Long stock + long put = synthetic long call
4. Short stock + short put = synthetic short call
5. Long call + short stock = synthetic long put
6. Short call + long stock = synthetic short put
7. Cost to carry = applicable interest rate $\times$ strike price $\times$ days until expiration/360

Synthetic pricing formulas:

1. Synthetic long call price = (+put price + stock price + cost to carry) − strike price
2. Synthetic long put price = (+call price + strike price − cost to carry) − stock price
3. Synthetic short call price = (−put price − stock price − cost to carry) + strike price
4. Synthetic short put price = (−call price − strike price + cost to carry) + stock price
5. A reversal consists of short stock plus a short put plus a long call.
6. A conversion consists of long stock plus a long put plus a short call.
7. PIN and interest-rate risks are the risks associated with a reversal/conversion.

Chapter 9 Quiz

1. An investor who has a pessimistic market outlook is bearish.
2. Buying one ABC July 80 call and selling two ABC July 85 calls is referred to as a ratio spread.
3. You are long 10 March 60 calls and short 10 April 60 calls, so you have a calendar spread.
4. With XYZ trading at $50, you purchased two October 50 puts that were trading for $3 (for a total investment of $600). The stock almost immediately has fallen to $45, and the October 50 puts are now trading for $6. The October 45 puts are trading for $3, and the October 40 puts are trading for $1. What are your alternatives?

    a. Liquidate the position—your puts are now worth $6. If you sell them, you will receive $1,200 for a net profit of $600.
    b. Let it ride—as long as you keep the puts, you own the down side.
    c. Sell further-out puts—two candidates to be strongly considered are 1) selling two October 45 puts and 2) selling four October 45 puts and buying two October 40 puts.

5. Predicted stock move < option premium = short straddle
6. The following position:

    a. Sell two May 70 calls at $4
    b. Buy 100 shares of stock at $71

    The purchase of 100 shares of stock combined with the sale of one May 70 call creates a synthetic short put for $3 (call price of $4 plus the strike price of $70 equals $74 minus the stock price of $71, which equals $3).

7. The short straddle risk = unlimited (stock rises or falls beyond the break-even points)

8. The short ratio bear spread risk = unlimited (stock falls below the
   break-even point)
9. If the predicted stock move > the option's premium = volatile strategy
10. Identify the following figure:

Black line = long 1 July 55 call.
Long 1 July 45 put at expiration.
Thin gray line = 21 days to expiration.

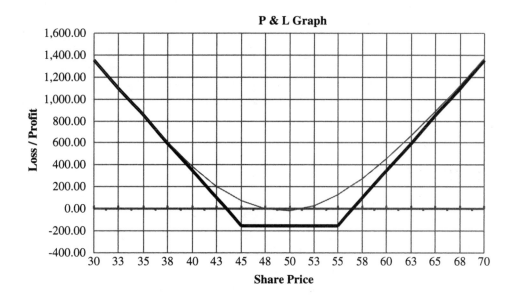

11. Identify the following figure:

Black line = 40-50-55-60 Condor.

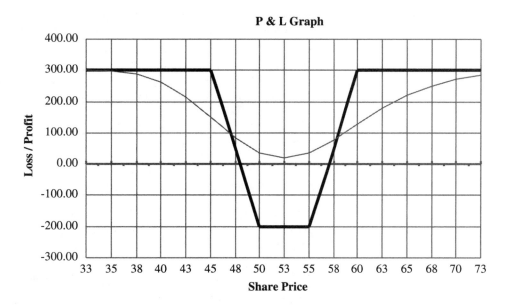

12. Identify the following figure:

Black line = short the 50 level straddle at expiration.
Thin gray line = short straddle with 21 days to expiration.

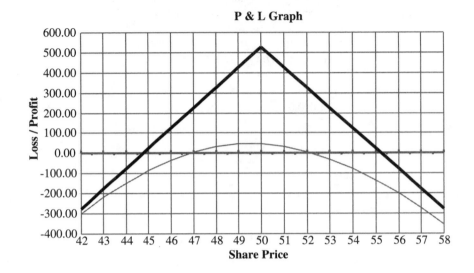

Glossary

A

All-or-None (AON) order—An order that must be completely filled or not filled at all

American-style option—An option contract that can be exercised at any time between the date of purchase and the expiration date. Most exchange-traded options are American-style. All stock options are American style.

Asset—A resource that has economic value to its owner. Cash, accounts receivable, inventory, real estate, and securities are examples of assets.

Assignment—The receipt of an exercise notice by an option seller (writer) that obligates him or her to sell (in the case of a call) or purchase (in the case of a put) the underlying security at the specified strike price

Ask—The price that a seller is willing to accept for the security; also called the offer price

At-the-Money (ATM)—An option is ATM if the strike price of the option is equal to the market price of the underlying security.

Arbitrage—The simultaneous purchase and sale of identical or equivalent financial instruments in order to benefit from the discrepancy in their price relationship

Automatic exercise—A protection procedure in which the *Options Clearing Corporation* (OCC) attempts to protect the holder of an expiring ITM option by automatically exercising the option

B

Bear market—A market in which prices are in a general down trend

Bearish—An outlook that anticipates lower prices in the underlying security —(a negative or pessimistic outlook)

Bear (or bearish) spread—A strategy involving two or more options (or options combined with a position in the underlying stock) that will profit from a fall in the price of the underlying stock

Bear spread (call)—The simultaneous writing of one call option with a lower strike price and the purchase of another call option with a higher strike price

Bear spread (put)—The simultaneous purchase of one put option with a higher strike price and the writing of another put option with a lower strike price

Bid—The highest price that any potential buyer is willing to pay for a particular option

Bid/ask—The latest available bid and ask prices for a particular option contract or stock

Bid/ask spread—The difference in price between the available bid and ask quotations for a particular option contract

Break-even point—The stock price at which a particular strategy neither gains nor loses money

Bull market—A market in which the general trend is rising prices

Bullish—A market outlook that anticipates higher prices in the underlying security (a positive or optimistic outlook)

Bull (or bullish) spread—A strategy involving two or more options (or options combined with an underlying stock position) that will profit from a rise in the price of the underlying stock

Bull spread (call)—The simultaneous purchase of one call option with a lower strike price and the writing of another call option with a higher strike price

Bull spread (put)—The simultaneous writing of one put option with a higher strike price and the purchase of another put option with a lower strike price

Butterfly spread—A strategy involving four options with three different strike prices. The butterfly has both limited risk and limited profit potential. A long call butterfly is established by buying one call at the lowest strike price, writing two calls at the middle strike price, and buying one call at the highest strike price. A long put butterfly is established by buying one put at the highest strike price, writing two puts at the middle strike price, and buying one put at the lowest strike price.

Buy on close—To buy at the end of the trading day on the closing price

Buy on opening—To buy at the beginning of the trading session at a price within the opening range

Buy-write—A covered call position in which stock is purchased and an equivalent number of calls are written at the same time. This position is generally transacted as a spread order, with both sides (buying stock and writing calls) being executed simultaneously.

C

Call—An option contract that gives the buyer (holder) the right to purchase and gives the seller (the writer) the obligation to sell a specified number of shares of the underlying stock at the given strike price on or before the expiration date of the contract

Called away—The process in which a call option writer (seller) is obligated to surrender the underlying stock to the option buyer at a price that is equal to the strike price of the call that is written

Class of options—Options contracts of the same type (call or put) and style (American, European, FLEX, or capped) that cover the same underlying security

Clearinghouse—An agency that is associated with an exchange that guarantees all trades, thus assuring contract delivery and/or financial settlement. The clearinghouse becomes the buyer for every seller and the seller for every buyer.

Close—The period at the end of the trading session when final prices are determined

Closing order—An investor buys or sells an option for which he or she has the opposite position (refer to Open Order).

Closing price—The price of a stock (or option) at the last transaction of the day

Closing purchase—A transaction in which an investor who had initially sold an option intends to liquidate his or her written (short) position by buying, in a closing purchase transaction, an option that has the same terms as the option that he or she wrote

Closing sale—A transaction in which an investor who had initially bought an option intends to liquidate his or her purchased position by selling, in a closing sale transaction, an option that has the same terms as the option that he or she purchased

Collar/risk collar—An option strategy in which an OTM call is sold and an ITM put is purchased. This technique is normally used as a long stock protective strategy. The opposite of this strategy, called a fence, could be applied as a protective measure in a short stock position.

Commission—The fee that clearinghouses charge their clients to buy and sell futures and futures options contracts. The fee that brokers charge their clients is also called a commission.

Condor spread—This strategy involves four options at four differing strike prices. The condor has both limited risk and limited profit potential. A long call condor spread is established by buying one call at the lowest strike, writing one call at the second strike, writing another call at the third strike, and buying one call at the fourth (highest) strike.

Contract—A call or put issued by the *Options Clearing Corporation* (OCC)

Contract size—The amount of the underlying asset covered by the options contract (generally 100 shares for one stock option unless adjusted for a special event, such as a stock split)

Conversion—A position that consists of a long put and a short call with the same strike price and expiration combined with long stock

Cost of carry charge—The interest expense on money that is borrowed to finance a margined securities position

Cover—Used to indicate the repurchase of previously sold contracts when the investor covered his or her short position. Short covering is synonymous with liquidating a short position or evening up a short position.

Covered call writing—A short option position in which the option seller (writer) owns an equal number of shares of the underlying stock represented by his or her option contracts

D

Day order—An order which, if not executed during the trading session the day it is entered, automatically expires at the end of the session. All orders are assumed to be day orders unless otherwise specified.

Day trader—Traders who usually initiate and offset positions during a single trading session

Delivery—The tender and receipt of an actual commodity of financial instrument, or cash in the settlement of an index contract

Delta—Measures the rate of change in an option's theoretical value for a one-unit change in the underlying stock's price. Calls have positive deltas, and puts have negative deltas. For example, a call option with a value of $2 and a delta of .50 would increase to $2.50 if the stock price increased by $1 (and would decrease to $1.50 if the stock price decreased by a dollar).

Derivative security—A financial security whose value is derived in part from the value and characteristics of another security (the underlying security)

Diagonal spread—A strategy involving the simultaneous purchase and writing of two options of the same class and the same underlying security (but they have different strike prices and different expiration dates)

Discount broker—A brokerage firm that offers low commission rates. These firms generally offer no inventment ideas and have no in-house investment research department.

Diversification—An investing or trading strategy in which positions are maintained in a variety of underlying stocks or stock options for the purpose of reducing risk and increasing bottom-line profits

Dividend—When a company pays some form of compensation to existing shareholders, this payment is known as a dividend. Dividends usually take the form of quarterly cash payments. These payments and the value of owning the stock attract investors who are seeking regular income. Dividends can also be in the form of additional stock or spin-offs of existing subsidiaries.

Down tick—A trade is said to be on a down tick when the last trade occurred at a price lower than the previous one.

E

Early exercise—A feature of American-style options that enables the owner to exercise an option at any time prior to its expiration date

Equity options—Refer to Stock Options.

European-style option—An option contract that can only be exercised on the expiration date

Exchange—An association of people who participate in the business of buying or selling stock, options, and or futures contracts; also known as a forum or place where traders (members) gather to buy or sell economic goods

Execution—The actual completion of a buy or sell order on the exchange floor

Exercise—To implement the right under which the buyer (holder) of an option is entitled to buy (in the case of a call) or sell (in the case of a put) the underlying security

Exercise price—Refer to Strike Price.

Ex-dividend date—On the ex-dividend date, the previous day's closing price is reduced by the amount of the dividend (rounded to the nearest eighth), because purchasers of the stock on the ex-dividend date will not receive the dividend payment. This date is sometimes referred to as simply the "ex-d."

Expiration calendar—A monthly calendar that contains important dates, such as market holidays, and expiration dates for expiring equity and index option classes

Expiration date—The last day that an option can be exercised under the underlying contract

Expiration cycle—An expiration cycle is related to the dates on which options of a particular underlying security expire. A stock option, other than LEAPS and long-term options, will be placed in one of three cycles: the January cycle, the February cycle, or the March cycle. At any point in time, an option will have contracts with four expiration dates outstanding: two in near-term months and two in far-term months.

Expiration date—The last day (in the case of American-style) or the only day (in the case of European-style) on which an option can be exercised. For stock options, this date is the third Friday of the expiration month; however, brokerage firms can set an earlier deadline for notification of an option buyer's (holder's) intention to exercise. If Friday is a holiday, the last trading day is the proceeding Thursday.

F

Fill—The price at which an order is executed

Fill-or-Kill **(FOK) order**—A trading order that is canceled unless the complete order is traded

Float—The number of shares outstanding that are available for public trading

Floor broker—An exchange member who is paid a fee for executing orders for clearing members or for their customers

Floor trader—An exchange member who generally trades only for his or her own account

Front month—The closest month to expiration for a futures or option contract

Full-service broker—A broker who provides investment research, information, and advice as well as the services that are involved with purchasing and selling securities. Full-service brokers usually charge the highest commission rates.

G

Gamma—The rate of change in an option's delta for a one-unit change in the price of the underlying stock

Gap—A term used by technicians to describe a jump or drop in prices

Good-Until-Canceled **(GTC) order**—A qualifier for any kind of order that extends its life indefinitely until filled or canceled

H

Halt—A halt ceases all trading activity on a stock.

Hedge—A conservative strategy that is used to limit investment loss by effecting a transaction that offsets an existing position

Hedged portfolio—A portfolio that consists of positions in the underlying securities that are covered by offsetting positions. In other words, this portfolio involves a long stock position and a long put option, which protects down-side movement in the long stock position.

High price—The highest (intra-day) price of a stock over the past 52 weeks; adjusted for any stock splits

Holder—The buyer of an option

I

Improving the market—An order that either raises the bid price or lowers the offering price is said to be improving the market. The market improves because the spread between the bid and the offer decreases.

Index—A statistical measure of the changes in a portfolio that represents a market. The *Standard & Poor's 500* (S&P 500) is a well-known index. It measures the overall change in the value of the 500 stocks of the largest companies in the United States.

Initial Public Offering (**IPO**)—A company's first sale of stock to the public.

Institutional investors—Organizations that invest, including insurance companies, depository institutions, pension funds, investment companies, mutual funds, and endowment funds

In-the-Money (**ITM**)—An option is ITM if it has intrinsic value. The call option is ITM if the strike is less than the market price of the underlying security. A put option is ITM if the strike price is greater than the market price of the underlying security.

Internet broker—A broker who offers online trading over the Internet. Commission rates are typically competitive and are in line with discount brokers.

Intrinsic value—The differences between an ITM option strike price and the current market price of a share of the underlying security

Iron butterfly—An option strategy that has limited risk and limited profit potential and that involves both a long (or short) straddle and a short (or long) combination. An iron butterfly contains four option strikes (versus the regular butterfly spread, which contains only three option strikes).

L

Last sale price—The price of a stock or option at the most recent transaction consummated

Last trading day—The final day under an exchange's rules during which trading can take place for a particular futures or options contract. Contracts that are outstanding at the end of the last trading day must be settled by the delivery of underlying physical commodities or financial instruments or by an agreement for a monetary settlement, depending on the futures contract specifications.

Long-Term Equity Anticipation Securities (LEAPS)—LEAPS are put or call options that have expiration dates that are one year or more in the future. Like standard options, each LEAPS contract represents 100 shares of the underlying stock.

Leg—A term describing one side of a spread position. When a trader legs into a spread, he or she establishes one side first—hoping for a favorable price movement so that the other side can be executed at a better price. This method is, of course, a higher-risk method of establishing a spread position. A leg can also be defined as a sustained trend in the stock market.

Leverage—The control of a larger sum of money with a smaller amount. By accepting the liability to purchase or deliver the total value of a contract, a smaller sum can be used as earnest money in order to guarantee performance. If prices move favorably, a large return on the contract can be earned from the leverage. The loss is limited to the total contract investment.

Limit orders—A customer sets a limit on the price of execution of a trade. For example, a buy limit order is placed below the market price. A sell limit order is placed above the market price. A sell limit is executed only at the limit price or higher. A buy limit is executed only at the limit price or lower.

Limited risk—A concept that is often used to describe the option buyer's position. Because the option buyer's loss can be no greater than the premium that he or she pays for the option, his or her risk of loss is limited.

Liquid or liquidity—The ease with which a purchase or sale can be made without disrupting existing market prices

Liquidating order—An order to close an existing open futures or options contract; the sale of a contract that has been purchased or the purchase of a contract that has been sold

Listed company—A listed company is one whose shares are publicly traded on a stock exchange.

Listed options—Options that are traded on one or more of the option exchanges. They are regulated by the U.S. government and the *Securities and Exchange Commission* (SEC) and are guaranteed by the *Options Clearing Corporation* (OCC).

Long position—A position in which a person's interest in a particular series of options is as a net holder (when the number of contracts bought exceeds the number of contracts sold). An investor is in long when taking ownership of a stock. The investor is looking for the stock to appreciate in value.

Long-term option (LEAPS)—Long-term options are available in two types: calls and puts. Both have expiration dates up to three years in the future.

M

Margin call—A call from a broker to a customer (maintenance margin call) to add funds to the margin account in order to cover an adverse price movement. The added margin assures the brokerage firm and the clearinghouse that the customer can purchase or deliver the entire contract (if necessary).

Margin requirement (for options)—The amount that an uncovered (naked) option seller (writer) is required to deposit and maintain in order to cover his or her daily position valuation and reasonably foreseeable intra-day price changes

Market maker—Those who maintain the best bid and ask prices on the option floors of the *Chicago Board of Options Exchange* (CBOE) and the *Pacific Exchange* (PCX). Market makers compete with each other on the same underlying securities option pricing in order to provide the best bid and ask prices at any time.

Mark-to-Market—The daily adjustment of margin accounts to reflect profits and losses

Market order—An order to purchase or sell at the best available price. At-the-market orders must be executed immediately and therefore take precedence over all other orders. Market orders to buy tend to be executed at the ask price, and market orders to sell tend to be executed at the bid price.

Married put—The simultaneous purchase of stock and put options representing an equivalent number of shares. This strategy is a limited-risk strategy during the life of the puts, because the stock can always be sold for at least the strike price of the purchased puts.

Money management—The principles that are involved with creating a plan to manage losses (as well as gains) in order to withstand market fluctuations

Market-If-Touched **(MIT) order**—A price order that automatically becomes a market order if the price is reached

Multiply listed options—Options on the same underlying security that are traded on more than one options exchange

N

Naked call writer—A short call option in which the seller (writer) does not own the shares of underlying stock represented by his or her options contracts (also known as uncovered call writing)

National Association of Securities Dealers Automatic Quotation System **(NASDAQ)**—An electronic quotation system that provides price quotations to market participants concerning the more actively traded common stock issues in the OTC market. About 4,000 common stock issues are included in the NASDAQ system.

Near-term—The nearest trading month of an options contract

Neutral—A term that is used to describe the belief that a stock or the market in general will neither rise nor decline significantly

Neutral strategy—An option strategy (or stock and option position) that is neither bullish nor bearish

New York Stock Exchange **(NYSE)**—Also known as the Big Board or The Exchange. More than 2,000 common and preferred stocks are traded on the NYSE. The exchange is the oldest in the United States, founded in 1792, and is the largest exchange in the United States. It is located on Wall Street in New York City.

Not-held order—An order that gives the broker discretion as to the price and timing in executing the best-possible trade. By placing this order, a customer agrees to not hold the broker responsible if the best deal is not obtained.

O

Offer (also ask price)—The lowest price that any potential seller is willing to accept for a particular option

Offset—Selling if one has bought or buying if one has sold an options contract

Open interest—The number of outstanding option contracts in a particular class or series. Open interest is considered an indicator of the depth or liquidity of a market (the ability to buy or sell at or near a given price).

Opening—The period at the beginning of the trading day during which all transactions are considered made or when first transactions were completed

Open outcry—An aucutionary trading method by which competing market makers and floor brokers who represent public orders short their bids and offers on the trading floor

Open order—An investor buys or sells an option without having a position in that option.

Opening price—The price of a stock or option at the first transaction of the day

Opening purchase—A transaction in which an investor becomes the holder of an option

Opening sale—A transaction in which an investor becomes the writer of an option

Options—A contract that entitles the holder to buy or sell a number of shares (usually 100) of a particular common stock at a predetermined price (refer to strike price) on or before a fixed expiration date

Options Clearing Corporation **(OCC)**—The issuer of all options contracts that are traded on the *American Stock Exchange* (ASE), the *Chicago Board of Option Exchange* (CBOE), the *Pacific Exchange* (PCX), *Philadelphia Stock Exchange* (PSE), and the *International Securities Exchange* (ISE).

Options contract—A contract that, in exchange for the option price, gives the option buyer the right (but not the obligation) to buy (or sell) a financial asset at the exercise price from (or to) the option seller within a specified time period or on a specified date (the expiration date)

Option cycle—A set pattern of months in which a class of options expires

Options exchange—Any exhange where options are publicly traded. The American Stock Exchange, Chicago Board of Options Exchange, Pacific Exchange, and Philadelphia Stock Exchange are the options exchanges in the United States.

Options price—The price paid by the buyer of the options contract for the right to buy or sell a security at a specified price in the future

Options writing—The result of selling options in an opening transaction (also refer to covered writing and naked writing)

Order—An instruction to purchase or sell an option; first transmitted to a broker's office and then submitted to the exchange floor for execution. Electronic orders are automatically executed with a market maker (without a broker).

Out-of-the-Money **(OTM)**—A call option is OTM if the strike price is greater than the market price of the underlying security. A put option is OTM if the strike price is less than the market price of the underlying security.

Out-trade—An error in which one trader believes that one trade occurred and the other believes that another trade occurred. This discrepancy could entail price, strike, month, and so on. An out-trade results in an unmatched trade.

P

Pacific Exchange **(PCX)**—The PCX trades equities, equity options, index options, bonds, and warrants.

Parity—A term used to describe an option contract's total premium when that premium is the same amount as its intrinsic value. For example, when an option's value is equal to its intrinsic value, it is said to be worth parity.

Pin risk—The risk to an investor (option writer) that the stock price will exactly equal the strike price of a written option at expiration (in other words, that option will be exactly ATM). The investor will not know how many of his or her written (short) options that he or she will be assigned. The risk is that on the following Monday, he or she might have an unexpected long (in the case of a written put) or short (in the case of a written call) stock position and thus will be subject to the risk of an adverse price move.

Position—Established when an investor makes an opening purchase or sale of an option

Position limit—The maximum number of futures or options contracts that any individual or group of individuals acting in concert can hold at one time

Premium—The price of an option contract over that option's intrinsic value

Put—An option contract that gives the buyer (holder) the right to sell and that places on the writer the obligation to buy a specified number of shares of the underlying stock at the given strike price on or before the expiration date of the contract

R

Ratio spread—A term that is most commonly used to describe the purchase of an option(s), call, or put and the writing of a greater number of the same type of options that are OTM with respect to those that are purchased. All options involved have the same expiration date.

Record date—The date on which a shareholder must own shares in order to be entitled to a dividend payment

Reversal—The exact opposite of a conversion. A reversal consists of a short put and a long call with the same strike price and expiration date combined with short stock.

Rho—The sensitivity of theoretical option prices with regard to small changes in interest rates. Increases in interest rates lead to higher call values and lower put values. Decreases in interest rates lead to lower call values and higher put values.

Risk/reward management—Understanding the inherent risks of a portfolio, taking the necessary steps to reduce it, and still maximizing the reward potential of the overall position

S

Series—All option contracts of the same class, unit of trade, expiration date, and exercise price

Short position—A position that has a bearish reward potential. Short stock, long puts, and short calls are three ways of obtaining a short position.

Short—To sell something that you do not own, generally in the hopes that the price will fall and that you will be able to purchase the asset for a lower price than the price at which you sold initially sold it.

Specialist—An exchange member whose function is to maintain a fair and orderly market in a given stock or class of options

Stock options—Options on shares of a stock

Stop loss—A price threshold that is reached and triggers the liquidation of a position. A stop loss order can be placed in the market in advance of that level being reached, or it can be monitored by a trader as a mental stop-loss level (which would trigger the action to enter a sell order in order to exit the position).

Stop-limit order—A contingency order that can be placed in order to trigger an entry or exit if a stock trades at a certain price

Strike price—The stated price per share for which the underlying stock can be purchased (in the case of a call) or sold (in the case of a put) by the option buyer (holder) upon exercise of the option contract

T

Time decay—The nonlinear loss of value of an option over time when all other factors are constant. Time decay increases greatly as the option reaches expiration.

Time value—The portion of the premium that is attributable to the amount of time remaining until the expiration of the option contract and that is attributable to the fact that the underlying components that determine the value of the option can change during that time.

Time value is generally equal to the difference between the premium and the intrinsic value.

Trading floor—The location at the options exchange where the contracts are actually bought and sold

Type—The classification of an option contract as either a put or a call

U

Uncovered call options—A short call option in which the seller (writer) does not own the shares of underlying stock represented by his or her options contracts

Uncovered put options—A short call option in which the seller (writer) does not have a corresponding short stock position or has not deposited in a cash account cash or cash equivalents to the exercise of the put

Underlying stock or security—The security that would be purchased or sold if the option was exercised. Underlying securities can include stock, futures, and indices.

Unit of trading—The minimum quantity or amount that is permitted when trading a security. The minimum for options is one contract (that generally covers 100 shares of stock).

Up tick—A stock is said to be on an up tick when the last trade occurred at a higher price than the one before it.

V

Volatility—The propensity of the market price of the underlying security to change in either direction

Volume—For options, the number of contracts that have been traded within a specific time period (usually a day or a week)

W

Writer—The seller of an option contract

Index